CONTEMPORARY CIRCUS

In this volume, twenty-four creators come together with three scholars to discuss Contemporary Circus, bridging the divide between practice and theory.

Lavers, Leroux, and Burtt offer conversations across four key themes: Apparatus, Politics, Performers, and New Work. Extensively illustrated with fifty photos of Contemporary Circus productions, and extensively annotated, *Contemporary Circus* thematically groups and contextualises extracts of conversations to provide a sophisticated and wide-ranging study supported by critical theory.

Of interest to both practitioners and scholars, *Contemporary Circus* uses the lens of 'contestation,' or calling things into question, to provide a portal into ways of seeing today's circus performance.

Katie Lavers is an Adjunct Senior Lecturer at the Western Australian Academy of Performing Arts, Edith Cowan University, Western Australia. Her research interests are Circus Studies, Performance Studies, Animal Studies, and Ecofeminism. She is the Co-Editor of *The Routledge Circus Studies Reader* (2016).

Louis Patrick Leroux is a Professor and Associate Dean of Research, Faculty of Arts and Science at Concordia University, Montreal. He is the Director of the Montreal Working Group on Circus Research and Co-Editor of *Cirque Global: Québec's Expanding Circus Boundaries* (2016).

Jon Burtt is a Lecturer in the Department of Media, Music, Communication and Cultural Studies at Macquarie University in Sydney, Australia. He teaches across dance, theatre, and circus. His research interests are Contemporary Circus Practice and Training; and Circus for Social Change. He is the Associate Editor of *The Routledge Circus Studies Reader* (2016).

CONTEMPORARY CIRCUS

*Katie Lavers, Louis Patrick Leroux,
and Jon Burtt*

Routledge
Taylor & Francis Group

LONDON AND NEW YORK

First published 2020
by Routledge
2 Park Square, Milton Park, Abingdon, Oxon OX14 4RN

and by Routledge
52 Vanderbilt Avenue, New York, NY 10017

Routledge is an imprint of the Taylor & Francis Group, an informa business

British Library Cataloguing-in-Publication Data
A catalogue record for this book is available from the British Library

Library of Congress Cataloging-in-Publication Data
Names: Lavers, Katie, editor of compilation. |
Leroux, Louis Patrick, 1971– editor of compilation. |
Burtt, John, editor of compilation.
Title: Contemporary circus / [selected and edited by] Katie Lavers,
Louis Patrick Leroux, and John Burtt.
Description: Milton Park, Abingdon, Oxon; New York,
NY: Routledge, 2019.
Identifiers: LCCN 2019011820 | ISBN 9781138680715 (hardback) |
ISBN 9781138680722 (paperback) | ISBN 9781315564074 (ebook)
Subjects: LCSH: Circus.
Classification: LCC GV1801 .C645 2019 | DDC 791.3—dc23
LC record available at https://lccn.loc.gov/2019011820

ISBN: 978-1-138-68071-5 (hbk)
ISBN: 978-1-138-68072-2 (pbk)
ISBN: 978-1-315-56407-4 (ebk)

Typeset in Bembo
by codeMantra

MIX
Paper from
responsible sources
FSC
www.fsc.org   FSC™ C013985

Printed in the United Kingdom
by Henry Ling Limited

CONTENTS

FIGURES

CONTRIBUTORS

Biographies: Authors

Dr Katie Lavers is an Adjunct Senior Lecturer in the Western Australian Academy of Performing Arts (WAAPA) at Edith Cowan University. She is a writer and scholar with a doctorate in the cultural history of Contemporary Circus. She is Co-Editor with Peta Tait of *The Routledge Circus Studies Reader* (2016) and has published on circus in academic journals such as *New Theatre Quarterly*; *Theatre, Dance and Performance Training*; *Journal of Theatre and Performing Arts*; and *Animal Studies Journal*. Her latest book chapter, co-authored with Louis Patrick Leroux, 'The Multiple Narratives of Cirque du Soleil,' can be found in *Narrative in Performance*, Macmillan (2018). Her research interests include Performance Studies, Circus Studies, Animal Studies, and Ecofeminism. She is a circus, dance, and physical theatre reviewer for ArtsHub, Australia.

With a background in performance as a director and producer of intermedia circus, her performance works combining circus, dance, interactives, video, text, electronic sound, and live music have toured throughout Australia and Asia.

She has received numerous awards and fellowships including an ArtsWA (Western Australia) Creative Fellowship (2010), numerous Australia Council for the Arts awards, an Australian Academy of the Humanities Travelling Fellowship (2016), and a Varuna Residential Writing Fellowship (2018).

Professor Louis Patrick Leroux is the Associate Dean of Research, Faculty of Arts and Science at Concordia University, Montreal. He is the Director of the Montreal Working Group on Circus Research and Associate Researcher at the

National Circus School in Montreal. In 2017, he was elected to the Royal Society of Canada's College of New Scholars, Artists and Scientists.

He is a playwright and a director, has published extensively and given many international talks on Contemporary Circus, and is closely involved with the Quebec circus scene as a researcher, collaborator, and teacher. He is in high demand as a speaker and has been Visiting Scholar or Professor in the following universities – Duke University, Charles University (Prague), the Centre National des Arts du Cirque in France, and the University of Chile.

He is currently involved in simultaneous research projects, all team-based, including a Quebec-funded project exploring circus dramaturgy; a Canadian-funded project studying physical literacy, creativity, and resilience; and a Canadian-funded historical synthesis and socio-aesthetic analysis of Quebec theatre.

Recent scholarly collections include *Cirque Global: Québec's Expanding Circus Boundaries*, co-edited with Charles Batson (McGill-Queen's UP, 2016); 'North-South Circus Circulations' in the edited issue of *Québec Studies* (2014); 'Le Québec à Las Vegas' in the edited issue of *L'Annuaire théâtral* (2010); and *Le jeu des positions. Discours du théâtre québécois*, co-edited with Hervé Guay (Nota Bene, 2014).

Dr Jon Burtt is a researcher and Lecturer in Dance and Performance Studies at Macquarie University, Sydney. He teaches across dance, theatre, and circus in the Department of Media, Music, Communication, and Cultural Studies. He has a doctorate in Circus Studies, and a masters in the cultural history of Mallakhamb, the traditional Indian yogic aerial rope. As a teacher and practitioner he works across the interdisciplinary areas between dance, circus, and theatre in a wide range of contexts from community-based to professional within Australia and internationally.

His research interests include Circus for Social Change, and Contemporary Circus Practice and Performer Development. He was Associate Editor for *The Routledge Circus Studies Reader* (2016) and has published on circus in numerous academic journals including *Theatre, Dance and Performance Training*; *Journal of Arts and Communities*; *International Journal of the Arts in Society*; and *New Theatre Quarterly*. His book chapter, co-authored with Sylvain Lafortune and Patrice Aubertin, 'Introducing Decision Training into an Elite Circus Arts Training Program,' based on his PhD research, can be found in *Cirque Global: Québec's Expanding Circus Boundaries* (McGill-Queen's UP, 2016). He was Researcher-in-Residence at the National Circus School in Montreal (2011–2012) and is a Cirque du Monde Instructor in Social Circus.

He has been the recipient of two ArtsWA (Western Australia) Creative Fellowships, numerous Australia Council for the Arts awards, and the Macquarie University Faculty of Arts Learning and Teaching Award, and the Vice-Chancellor's Citation for Outstanding Contribution to Student Learning.

Biographies: Creators

Lachlan Binns and Jascha Boyce began recreational circus classes at a young age with Cirkidz, the youth circus based in Adelaide, South Australia. On leaving Cirkidz in 2009 the two joined forces with five other friends and co-founded Gravity and Other Myths (GOM). Binns and Boyce are now both core performers and Co-Directors of GOM.

Freefall (2009), GOM's first show, toured Australia for two years. GOM's next work *A Simple Space* (2013) has achieved international success, and has been performed more than 500 times at 76 festivals, across 24 countries, over the past five years. GOM's follow-up work *Backbone* (2017) headlined Montreal's 2018 Complètement Cirque Festival, as well as being presented in other arts festivals around the world. GOM has won an Australian Dance Award for 'Best Physical Theatre' (2018); an Australian Green Room Award for 'Outstanding Contemporary Circus' (2015); and the Adelaide Fringe Festival 'Best Circus' Award (2014). The company now tours 10 to 11 months a year sometimes with two casts performing simultaneously.

Ampersand, a new production company launched recently under the umbrella of GOM, offers financial and creative support to both emerging and established artists to develop new work, and creates a platform to launch established work into the market.

http://www.gravityandothermyths.com.au/the-company

Tilde Björfors is the Artistic Director of Cirkus Cirkör which she co-founded in 1995 in Stockholm, Sweden. Circus Cirkör's performances are seen annually by between 70,000 to 100,000 people nationally and internationally, and 30,000 people undertake circus training with the company every year.

In 1997, Cirkus Cirkör created the first Contemporary Circus school in Scandinavia, Cirkuspiloterna, which in 2005 became part of Dans och Cirkushögskolan (DOCH), the University of Dance and Circus in Stockholm. Tilde Björfors was Guest Professor of Contemporary Circus at DOCH from 2005 to 2010.

Björfors has directed numerous works for Cirkus Cirkör including *Inside Out* (2008), *Wear it like a Crown* (2010), and *Knitting Peace* (2013). Her most recent works for the company are politically activist in nature. These include the trilogy *Borders* (2015), *Limits* (2016), and *Movements* (2017) which examines the topic of refugees; a circus opera version of Philip Glass' opera *Satyagraha* (2016) which looks at the political activism of Mahatma Gandhi in South Africa; and *Epifónima* (2018), a feminist work which tackles patriarchal hierarchies, featuring a cast of seven female circus artists.

In 2018, Cirkus Cirkör, with Tilde Björfors named as its Artistic Director, was awarded the XV Europe Prize, Theatrical Realities (The European Theatre Prize / Premio europa per il teatro).

https://cirkor.se/en

Kim 'Busty Beatz' Bowers is the Co-Founder, Co-Creator, and Musical Director of Hot Brown Honey. She also performs with the company as the 'Queen Bee.' Hot Brown Honey features performers who are all women of colour from diverse backgrounds, including Samoan, Aboriginal Australian, Tongan, Maori, Indonesian, and South African. Since its formation in 2011 the company has toured the UK, Europe, New Zealand, and Canada, winning the Total Theatre UK Award for Experimentation, Innovation, and Playing with Form in the 2016 Edinburgh Fringe Festival, and in Australia, a Helpmann Award, two Green Room Awards, and a Sydney Theatre Award.

As a sound designer and composer for theatre, she has worked with Belvoir St Theatre, Sydney; Queensland Theatre Company; Australian Theatre for Young People (ATYP); Debase; Jute Theatre Company; La Boite; The Roundhouse (UK) and I.C.E. She works across forms working with *Jarjum's Life Museum* for Out of The Box Children's Festival; London's Wellcome Collection; and The Sick of The Fringe for the multimedia commission *We Are the Latest Models of Our Ancestry*; and she was invited to be a part of Barby Asante's work *As Always a Painful Declaration of Independence* for the Venice Biennale's Diaspora Pavilion.

She has also created sound for circus and dance theatre including for Polytoxic, Flipside, Casus, *Chasing Smoke*, Strut'n'Fret, and is currently the resident Musical Director for the boylesque show *Briefs*. Kim Bowers is also Co-Director of the production company Black Honey which she co-founded with her sister, performer Candy Bowers.
https://www.hotbrownhoney.com/

Shana Carroll is a Co-Founder and Co-Artistic Director of the Montreal circus collective, The 7 Fingers (Les 7 Doigts de la Main). Originally from Berkeley, California, she began her career as a trapeze artist with San Francisco's Pickle Family Circus. She then studied at Montreal's National Circus School (1991–1993) and France's École Nationale de Arts du Cirque de Rosny-sous-Bois (1993–1994). She performed as an aerialist for over 20 years, performing the trapeze solo in Cirque du Soleil's *Saltimbanco* from 1994 to 2001.

She founded The 7 Fingers in 2002 with six other circus artists, Isabelle Chassé, Patrick Léonard, Faon Shane, Gypsy Snider, Sébastien Soldevila, and Samuel Tétreault. Shana Carroll co-directed and performed in The 7 Fingers' first show *Loft* (2002) which went on to be performed over 900 times to over 300,000 people. She also co-directed and performed in *La Vie* (2007). She co-directed *Traces* (2006) with Gypsy Snider, a show which has been performed to over a million people in 25 countries with a one-year season in 2011 at Union Square Theatre in New York. Carroll has also directed or co-directed The 7 Fingers' shows, *Psy* (2009), *Cabaret* (2010), *Sequence 8* (2012), *Le murmure du coquelicot* (2013), *Cuisine & Confessions* (2014), and *Passagers* (2018).

Carroll created the circus component of *Queen of the Night*, at Diamond Horseshoe in New York, which won a Drama Desk award (2013) for 'Unique Theatrical Experience,' and she co-designed the medieval segment of the Sochi Winter Olympics Opening Ceremony.

She has frequently collaborated with Cirque du Soleil, most recently as Co-Director with Sébastien Soldevila for Cirque du Soleil's first show on ice *Crystal* (2017), and previously as Acrobatic Designer and Choreographer of *Iris* (2011) and *Paramour* (2016), and she was Choreographer of the Cirque du Soleil performance at the 2012 Academy Awards. The 7 Fingers was awarded the Grand Prix du Conseil des Arts de Montreal in 2015.
http://7fingers.com/

David Clarkson is a physical performer and the Artistic Director of Stalker Theatre, which he co-founded in Sydney, Australia in 1988. Stalker's work combines Contemporary Circus, contemporary dance, martial arts, interdisciplinary and intercultural practices and processes, and the use of innovative interactive technologies. Clarkson has conceived and directed numerous Stalker shows, with performances in locations and venues ranging from street performances to large opera houses, with work ranging from solo performances, to ensemble works, to large and small-scale community outreach projects, to Olympic Opening Ceremonies.

He has undertaken numerous residencies across Australia and America, including a period as Artist in Residence at the Miami Performing Arts Centre, and he has been involved in intercultural exchanges including in Bogotá, Colombia; Boulder, Colorado; and Seoul, South Korea.

Clarkson's works for Stalker include *Fast Ground* (1989), *Toy Cart* (1990), *Angels ex Machina* (1993), *Blood Vessel* (1997), *Four Riders* (2001), *Incognita* (2002), *Red* (2004), *Stiltbreak* (2006), *Sugar* (2007), *Flexion* (2007), *MirrorMirror* (2009), *Shanghai Lady Killer* (2010), *Elevate* (2010), *Encoded* (2012), *Pixel Mountain* (2013), *Phospori* (2013), *Compartmentalised* (2014), *Creature – the Installation* (2016), *Frameshift* (2016), and *Creature – Dot and the Kangaroo* (2016) which toured to China and throughout Australia in 2018. He is currently developing a space-themed immersive theatre experience *Big Skies* for the 50th anniversary of the Apollo 11 moon landing in 2019.

In 2007, David Clarkson was awarded the Rex Cramphorn Scholarship, one of Australia's top awards, for an outstanding, lifelong commitment to innovative performance, and in 2015, he received the inaugural Arts NSW Art and Technology Fellowship for his research into the use of interactive and digital technology in performance.
https://www.stalker.com.au/

Philippe Decouflé is a performer and choreographer, and Director of the Paris-based Compagnie DCA which he founded in 1983. Decouflé studied circus arts at the École Nationale du Cirque Annie Fratellini in Paris before studying dance. As a dancer he worked with many notable choreographers including Alwin Nikolais, Karole Armitage, François Verret, and Régine Chopinot.

Decouflé has created and directed many different kinds of work. His dance-based works include *Codex* (1986), *Petites Pièces Montées* (1993), *Decodex* (1998), *Shazam!* (1998), *Tricodex* (2004), *Désirs* (2009) for the Parisian cabaret Crazy Horse, *Octopus* (2010), *Panorama* (2012), *Contact* (2014), *Courtepointe* (2016), and *Nouvelles Pièces Courtes* (2017). He has choreographed dance videos, including *True Faith* for the band New Order which won the 1988 Best Music Video prize at the BRIT Awards; an advertisement for Polaroid which won a Silver Lion Prize at the Venice Film Festival (1989); films including *Jump (Hystérique bourée)* in collaboration with Charles Atlas (1984); and interactive video installations including *Opticon* (2012).

He has directed large-scale works including the Opening and Closing Ceremonies of the 1992 Winter Olympic Games in France; and musicals including *Dora* (1996), and *Watashi Wa Shingo* (2016), a musical adaptation of Kazuo Umezu's manga made in collaboration with Japanese artists. Decouflé created and directed *Iris* (2011) and also directed *Paramour* (2016) for Cirque du Soleil.

Philippe Decouflé won the Prix Bagnolet for Choreography at 21 years of age, and in 2015 was made a Commander of the Order of Arts and Letters from the Ministry of Culture, France, to recognize his contribution to the arts.
https://www.cie-dca.com/en/the-company

Fez Faanana is a performer and director, and the Co-Founder and Co-Artistic Director of the Brisbane-based boylesque company Briefs. The company, which evolved out of warehouse parties and late-night speakeasies in the Brisbane club scene, was founded in 2008.

Briefs' shows combine circus, cabaret, dance, and drag, with sharp political commentary. Faanana plays Mistress of Ceremonies Shivannah, a character he describes as, 'the love child of the bearded lady and the ring master.'

The first show *Briefs: All Male. All Vaudeville. All Trash* toured for four years. The second show *Briefs: The Second Coming* was an international breakthrough, receiving the 'Best Circus Award' from Fringe World at the Edinburgh Fringe Festival (2014), and two Green Room Awards in Australia in 2015.

Briefs' third show *Briefs: Close Encounters* has also been an international success with audiences and critics, playing a two-month season in London's West End, 2018–2019.

Fez Faanana is also Artistic Director of Briefs Factory, a production house presenting Briefs, Hot Brown Honey, Club Briefs, Sweatshop, Brat Kids Carnival, and Yana Alana.
https://www.briefsfactory.com/

Mike Finch is a freelance director and consultant working across circus, video, film, and theatre. He began creating circus in 1996, when he co-founded Circus Monoxide, and then toured for a year throughout regional

Australia with eight other performers performing an outdoor show that folded off the side of a bus.

Finch became Artistic Director and Co-CEO of Circus Oz at the age of 28, and from 1997–2015 he was responsible for the artistic direction of all the company's work. Circus Oz toured annually across Australia and the world with numerous return seasons to New York, and major tours to the capital cities of Europe, Asia, and the Americas. He maintained and developed many of the radical political intentions of the company founders, upholding a policy of gender balance in all performances; helping to set up the BLAKflip programme to create career pathways into circus for emerging Indigenous performers; introducing the ongoing inclusion of Indigenous performers into Circus Oz ensembles; continuing annual seasons in remote Australian Indigenous communities; and conducting a major tour across Arnhem Land, Northern Australia, culminating in a performance at the Garma Festival of Traditional Cultures.

His recent creative works include co-creating the 12-hour non-stop Circus-Circus precinct for Melbourne White Night (2016); and directing two *Funatorium* shows for the Sydney Opera House (2017, 2018).

As a consultant, Mike Finch has worked with Spaghetti Circus and the National Circus Festival in Mullumbimby; with Cirkidz and the South Australian Circus Centre; and on strategic planning and site-specific projects for Northern Rivers Performing Arts (NORPA).
www.carnivalcinema.com.au
http://archive.circusoz.com/

Daniele Finzi Pasca is a performer, and the Founder and Director of Compagnia Finzi Pasca based in Lugano, Switzerland. He was initially introduced to circus through gymnastics and then guided by the clown, Fery Rivelinos.

In 1983, at the age of 19, Finzi Pasca went to India with a volunteer program to help the terminally ill. On his return to Switzerland he founded Teatro Sunil and, with his brother Marco Finzi Pasca and Maria Bonzanigo, created a new form of theatre combining clowning, dance, and acting, called 'Theatre of the Caress.'

Sentenced to prison as a conscientious objector, Finzi Pasca finished the writing of his solo show, *Icaro*, in jail. The show, which forms the foundation of Finzi Pasca and Teatro Sunil's approach to theatre, has now been performed by Finzi Pasca for over 27 years, in six different languages, in 25 countries around the world.

Finzi Pasca created many shows for Teatro Sunil including *Rituale, Viaggio al Confine, Dialoghi col Sonno, Percossi Obbligati, Giacobbe, 1337, Aitestás,* and *Visitatio* (co-produced with Montreal's Carbone 14), and these have been performed in more than 20 countries. He has created and directed three shows for Cirque Éloise, *Nomade* (2002), *Rain* (2003), and *Nebbia* (2007); and two shows for Cirque du Soleil, *Corteo* (2005) which has been seen by over nine million spectators and is still performed as an arena show, and *Luzia* (2016).

He has created and directed numerous large-scale events including three Olympic Games ceremonies; and *Montréal Avudo* (2017), a multimedia event with large-scale video projections and water choreography to celebrate the 375th anniversary celebrations of Montreal. He has also directed numerous operas including *L'Amour de Loin* (2009) for the English National Opera; *Pagliacci* (2011) for Teatro San Carlo in Naples, restaged by Mariinsky Theatre, St. Petersburg; *Aida* (2011) and Verdi's *Requiem* (2014) for the Mariinsky Theatre, St. Petersburg; and *Carmen* (2016) for the Teatro San Carlo in Naples.

With his own company, Compagnia Finzi Pasca, he created and directed *Donka* (2010), based on the life and work of Chekov; *La Verità* (2013), based on Tristan and Isolde with a backdrop painted by Salvador Dali; and *Bianco su Bianco* (2014), a clown theatre show. After the death of his wife and creative partner Julie Hamelin Finzi in 2016, Finzi Pasca created *Per Te* (2016) in her memory. Along with *Icaro*, all five shows are currently on international tour.

Finzi Pasca was awarded the Swiss Theatre Prize in 2008.

https://finzipasca.com/

Sean Gandini is a juggler, choreographer, and the Co-Founder and Co-Director of Gandini Juggling. He began performing in the 1980s when he regularly performed in the street in London's Covent Garden, and also toured with a number of companies including the British New Circus company Ra-Ra Zoo. In 1991 he co-founded Gandini Juggling with Kati Ylä-Hokkala, the Finnish rhythmic gymnastics champion and juggler.

Gandini Juggling to date has performed over 5,000 shows in over 50 countries. Together Gandini and Ylä-Hokkala have created a diverse array of nearly 30 different shows including works combining juggling with different forms of dance, such as the hit show *Smashed*, a tribute to Pina Bausch (2010); *4 x 4: Ephemeral Architectures* (2015), combining juggling with ballet; and *Sigma* (2017) which combines juggling with Bharatanatyam classical Indian dance. *Sigma* was awarded The Edinburgh Fringe Total Theatre Award for Visual Theatre (2018) and the Asian Arts Award for Best Directing (2018). *Spring* (2018) is a collaboration with the Alexander Whitney Company and features juggling combined with contemporary ballet.

In 2012, Gandini created *The Sweet Life* for the celebration of the London Olympics, and in 2016, he collaborated as Juggling Choreographer on English National Opera's production of the Philip Glass opera *Akhnaten*, which won an Olivier Award for Best New Opera Production in 2017. In 2019, this production is being presented at the Metropolitan Opera House in New York.

Sean Gandini regularly teaches in many of the world's leading circus schools to inspire the next generation of jugglers.

http://www.gandinijuggling.com/

Firenza Guidi is a writer, performance creator, and an independent director who has created and directed performance works around the world in the UK, Europe, India, the USA, and Cuba. She has been Director-in-Residence for the National Youth Theatre of Wales and also for NoFit State Circus, one of the United Kingdom's longest-running Contemporary Circus companies. Her works for NoFit State include *ImMortal* (2004); *Tabú* (2006), inspired by the writings of Gabriel Garcìa Márquez; the immersive promenade show *Bianco* (2012); and *Lexicon* (2018). Other works include *Hybrids* (2000); *3 x Hamlet* (2001); *wwWoyzeck* (2002); *The Machine – when is a man-woman free?* (2003); *Out of Place*, inspired by the writings of José Saramago (2004); and *Borders* (2005) inspired by Kurt Vonnegut's novels.

Guidi has studied with many international masters including Dario Fo, Philippe Gaulier, Ludwig Flaszen, and Ida Kelarova, and trained as an actress and singer at the Royal Welsh College of Music and Drama, where since 1995 she has been a guest teacher and director. She has a doctorate in Sixteenth Century Tragedy from Queen's University, Belfast, and has presented scholarly papers all around the world.

Guidi co-founded the Wales-based European Live Arts Network (ELAN) with David Murray in 1989. Since 2004 she has also directed the International Performance School, Frantoio, ELAN's sister organisation in Fucecchio, Italy. http://www.elanfrantoio.org/en/about/firenza-guidi https://www.nofitstate.org/en/

Jo Lancaster and Simon Yates are the Co-Founders of Acrobat, the Australian performance company based in Albury-Wodonga, which was founded in 1995. Since then Acrobat has been at the forefront of experimental, uncompromising performance work combining circus, physical theatre, and performance art.

Their first show, the eponymous *Acrobat* (1996–2004), presented in different versions over a period of eight years, received a number of prestigious awards. The next work *Smaller, Poorer, Cheaper* (2007) featured performers Lancaster and Yates joined by fellow circus artist Mozes along with ongoing collaborator, sound scientist Tim Barrass. In their following show *Propaganda* (2010) Lancaster and Yates performed alongside their two children. Acrobat's most recent show *It's Not for Everyone* (2015) features Lancaster and Yates on-stage with collaborator Tim Barrass off-stage creating sound. The show is an examination of clowning and circus, and contests the status quo with wry black humour, 'This is bitter clowning and the meanings are sinister and unflinching. No wonder Samuel Beckett loved clowns so much. He would have loved Acrobat' (Murray Bramwell, 2017, The Best (So Far) of the Adelaide Fringe Festival. *Daily Review.* https://daily review.com.au/adelaide-fringe-festival-round/56256/).

Acrobat has been performing and touring for 23 years throughout the world and so far has toured to more than 20 countries. https://www.acrobat.net.au/about

Johann Le Guillerm is a juggler, performance creator, and Founder of Cirque Ici in Paris, France. Le Guillerm originally studied clowning, tight wire, and object manipulation at the École Supérieure des Arts du Cirque de Châlons-en-Champagne, graduating in 1989. He went on to work with the French New Circus company Archaos. He developed new works with Théâtre Dromesko, and then co-founded Le Cirque O.

In 1994, he founded his own company Cirque Ici, and created his solo show *Où ça?* which toured the world for five years. In 2001, he began a series of works entitled the *Attraction* project with the aim of taking 'a 360 degree look at the world.' The project led him to explore this idea through sculpture, installation, performance, and exhibitions.

Johann Le Guillerm often performs with sculptural objects that he creates, which he sees as tools enabling him to interrogate elements of balance, movement, and points of view. Key works include *Secret* (2003–2011) and the show's second iteration *Secret II* (2012–2016) which have toured around the world and have been described as lying 'somewhere between circus, art installations and object theatre' (La Transumante, 2017, http://www.lestombeesdelanuit.com/en/spectacles/la-transumante-en/).

Since 2011 Johann Le Guillerm has been supported and hosted by the Paris City Hall at the Jardin d'Agronomie Tropicale, Paris in a creative research residency. Le Guillerm has been the recipient of multiple awards including recognition by the French Government with the Grand Prix National du Cirque (1996); and by the SACD (Société des Auteurs et Compositeurs Dramatiques) with the Prix Arts du Cirque (2005); and the SACD Grand Prix (2017). http://www.johannleguillerm.com

Yaron Lifschitz is Artistic Director and CEO of Circa, the Brisbane-based Contemporary Circus company. Lifschitz has created more than thirty works for Circa and these have been performed in 40 countries, and have been seen by over one million people. His work for Circa has received numerous awards including six Helpmann Awards in Australia.

Since graduating from the Graduate Director's Course at the National Institute of Dramatic Arts (NIDA) in Sydney, Lifschitz has directed over 60 productions including large-scale events, opera, theatre, physical theatre, and circus. His productions have been presented at major festivals and venues around the world including the Brooklyn Academy of Music, New York; the Barbican, London; Les Nuits de Fourvière, France; Chamäleon Theater, Berlin; and all the major Australian international arts festivals.

Recent shows created for Circa include *Il Ritorno* (2015), *Reclaimed Pianos (2016), Humans* (2017), *En Masse* (2018), *Circa's Peepshow* (2018), and *Wolfgang's Magical Musical Circus* (2018). Yaron Lifschitz was Creative Director of *Festival 2018*, the Arts and Cultural Program of the 21st Commonwealth Games. As well as directing new Circa creations in 2018, Lifschitz also directed a new production

of the Mozart Opera *Idomeneo* which opened in Lisbon, Portugal at The Teatro Nacional de São Carlos.
https://circa.org.au/about-circa/

Chelsea McGuffin is the Co-Director of Brisbane-based Company 2 which she co-founded with musician and performer David Carberry in 2009.

McGuffin originally trained as a dancer at the Adelaide Centre for Performing Arts before moving into circus training with Circus Monoxide and learning the Toss the Girl act from Cletus Ball. She worked with Circa, Queensland Theatre Company, and Circus Monoxide, and toured with these companies to the UK, Europe, Canada, South America, and Asia. She was also Director and Head Trainer of Flipside Circus, the largest youth circus in Brisbane, before co-founding Company 2.

She has directed or co-directed many works for Company 2 including *Cantina* (2010) which won numerous awards including 'Best Overall' from the Adelaide Fringe Festival (2011); *Scotch and Soda*, (2013), mixing circus and jazz, which won 'Best Circus' in the Adelaide Fringe Festival (2015) and was performed most recently at the 2018 Montreal Complètement Cirque Festival; *She Would Walk the Sky* (2014), a collaboration with Tasmanian writer Finegan Kruckemeyer commissioned for the World Theatre Festival; *Kaleidoscope* (2016), a circus theatre work exploring the inner world of the central performer, a young boy diagnosed as having Asperger Syndrome; *Fallot* (2017), a collaboration with Marianna Joslin, a circus artist born with a rare heart condition; and most recently *Le Coup* (2019), a new work inspired by the Brophy Boxing Tents that tour the Australian outback. Chelsea McGuffin is currently researching and developing a new collaborative project between Company 2 and Circus Oz, *Wunderage*, to be presented in 2019.
http://www.company2.com.au

Phia Ménard was born into the body of a boy in France in 1971 when he was named Philippe, the future Phia Ménard began as a juggler, originally studying with renowned juggler Jérôme Thomas, then joining his company as a performer, and as a creator of several shows until 2003. Ménard also studied dance with the choreographers Valérie Lamielle and Hervé Diasnas and performed in two of their works.

In 1998, Ménard founded her own company, Compagnie Non Nova, and began her move away from juggling virtuosity, aiming instead to create work combining dance and performance art with circus. The solo show *Ascenseur, fantasmagorie pour élever les gens et les fardeaux* (2001) gained her widespread recognition. Compagnie Non Nova was invited to be Associate Artistic Company at the National Théâtre Le Carré in Chateau-Gontier in France for three years creating several works in that period. Ménard then went on to create *Zapptime#Remix* (2005) and *Doggy Bag* (2007).

It was in 2008 that Philippe revealed the decision to become a woman and to continue life as Phia Ménard. The show *P.P.P.* (*Position Parallele au Plancher*) (2008) explored the 'unjugglability' of ice in relation to the changing nature of her body. *P.P.P.* was part of her long-term project *ICE* (an exploration into the 'unjugglability' of natural elements). Her works since then include *Black Monodie* (2010), *Vortex* (2011), *L'Après-midi d'un Foehn* (2011), *Belle d'Hier* (2015), *Les Os Noirs* (2017), and *Et in Arcadia Ego* (2017), directed for the Opera Comique. Her most recent work, *Saison Sèche (Dry Season)*, created for the 2018 Avignon Festival, featured an all-women cast, and investigated gender and the struggle to contest patriarchal norms. In 2014, Ménard was made a Chevalier de l'Ordre des Arts et des Lettres (Knight of the Order of Arts and Letters) by the French Minister of Culture and Communication.
http://www.cienonnova.com/en

Jennifer Miller is a theatre artist, director, and juggler, and Founder and Director of Circus Amok.

As a dancer researching improvisational strategies, Miller worked with Screw's Loose, They Won't Shut Up, and other informal collaborations in New York in the mid-1980s and early-1990s. She also appeared in many of Sarah Schulman and Robin Epstein's early plays; in a wide range of ensemble projects including San Francisco's Make-A-Circus, and Hartford's Protean Theater; and in solo shows including *Morphadyke* and *Free Toasters Everyday*. She also spent seven seasons working at Coney Island Sideshow by the Seashore.

In 1989, she co-founded the political, queer circus, theatre extravaganza Circus Amok. Since then she has directed and performed with Circus Amok annually, outdoors, in the parks of New York City. Circus Amok embodies Miller's political and aesthetic desires – free and open to all comers, it engages many theatrical languages at once, deploying tropes of old-school popular theatre, juggling and acrobatics, alongside high camp, dance, drag, and puppetry. For over two decades this project has brought people together across class, community, and political lines in shared public spaces.

As a playwright Miller has created work such as *Cracked Ice* (2009) and *The Golden Racket* (2011) which were produced at La Mama and Performance Space 122, and she maintains ongoing collaborations with dance makers and performance artists including Vaginal Davis, Jennifer Monson, Jon Kinzel, and Cathy Weis.

Miller has received numerous awards, including a 'Bessie,' an OBIE, a BAX 10, and the Ethyl Eichelberger award, and is the subject of the 1992 documentary *Juggling Gender*. She is also Professor in Humanities and Media Studies at the Pratt Institute in New York.
http://www.circusamok.org

Adrien Mondot is a multidisciplinary artist, computer scientist, and juggler, and Co-Founder of Compagnie Adrien M & Claire B with artist Claire Bardainne.

He creates stage performances involving digital and interactive artforms, juggling, dance, and music.

In 2004, Adrien Mondot founded his own company Adrien M. His first show *Convergence 1.0* took out the top prize at Jeunes Talents Cirque 2004. He then went on to win numerous other awards including the Grand Jury Prize at the International Dance and New Technologies Competition in Enghien-les-Bains, France in June 2009 for his performance work *Cinématique*.

In 2010 he met visual artist, graphic designer, and scenographer Claire Bardainne. A graduate from the Estienne and Paris Arts Déco schools, her approach focuses on imaginary realms portrayed in visual form, particularly in their capacity to reconstruct space. She co-founded the BW Studio in 2004 and works with a research team in Sociology of the Imaginary at CEAQ (Sorbonne, Paris).

After joining forces on their shared creative vision in 2011, Adrien Mondot and Claire Bardainne restructured the company to become Compagnie Adrien M & Claire B. Together they create digital and live artforms, ranging from stage performance to installations. Their approach puts the human experience at the centre of technological issues with a strong visual focus on the body, and with unique technology created in-house.

Their latest works include exhibitions *XYZT: Abstract Landscapes* (2011) and *Mirages & Miracles* (2017); installations such as *The shadow of the vapor* (2018); a monograph book entitled *Snow does not make sense* (2016); performances such as *Hakanaï* (2013), *The movement of air* (2015), and their upcoming project *Acqua Alta* (2019); as well as collaborations such as the performance *Pixel* (2014) created with choreographer Mourad Merzouki.

In 2015, Adrien Mondot and Claire Bardainne were jointly awarded the SACD Interactive Digital Creation Award.
https://www.am-cb.net/

Charlotte Mooney and Tina Koch are Co-Founders and Co-Directors of Ockham's Razor, the Contemporary Circus and physical theatre company based in London, UK. The two artists, together with Alex Harvey, the other Co-Founder of the company, are graduates of Circomedia, Centre for Contemporary Circus and Physical Theatre in Bristol, UK. On leaving Circomedia in 2004 the three artists co-founded Ockham's Razor.

The company combines aerials, acrobatics, and visual theatre with innovative bespoke apparatus designed by company members. After their breakthrough performance *Arc* (2007), a piece performed above the stage on an aluminium aerial raft for the London International Mime Festival, the company has gone on to perform extensively at international arts festivals throughout the world. Key works include *Memento Mori* (2004), an aerial duet that takes place on a suspended metal frame rather than a traditional trapeze bar; *The Mill* (2010–2015), first performed at the London International Mime Festival in 2010, an aerial performance featuring a large suspended wheel operated by a system of ropes and drums controlled by the performers; *Not Until We Are Lost* (2012–2016), an immersive work performed on aerial structures in and around the audience; and *Tipping Point* (2015-present), a work featuring five-metre metal poles which are transformed from traditional Chinese poles into inventive aerial and acrobatic apparatus. Their most recent work is *Belly of the Whale* (2018), an outdoor show featuring a giant semi-circular see-saw made of wood and steel that is controlled by the body weight of the performers.

Ockham's Razor received The Total Theatre and Jackson's Lane Award for Circus for *Tipping Point* at the Edinburgh Festival 2016.

https://www.ockhamsrazor.co.uk/

Philippe Petit is the high wire artist whose iconic walks have been celebrated in TV shows, films, books, songs, and major documentaries. His high wire walks include his notable 'illegal walks' staged without permission from the authorities. These include a walk between two towers of Notre Dame Cathedral (1971); a walk between the pylons on the North End of Sydney Harbour Bridge (1973); as well as his iconic walk between the Twin Towers of the World Trade Center (1974) which was the subject of the Academy Award winning documentary *Man on Wire* (2008) directed by James Marsh. In 2015, a 3D/IMAX biographical drama about Petit's Twin Towers walk entitled *The Walk,* starred Joseph Gordon-Levitt as Petit and was directed by Robert Zemeckis. In 1986, Petit re-enacted the famous 1859 walk made by the French Funambulist Blondin across Niagara Falls for an IMAX movie.

In 1989, at the invitation of the Mayor of Paris Jacques Chirac to make a walk to commemorate the French Bicentennial and Anniversary of the Declaration of the Rights of the Man and of the Citizen, Petit staged an inclined 700 metre walk from the Palais de Chaillot, crossing the Seine, to the second storey of the Eiffel Tower, in front of an audience of 250,000 people. Petit's other works include concerts, operas, and choreographed works for, or including, high wire performances.

Philippe Petit has published ten books, including *On the High Wire* (1983), *Funambule* (1991), *To Reach the Clouds: My Highwire Walk Between the Twin Towers* (2002), *Man on Wire* (2008), and *Creativity: The Perfect Crime* (2014). Petit has also created an ebook for TED Books, *Cheating the Impossible: Ideas and Recipes from a Rebellious High-Wire Artist.*

Petit has also performed numerous wire-walks inside the Cathedral of St John the Divine in New York City where he has been Artist-in-Residence for the last forty years. In 2006, Petit was awarded the first STREB Action Maverick Award, an award established by Elizabeth Streb to celebrate 'action specialists whose seemingly reckless journeys are, in reality, a society's insignia for bravery and courage' (Action Maverick, 2019, http://streb.org/action-maverick/).

Philippe Petit continues to practice each day and to have ongoing wire-walking projects.

https://www.youtube.com/channel/UCLczgJc_VokuACXvK8gK2gQ

Elizabeth Streb has dived through glass, walked down London's City Hall, dumped a ton of dirt on her head, and set herself on fire, among many other feats of extreme action. She founded the STREB EXTREME ACTION COMPANY in 1979 and established SLAM (STREB Lab for Action Mechanics) in Brooklyn, NY in 2003. Streb holds a Master of Arts in Humanities and Social Thought from New York University, a Bachelor of Science in Modern Dance from SUNY Brockport, and two honorary doctorates. She has received numerous awards and fellowships including the John D. and Catherine T. MacArthur Foundation 'Genius' Award, the Guggenheim Fellowship and a Doris Duke Artist Award. She is a member of the board of The Jerome and Camargo Foundations and has been a featured speaker at TEDxMET, the Institute for Technology and Education (ISTE), POPTECH, the Institute of Contemporary Art, The Brooklyn Museum of Art, the Rochester Institute of Technology, the Association of Performing Arts Presenters (APAP), the Penny Stamps Speaker Series, Chorus America, the University of Utah, as a Caroline Werner Gannett Project speaker in Rochester NY, and on NPR's Science Friday. Streb was the subject of Alec Wilkinson's profile in *The New Yorker* magazine. In 2010, Feminist Press published her book, *STREB: How to Become an Extreme Action Hero*. She is the subject of two recent documentaries. *Born to Fly*, directed by Catherine Gund (Aubin Pictures), is currently available on Netflix and iTunes. *OXD*, directed by Craig Lowy, follows STREB at the 2012 London Olympics and premiered at Doc NYC. In Spring 2018, Streb was invited to present a talk at TED 2018: THE AGE OF AMAZEMENT.
http://streb.org

Translations, Transcriptions, and Interpreting

Alice Brand transcribed and translated the conversations with Daniele Finzi Pasca and Phia Ménard with revisions by Louis Patrick Leroux.

Athena Pierquet transcribed and translated the conversations with Adrien Mondot, Johann Le Guillerm, and Philippe Decouflé with additional translation and revisions by Louis Patrick Leroux.

Dr Bénédicte André interpreted the conversation with Phia Ménard.

ACKNOWLEDGMENTS

Katie Lavers

Many thanks are due for the support I received in writing this book; in particular I would like to thank the Australian Academy of the Humanities for the Humanities Travelling Fellowship which supported the initial research for this book; the Western Australian Academy of Performing Arts (WAAPA) at Edith Cowan University for a research grant supporting transcriptions of many of the circus conversations; and also WAAPA for their ongoing support of the research which informs this book.

I would also like to thank all the Contemporary Circus creators we spoke to in writing this book for their generosity of spirit and for all the stimulating conversations. Thanks also to my co-writers Professor Louis Patrick Leroux and Dr Jon Burtt for all their work on the project and for the interchange of ideas and the discussions that have proved so inspiring. Lastly, thanks to the Editors at Routledge for their support in bringing this project to fruition.

Louis Patrick Leroux

I would like to acknowledge Concordia University and the National Circus School of Montreal through its Canada Industrial Research Chair in Circus Arts for their constant support of this research. A special thanks to Cyril Thomas at the Centre National des Arts du Cirque in France for facilitating certain continental conversations. Thanks to the artists who gave their time and candor for their interviews and also for other conversations and exchanges along the way. Many thanks are due to Katie Lavers and Jon Burtt for leading and driving this project.

Funding for travel and transcriptions of some of the interviews came from the *Fonds de recherche du Québec – Société et culture* (FRQ-SC). Interview transcriptions were by Alice Brand and Athena Pierquet, and translations into English by Alice Brand, Athena Pierquet, and Louis Patrick Leroux. Thanks to Alison Bowie and Alisan Funk, my research assistants on many intersecting projects during the past few years, for their consistency and ongoing conversation about what matters in research and how research matters.

Jon Burtt

I would like to acknowledge the contribution of Macquarie University for their ongoing support of this research. In particular, I would like to thank Professor Nicole Anderson, Head of the Department of Media, Music, Communication and Cultural Studies, for her continuous support and advice. In addition to all the other translators and transcribers of interviews acknowledged elsewhere in this book, I would also like to thank Dr Bénédicte André from Macquarie University for her work as an interpreter for the interview with Phia Ménard. A very big thank you to all the contributors to this volume. It was through the generosity of these busy artists that such a project was made to happen. The breadth of ideas that have emerged out of our conversations with these circus creators is inspiring and sheds light on the sheer diversity of practice happening in Contemporary Circus today. I would also like to acknowledge the editors and staff at Routledge for their ongoing support of the academic discipline of Circus Studies.

INTRODUCTION

Contemporary Circus provides a new and engaging point of entry for readers to explore the artform.

Although Contemporary Circus is now firmly established as one of the most popular forms of live performance, with shows featured as a major part of many arts festivals, there has as yet been comparatively little written about it. Much of the Circus Studies scholarship to date has been focused on the predecessors of Contemporary Circus, namely Traditional Circus and New Circus.[1] In particular, little attention has been paid to the voices of Contemporary Circus practitioners actively working in the field.

Contemporary Circus sets out to begin to redress this gap in the body of knowledge. The book centres on conversations that took place between 24 creative practitioners in Contemporary Circus, and three circus scholars. Extracts from these conversations form part of this book and sit alongside inductive critical theory and contextualising histories that the scholars developed in response to the conversations. Contemporary Circus is an increasingly hybrid artform, in which circus skills are melding with diverse disciplines from opera, to dance, to postdramatic theatre, physical theatre, through to commedia dell'arte. This book sets out to actively engage with this hybridity and, by bringing together the voices of practitioners in the field and combining them with critical theory from three Circus Studies scholars, to celebrate the inherent hybridity of the field in both form and content.

The three Circus Studies scholars who have co-authored this book, Katie Lavers, Louis Patrick Leroux, and Jon Burtt, have all published widely in the field, edited foundational Circus Studies books,[2] and, as creators and directors, have all produced and directed their own Contemporary Circus work.

The boundaries of Contemporary Circus are continually reshaping as the artform hybridises with different genres, and one book can only reflect a specific and limited range of practice within such a diverse field. For reasons of necessity and length the Contemporary Circus work represented in this book is restricted in geographical reach to Scandinavia, Europe, America, Canada, and Australia. The authors have chosen to speak with artists who themselves see their work either as being circus, or who see circus as an informing presence in their work. Above all, the authors have chosen to speak with artists whose work they find stimulating and inspiring.

Conversations took place with 24 creators from France, Australia, South Africa/Australia, Canada, England, the USA, Italy/Wales, Samoa/Australia, Switzerland, and Sweden, namely: Lachlan Binns and Jascha Boyce (Gravity and Other Myths), Tilde Björfors (Cirkus Cirkör), Kim 'Busty Beatz' Bowers (Hot Brown Honey), Shana Carroll (The 7 Fingers), David Clarkson (Stalker), Philippe Decouflé (Compagnie DCA), Fez Faanana (Briefs), Mike Finch (Circus Oz), Daniele Finzi Pasca (Compagnia Finzi Pasca), Sean Gandini (Gandini Juggling), Firenza Guidi (Elan Frantoio; NoFit State), Tina Koch and Charlotte Mooney (Ockham's Razor), Jo Lancaster and Simon Yates (Acrobat), Johann Le Guillerm (Cirque Ici), Yaron Lifschitz (Circa), Chelsea McGuffin (Company 2), Phia Ménard (Compagnie Non Nova), Jennifer Miller (Circus Amok), Adrien Mondot (Compagnie Adrien M & Claire B), Philippe Petit (High Wire Artist), and Elizabeth Streb (STREB Extreme Action).

Conversations were conducted in English or French, then transcribed and, where necessary, translated into English. After the initial conversations the artists were given the chance to reflect on the text of their transcribed conversations, and to edit, delete, or develop their ideas in the transcriptions as they wished. In the extracts of conversations included in this book, the voices of the authors have been edited in order to give more space to the voices of the Contemporary Circus creators.

The critical theory then emerged from the exploration of these transcribed conversations, and was built-up through cycles of discussion and reflection in response to the ideas and practices of the practitioners themselves. By placing the voices of these creators at the heart of this book, and introducing their ideas and knowledge into the critical discourse about Contemporary Circus in Circus Studies, the authors aim to address the absence of the voices of practitioners that currently exists; to bring attention to their ideas and particular approaches to practice; to respond with inductive critical theory and historical points of reference generated through reflection and discussion; and in this way to contribute to bridging the divide between practice and theory in Contemporary Circus.

Although there are numerous ways in which scholars could respond to these transcribed conversations, it is beyond the scope of this book to engage with all the ideas which have emerged, and as a result the authors see these conversations as having the potential to inspire further research. The critical theory and contextualisation in Part 1 of each chapter is intended to act as a focal point to initiate further dialogue and debate in the field.

The authors have chosen as a focusing device the lens of 'contestation' as a way of exploring, analysing, and interacting with some of the ideas contained in the extracts of conversations included in each particular section.

Circus Studies scholars often point to the unrest in Paris in May 1968 as the beginnings of New Circus. Julia Kristeva, the Bulgarian literary theorist and philosopher, who was present during the unrest in Paris in May that year, identifies the spirit of 'contestation' as the prevailing ethos at that time, and she defines this as the 'freedom to revolt, to call things into question.'[3] French Circus Studies scholar, Pascal Jacob, picks up on this quote from Kristeva when referring to the emergence of New Circus, writing, 'Everything which once defined the circus has been called into question, either patiently or with brutality.'[4] Although the word 'problematise' might be more widely used in English, the authors have chosen to also use the words 'contest' and 'contestation' in the sense of 'calling things into question' in the critical discourse in this book in order to retain this link with the ethos identified by Kristeva in relation to 1968 and the origins of New Circus.

As the authors studied the conversations, key themes became apparent which emerged as entry points to consider and engage with the field: *Apparatus, Politics, Performers,* and *New Work* and these themes form the basis of the four chapters. Each chapter is divided into two parts, Part 1 provides the inductive critical theory and historical framework which the authors have developed in response to the conversations with the creators which are included in Part 2. The critical theory and background have been placed first in order to provide context for the reader for the conversations that follow. These extracts of conversations are joined by short segues to provide linking ideas and some biographical information about the upcoming speaker.

Chapter 1, *Apparatus in Contemporary Circus,* explores new understandings of what may constitute circus apparatus, and the ways in which the idea of mastery over the apparatus is being problematised. An array of new forms of apparatus are being developed ranging from the traditional, to the bespoke, to the mutable, to the sculptural, and the virtual. Alongside this expanding notion of what can constitute circus apparatus, the notion of physical mastery over objects is being called into question. A newly emerging emphasis on more complex forms of interaction is allowing more nuanced readings of the work. 'Unjugglable' apparatus for jugglers, such as cacti and heavy tyres, are being used to call into question the notion of the performer's mastery over the apparatus;[5] in the same way mutable forms of apparatus, made from materials such as ice and soft clay that change form as they are handled, also contest notions of mastery. Different forms of interactive or virtual apparatus allow the performer to work with invisible forces such as infrared beams, air currents, or electricity, and in other instances control of the apparatus is being handed over to audience members and 'democratised' in new ways.[6]

In Part 2, the *Voices* section, conversations are included with the following nine creators, all of whom are noted for their distinctive approaches to working with apparatus: Philippe Petit (High Wire Artist), Shana Carroll (The 7 Fingers), Tina Koch and Charlotte Mooney (Ockham's Razor), Elizabeth Streb (STREB Extreme Action), Johann Le Guillerm (Cirque Ici), Phia Ménard (Compagnie Non Nova), David Clarkson (Stalker), and Adrien Mondot (Compagnie Adrien M & Claire B).

Chapter 2, *Politics in Contemporary Circus*, explores the ways in which the 'normate' is being contested in politically-driven work within the field. Disability Studies scholar Rosemarie Garland-Thomson defines the normate as the deeply hidden, internalised, socially-constructed figure which accrues cultural capital, and, as a result, is able to step easily into positions of authority. Garland-Thomson posits that the form of the normate is made visible through 'the array of deviant others whose marked bodies shore up the normate's boundaries.'[7]

When P. T. Barnum divided his circus into two parts, the big top and the side-show annexe, he situated the 'human menagerie' (a term popularised by Barnum) alongside the animal menagerie in the sideshow. In the sideshow annexe were the freaks or 'human curiosities,' the ethnographic displays of First Nations people, and the African American performers, all of whom were effectively excluded from the big top. This architectonic division of space and the subsequent division of the performers created by it were intrinsic to the development of the normate, which now, it can be argued, remains deeply internalised in Contemporary Circus. Performers of colour, First Nations performers, performers with adaptive bodies, and queer performers mark out the boundaries of this pervasive, still active normate, and they are joined by female performers who are now also often increasingly marginalised in much Contemporary Circus performance.

In Part 2, the *Voices* section, conversations are included with eight creators who are known for their engagement with political issues: Mike Finch (Circus Oz), Jennifer Miller (Circus Amok), Tilde Björfors (Cirkus Cirkör), Kim 'Busty Beatz' Bowers (Hot Brown Honey), Phia Ménard (Compagnie Non Nova), Jo Lancaster and Simon Yates (Acrobat), and Fez Faanana (Briefs).

Chapter 3, *Performers in Contemporary Circus*, explores the ways in which the presentation of bodily prowess in circus is being contested. In Traditional Circus, circus performers are often presented as being almost superhuman. Performers generally display their bodily prowess in order to elicit feelings of awe and wonder and also, with some acts, a visceral or kinaesthetic response from audience members. Now, in much Contemporary Circus, this presentation of bodily physical prowess is being contested, with many creators becoming increasingly interested in presenting the performer as being vulnerable, with the aim of revealing their essential humanity and weaknesses, and connecting with audience members on a human-to-human level. The range of approaches in relation to the presentation of prowess in performance is one of the many challenges that performers now face in Contemporary Circus. The diversity of practice presents challenges not only for performers, but also for circus schools, in deciding how best to equip graduates for the complexities of the field.

In Part 2, the *Voices* section, conversations are included with the following 10 creators working in the field of Contemporary Circus, many of whom are, or have been, performers themselves, speaking about what they look for in performers, and how they develop performers for their own work: Shana Carroll (The 7 Fingers), Yaron Lifschitz (Circa), Firenza Guidi (Elan Frantoio; NoFit State), Mike Finch (Circus Oz), Elizabeth Streb (STREB Extreme Action), Phia Ménard (Compagnie

Non Nova), Daniele Finzi Pasca (Compagnia Finzi Pasca), Philippe Decouflé (Compagnie DCA), Lachlan Binns and Jascha Boyce (Gravity and Other Myths).

Chapter 4, *New Work in Contemporary Circus*, explores the ways in which the choreographed circus act, the traditional structural unit of circus, is currently being problematised. Traditionally circus artists often had their own unique act created to display their particular skills and bodily prowess, and they often performed the same act for most of their performing lives, and this remains the case in some New Circus and some Contemporary Circus. Although some performers enjoy the repetition and familiarity of continually performing the same act, it can lead others to experience their act as a form of imprisonment.

With the influx of artists from different disciplines into New Circus, the drive to create new work emerged as a vital way of contesting the 'imprisonment' of the act. New approaches to the creation of work came into Contemporary Circus from fields such as postmodern dance, postdramatic theatre, and site-specific performance. Group-devising processes and improvisational tasks became a way of enabling the circus artist to become a contributing creator involved in the creation of new work.

Many Contemporary Circus creators are contesting the sole function of the circus act as being a vehicle for the display of prowess, and are instead developing new kinds of circus acts designed to hold meaning. These new kinds of circus acts are often embedded in a wide range of innovative contexts, for example within performance material such as floor-based movement or autobiographical text often created through group-devising processes involving the performers as co-creators of the work. Other creators are now contesting the structure of the act altogether and have begun creating work which focuses on flows of performance material rather than the stop-start rhythm of traditional act-based structures.

In Part 2, the *Voices* section, conversations are included with 12 creators speaking about their approaches to the circus act, and to the making of new work: Shana Carroll (The 7 Fingers), Chelsea McGuffin (Company 2), Lachlan Binns and Jascha Boyce (Gravity and Other Myths), Sean Gandini (Gandini Juggling), Yaron Lifschitz (Circa), Firenza Guidi (Elan Frantoio; NoFit State), Johann Le Guillerm (Cirque Ici), Philippe Decouflé (Compagnie DCA), Jo Lancaster and Simon Yates (Acrobat), and Jennifer Miller (Circus Amok).

This book, *Contemporary Circus,* is non-linear in structure and readers may enter at any point and proceed as they wish. Each chapter is stand alone with the relevant references and endnotes included. The book is extensively annotated and indexed to provide a comprehensive guide to the field with links provided to relevant videos of work, newspaper articles, blogs, and related scholarly journals and books. It is envisaged that the book will act as a foundational resource in the field of Circus Studies for artists, practitioners, researchers, students, and teachers in schools, colleges, circus schools, and universities.

Contemporary Circus is designed to be a stimulating launch pad into discussion and further reading, allowing readers to engage with the field in ways that give new insights into this absorbing artform.

Notes

1 Traditional Circus, or Modern Circus as it is sometimes called, was first created by Philip Astley in London in 1768, and was centred around horse-riding displays performed in a specially designed circus ring to a paying audience. The equestrian acts were interspersed with episodic acts such as juggling, clowning, and acrobatics. New Circus is the term used to describe the form of circus that is widely considered to have emerged out of the widespread social unrest in 1968. It contested the iconic elements of Traditional Circus such as the animals acts, the circus ring, and the ringmaster, and hybridised with different artforms. In the context of this book, Contemporary Circus as a term is used to describe forms of circus that were a continuation of New Circus after the late 1990s. Companies identifying as New Circus and Traditional Circus still continue around the world. For commentaries and approaches to definitions of the terms Contemporary Circus and New Circus, see also Martine Maleval (2014). *Sur la piste des cirques actuels*, Paris: L'Harmattan; Tomi Purovaara, Camilla Damkjær et al. (2012). *Introduction to contemporary circus*. Stockholm: Stuts/New Nordic Circus Network; and, Peta Tait and Katie Lavers (2016). Introduction. In P. Tait & K. Lavers (Eds.), *The Routledge Circus Studies reader* (pp. 1–11). Abingdon, Oxon & New York: Routledge.

The terms Contemporary Circus, Traditional Circus, Modern Circus, and New Circus have been capitalised to avoid contextual misinterpretation, i.e., 'This was a New Circus show…' as opposed to 'This was a new circus show…'
2 See Peta Tait and Katie Lavers (Eds.) (2016). *The Routledge Circus Studies reader*. Abingdon, Oxon & New York: Routledge; and, Louis Patrick Leroux and Charles R. Batson (Eds.) (2016). *Cirque global: Québec's expanding circus boundaries*. Montreal-Kingston: McGill-Queen's University Press.
3 Julia Kristeva (2002). *Revolt, she said* (Sylvère Lotringer, Ed., B. O'Keefe, Trans.). New York and Los Angeles: Semiotext(e), p. 12.
4 Pascal Jacob (2008). The circus artist today: Analysis of the key competences, p. 12. http://www.fedec.eu/en/articles/325-miroir01---part-1-the-circus-artist-today---analysis-of-the-key-competences-2008.
5 See Phia Ménard, 12; pp. 37–8.
6 See Adrien Mondot, 14; pp. 42–8; and David Clarkson, pp. 39–42.
7 Rosemarie Garland-Thomson (1997). *Extraordinary bodies: Figuring physical disability in American culture and literature*. New York, NY: Columbia University Press, p. 8.

References

Garland-Thomson, R. (1997). *Extraordinary bodies: Figuring physical disability in American culture and literature*. New York: Columbia University Press.

Jacob, P. (2008). The circus artist today: Analysis of the key competences. *FEDEC*, 1–49. Retrieved from http://www.fedec.eu/en/articles/325-miroir01---part-1-the-circus-artist-today---analysis-of-the-key-competences-2008

Kristeva, J. (2002). *Revolt, she said* (Sylvère Lotringer, Ed., B. O'Keefe, Trans.), New York and Los Angeles: Semiotext(e).

Leroux, L. P. & Batson, C. R. (Eds.) (2016). *Cirque global: Québec's expanding circus boundaries*. Montreal-Kingston: McGill-Queen's University Press.

Maleval, M. (2014). *Sur la piste des cirques actuels*. Paris: L'Harmattan.

Purovaara, T., Damkjær, C., Degerbøl, S., Muukkonen, K., Verwilt, K., & Waage, S. A. (2012). *An introduction to contemporary circus*. Stockholm: Stuts/New Nordic Circus Network.

Tait, P., & Lavers, K. (2016). Introduction. In P. Tait & K. Lavers (Eds.), *The Routledge Circus Studies reader* (pp. 1–11). Abingdon, Oxon & New York: Routledge.

Tait, P. & Lavers, K. (Eds.) (2016). *The Routledge Circus Studies reader*. Abingdon, Oxon & New York: Routledge.

1

APPARATUS IN CONTEMPORARY CIRCUS

Apparatus in Contemporary Circus – contesting mastery

Contemporary Circus performance is now no longer a unified field of practice but instead is an artform distinguished by the enormous variety of work it encompasses, ranging from the immersive work of NoFit State Circus under the artistic direction of Firenza Guidi, to the performance-art-based work of Phia Ménard who juggles with ice, to the stripped-back acrobatics of Circa, to the anarchic biting humour and commedia dell'arte of Acrobat.

Through the conversations that the authors have had with the creators included in the *Voices* section of this chapter, it has become clear that in relation to apparatus some major changes are occurring and that these mark some fundamental distinctions which are emerging between Traditional Circus and Contemporary Circus.[1] These distinctions are predicated on emerging extended definitions of what exactly can constitute a circus apparatus and what its function might be, and also on an evolving process of questioning and contesting the possible nature of the performer's relationship with their apparatus.[2]

In Traditional Circus, 'apparatus' could perhaps best be defined as a piece of equipment that enables the performer to demonstrate their own bodily prowess, their mastery over the object, and in addition their mastery over forces such as gravity. This Traditional Circus understanding of what constitutes apparatus is now being contested in a number of diverse ways in Contemporary Circus.

A radically extended definition of apparatus is proposed by the Italian philosopher Giorgio Agamben. In his 2009 essay 'What is an Apparatus?' he writes: 'I shall call an apparatus literally anything that has in some way the capacity to capture, orient, determine, intercept, model, control, or secure the gestures, behaviors, opinions, or discourses of living beings.'[3]

Agamben builds on Michel Foucault's work[4] listing apparatus as, 'Not only therefore prisons, madhouses, the panopticon, schools, confession, factories, disciplines, juridical measures, and so forth (whose connection with power is in a certain sense evident), but also the pen, writing, literature, philosophy, agriculture, cigarettes, navigation, computers, cellular telephones,'[5] and he continues, 'today there is not even a single instant in which the life of individuals is not modeled, contaminated, or controlled by some apparatus.'[6]

This extended definition of apparatus can be seen as radical and transformative and lies at the heart of many of the innovative developments in Contemporary Circus. New performance works using apparatus made from materials such as ice and clay, which are mutable and transform during the performance, or virtual apparatus which allow the performer and the audience to interact with invisible forces, such as infrared beams, are radically extending understandings of what circus apparatus can be.

In the same essay Giorgio Agamben goes on to propose that the world is split into two, that is into living beings and apparatus, and he suggests that subjectivity emerges as a third element arising from the interaction between the two.

Expanding on this idea further, Dance Studies scholar André Lepecki proposes that the possible relationships with apparatus are rapidly becoming more complex, and that

> as we produce objects, we produce apparatuses that subjugate and diminish our own capacity to produce non-subjugated subjectivities. As we produce objects, we find ourselves being produced by objects. In the struggle between the living and the inorganic, it is not only as if objects are taking command – subjectivity itself is becoming a kind of objecthood.[7]

This changing understanding of possible interrelationships with objects, has led some philosophers to describe one of the complex new kinds of subjectivities that can emerge as creating a form of 'extended self,' a term coined in 1998 by the philosophers Andy Clark and David Chalmers.[8] They argue that, 'essentially, the mind and the self are extended to those devices that help us perform what we ordinarily think of as our cognitive tasks.'[9] Philosopher Michael Lynch, speaking about this idea of the extended self, says that Clark and Chalmers are proposing that 'the shopping list, for example, becomes part of our memory, the mind spilling out beyond the confines of our skull to encompass anything that helps it think.'[10] This rethinking of the relationship with apparatus is emphasised still further by Lynch, who writes,

> Smartphones were only the first step towards the world we live in now – the 'internet of things.' More and more devices – from refrigerators to cars to socks – interact with the internet on a nearly constant basis, leaving a trail of digital exhaust. That means greater convenience, but increasingly it also means that our devices are becoming 'ready at hand' as Heidegger would have said. We've begun to see them as extensions of ourselves.[11]

Given this changing and increasingly complex understanding of the nature of the relationship between people and things, the Traditional Circus relationship in which the artist demonstrates mastery over the apparatus, can be seen as restricting and limiting the range of contemporary subjectivities that could be investigated through performance with objects.

Some Contemporary Circus creators and performers, by exploring an increasingly diverse range of possible relationships with apparatus, are beginning to negotiate new, more nuanced subjectivities. One interesting paradox which lies at the centre of these new forms of Contemporary Circus is that the mastery of the apparatus is, in and of itself, a pre-requisite – a vital element in the performative process of being able to effectively problematise the notion of mastery, and it is perhaps this tension which makes this area of development in Contemporary Circus so compelling.

Apparatus and training

The relationship between the circus performer and their particular apparatus has always been intense. It is often painful and is, for the most part, central to their circus practice, and the body of the circus performer is often marked, calloused, and scarred by the interaction. Contemporary Circus students in particular, until they become accustomed to working hours a day with their apparatus, often spend breaks between training sessions comparing, and sometimes documenting on social media, the blisters, scratches, and scars they have received from working on their own specific apparatus.

Circus performers spend years interacting with the particular objects that they use as props, or apparatus, in their acts, often working with the same piece of apparatus many hours a day, at least five days a week, over an extended period of many years. Their muscles change. Their body changes shape in response to the specialised physical demands placed on it by the interaction with their particular apparatus. This intense relationship between performer and apparatus in circus not only shapes the performer's body, changing the structure of their muscles and their physical appearance, but in some cases has also been proven to physically alter the structure of their brain.

Brain scans taken of 24 people who had practised juggling for half an hour a day over a period of six weeks showed radical change when compared with a control group of 24 non-jugglers over the same period. In this short six-week period of the trial, the brains of those learning juggling had increased not only in grey matter, as had been shown in previous studies of juggling, but also, as this study undertaken in 2009 by Jan Scholtz and colleagues at Oxford University shows, had increased in 'white matter,' a term used for 'mostly axons – outgrowths of nerve cells that connect different cells.'[12]

> Before and after this training period, the researchers scanned the brains of the jugglers along with those of 24 people who didn't do any juggling,

using a technique called diffusion tensor imaging that reveals the structure of white matter. They found that there was no change in the brains of the non-jugglers, but the jugglers grew more white matter in a part of the parietal lobe – an area involved in connecting what we see to how we move.[13]

Contemporary Circus performers now most often specialise in one form of circus apparatus. In many cases professional circus schools expect the student auditioning for entrance to already have a prior speciality with a particular apparatus. If accepted into the school, the student is often expected to commit to the same piece of circus apparatus, and to continue to specialise in it, dedicating themselves to mastering it. The student will spend the next three years developing the physical capacity to perform on or with that specific apparatus at peak level. They will focus on conditioning the body to best suit the apparatus of choice by, for example, developing the increased upper body strength necessary for aerial straps, or the particular extreme back and hip flexibility necessary for lyra (aerial hoop), as well as undertaking extended periods of training on the actual apparatus itself.

In Contemporary Circus, which also has an underlying pressure of innovation, training is undertaken first of all to master the pre-existing tricks already developed for the apparatus, and to work on the flow and transition between these skills, and then on developing new skills. In the professional circus schools this is all mostly undertaken with the ultimate aim of being able to create an innovative act through which to present mastery over the apparatus in the final performance at graduation.

New and emerging forms of apparatus

Innovative forms of circus apparatus have emerged in the last 50 years which have now been widely adopted in Contemporary Circus.

Acrobat Alexander Moiseev is credited as being the Concept Creator of the Russian Bar in 1978.[14] In the Russian Bar act a fibreglass bar is balanced between the shoulders of two porters (or bases). An acrobat stands on the bar, and in coordination with these porters, can be propelled up into the air to perform turns and tumbles high in the air above the bar.[15] Alexander Moiseev twice performed with the Russian Bar at the International Circus Festival of Monte-Carlo winning a Gold and a Silver Clown. He went on to become Head Coach and Acrobatic Advisor with Cirque Du Soleil, and Advisor on the show *Alegria* (1994).

André Simard, a former Olympic gymnast and then National Coach of the Canadian gymnastics team, worked as a coach at the National Circus School in Montreal for ten years, before going on to be a member of Cirque du Soleil's permanent creation team. In the early 1990s, Simard developed a new, secure safety line system enabling acrobats to perform complex aerial turns and tumbles safely during aerial high flying. His invention has revolutionised aerial acrobatics.

In 1995, Simard also created the tissu aérien or silks act.[16] This apparatus consists of two lengths of synthetic material suspended from a spinning shackle or ring. The performer climbs the silks wrapping the drapes around their body and is able to execute acrobatic moves such as tumbles or drops down the length of the fabric supported by the strength, stretch, and relative non-perishability of the synthetic material. The same apparatus can also be used to perform spectacular flying sequences and acrobatic aerial partnering acts.

The Cyr wheel is another relatively recent circus innovation.[17] This piece of circus equipment was created by Daniel Cyr, Co-Founder of Cirque Éloize, in Montreal.[18] An aluminium, or steel, mono-ring, it enables performers to execute spins, inversions, and acrobatic moves not possible with the German wheel, the traditional wheel with two rings. Daniel Cyr premiered the Cyr wheel at the Festival Mondial du Cirque de Demain in Paris in 2003, where he won the Silver Medal for his act. The Cyr wheel is now a staple piece of circus apparatus and has been seen in many major circus works, including the Cirque Éloize shows *Nomade, Rain, iD, Cirkopolis*, and *Saloon*, and Cirque du Soleil's *Luzia*.

More recently, however, some Contemporary Circus creators are beginning to call into question many of the existing assumptions about what can constitute circus apparatus, and also to contest the restrictions inherent in the conventional performed relationship of mastery over the apparatus by the performer. Some artists are asking whether the actual physical material of the apparatus itself needs to be stable; whether the performed relationship between the performer and the apparatus has to remain one of mastery; and, if the relationship of mastery is contested, how the new emerging subjectivities between people and objects can best be explored and identified through circus. Other artists are asking whether the apparatus itself actually needs to be visible or whether it can in fact consist of invisible forces. Through the exploration of existing assumptions in relation to apparatus, and through responding to some philosophical provocations, some remarkable new work has started to emerge in Contemporary Circus.

The changing complexity of contemporary interactions with objects is firstly visible in how performers are conceptualising and speaking about their relationship with their apparatus. Philippe Petit, the high wire artist, for example, instead of describing a relationship of mastery, speaks about the interaction with his wire as being one that requires him to actively listen to, and respond to, the apparatus. Petit also describes how he has created a daily ritual that he now performs 'to greet' his equipment.

Sean Gandini, Co-Founder of Gandini Juggling, describes the ever-present risk of the 'drop' in juggling, and how this element in the narrative of mastery over the apparatus can become an obsession in the mind of the juggler. He talks about how the company has explored numerous approaches to combating the fear of the drop, and how the drop itself has been contested in the company's work *Smashed*. Near the end of the show, there is a section where the stage is set with china teapots and teacups which cover the floor while the performers stand amongst them juggling with apples. In a decisive moment, the performers free themselves from the debilitating fear of the 'drop,' by allowing the apples to drop onto the floor smashing the china. In this way, the performers actively contest the restraints that denote conventional mastery in juggling and free themselves from the fear of the drop, and '*Smashed* finishes with ten minutes of furious dropping and breaking everything.'[19]

Phia Ménard, performer and Founder of Company Non Nova, contests the notion of mastery through her concept of 'unjugglability' in which she problematises her own mastery of apparatus by juggling with objects that are theoretically 'unjugglable,' for example cacti, or heavy tires. This decision to juggle with the 'unjugglable' brings the performer into a direct interaction with an object or force in which the limits of the performer's control are made clear to spectators, and the limits of mastery are revealed, and, through this process, the humanity and vulnerability of the artist also become clear. Ménard herself describes her work saying, 'Paradoxically, the juggler usually masters the object, but I am a juggler who does not master matter, but rather one who follows matter. By this I mean that I must comply with the laws of matter.'[20]

Other artists are contesting the traditional performance of mastery by the performer over their apparatus by focusing instead on the poetic and metaphorical potential inherent in the relationship between performer and apparatus. Shana Carroll, one of the Co-Founders of The 7 Fingers in Montreal, and herself a trapeze artist who performed for seven years with Cirque du Soleil, describes the metaphorical potential of swinging trapeze, saying that through the performer's efforts the trapeze swings upwards fighting the effects of gravity, hangs for a moment suspended in space, and then is drawn back down by the pull of gravity. She says that this movement can be read as having the metaphorical potential to suggest yearning, and a striving to attain something, only to be defeated, but then with the next swing a continued striving to achieve something against all the odds.[21]

In some of the more memorable Contemporary Circus work that is being developed, the performers reveal a unique physical narrative or poetics, which emerges through the particularity of their own body and their own lived experience, in relation to the metaphors inherent in the apparatus. This is the work where the interaction between the physical language, the performer, and the apparatus moves beyond spectacle and visceral or kinaesthetic response, and beyond a demonstration of mastery over the apparatus, into an area with the power to explore complex nuanced emotions and subjectivities.

Some artists are beginning to work with unconventional materials to extend the potential for new relationships to develop between the performer and the apparatus. Phia Ménard, in her work *P.P.P.* (*Position Parralèle au Plancher*) (2008), uses ice as the material for her juggling props. The apparatus proves highly mutable, with the balls of ice changing to water as she juggles with them. The show sets in place a powerful metaphorical interaction between performer and apparatus. *P.P.P.* was made at the same moment in time that Phia Ménard transitioned from male to female when her body was undergoing profound changes. The apparatus as it changes from ice into water reflects the changes that were taking place in the performer's body as she transitioned from male to female and can be seen as embodying a metaphor of mutability of the body and of identity. This work sets in place a new possibility for apparatus, one of material mutability.[22]

Other jugglers have continued investigating this idea of apparatus being mutable. Juggler Jimmy Gonzalez won the Gold Prize at Festival Mondial du Cirque de Demain in 2015 for his piece *D'Argile*, an act in which he juggles with wet clay.[23] In *D'Argile*, which was developed in part during an arts residency at Montreal's Museum of Fine Arts alongside a Rodin exhibition, Gonzalez creates a sense of play by altering his apparatus as he juggles, pulling and rolling the clay to create different-sized juggling balls, and constantly changing the numbers of balls he juggles with by remoulding the clay as he performs. At the end of the act he presses the clay over the surface of his face to form a mask, creating an archetypal image of clay as flesh.

Other creators are problematising the traditional understanding of the function of equipment as being a means to enable the performer to display their mastery over the apparatus, by developing new bespoke apparatus with entirely new functionalities. Tina Koch and Charlotte Mooney, directors of the UK circus company, Ockham's Razor, build new pieces of apparatus in order to destabilise the expectations of conventional circus equipment that spectators bring to a performance. Johann Le Guillerm builds unique sculptural apparatus for his solo performances which enable him to investigate three-dimensionality, spatiality, and understandings of different points of view, while Elizabeth Streb builds new forms of equipment in order to explore her performers' relationships with the apparatus and space in terms of rate, speed, and physical forces.

In Phia Ménard's work, *L'Après-Midi d'un Foehn*, the actual act of juggling itself and the manipulation of the apparatus are presented as having been handed to an external source of energy.[24] In this work, Ménard takes plastic bags and ties them into the shape of small human-like figures. A jet of air lifts them into the air, animates them, and effectively juggles with them, moving them through the space. This work presents the source of energy and the control of the apparatus as having been moved away from the human, to a natural force, to jets of air, which effectively juggle with the small human-like figures created from the plastic bags.

In the same way that Ménard questioned the solidity or unchangeable quiddity of the juggling prop in *P.P.P.*, in *L'Après-Midi d'un Foehn* she has moved the performance of control of the juggling pathways away from the human, to external forces to create a new form of juggling. The scene is post-apocalyptic in essence, as the audience sees the wind juggling with these small twisting human figures fashioned from plastic bags. The visible human control has been removed, and we see non-human forces juggling with apparatus formed from what is left of the human, their non-biodegradable detritus.

The French juggler Adrien Mondot also investigates new questions about the nature of apparatus as he explores the disappearance of the object and the emergence of the virtual. In the conversation with him in the *Voices* section of this chapter Mondot says that,

> the actual apparatus always seemed to me like a pretext – you could say a working aid to approaching movement … our working tool is actually forces, for all circus artists: we create with forces … Gravitational forces, but also muscular forces, the axes of rotations that permit us to do things. The forces that we have in play. For me in the beginning my focus was the juggling balls, but in fact I am more interested in it being these forces.[25]

In this way Mondot engages with apparatus as a means of approaching movement and allowing engagement with forces, and he manifests this in his performances which are created in interactive environments. The interface itself acts as a form of apparatus allowing the performers, and sometimes audience members, to interact with invisible forces.

Part 2 of this chapter, the *Voices* section, includes conversations with nine creators who are all known for their distinctive approaches to working with different kinds of apparatus: Philippe Petit, (High Wire Artist), Shana Carroll (The 7 Fingers), Tina Koch and Charlotte Mooney (Ockham's Razor), Elizabeth Streb (STREB Extreme Action), Johann Le Guillerm (Cirque Ici), Phia Ménard (Compagnie Non Nova), David Clarkson (Stalker), and Adrien Mondot (Compagnie Adrien M & Claire B).

Apparatus in Contemporary Circus – voices

This *Voices* section starts with a conversation with the French Contemporary Circus artist, Philippe Petit, the renowned high wire performer who has made many world-famous walks, including his walk between the Twin Towers in New York on 7 August 1974. This walk is one that has remained permanently seared into the collective psyche, and, since the destruction of the Twin Towers on 11 September 2001, seems to have only gained in iconic potency.[26]

Petit first imagined and conceived his walk between the Twin Towers at the age of 18 and he went on to plan it over a period of six years. Then, with the help of friends, he illegally rigged his wire between the Twin Towers and walked at the previously unheard of, and as yet unsurpassed, height of 1350 feet, or 411 metres above the ground. Petit walked untethered between the Twin Towers for 45 minutes making eight passes before eventually being called off the wire by police and being arrested.[27]

Petit describes himself as a rebellious inventor, an innovator, and, as he says in this interview, 'I think if I'd been born into a Traditional Circus family, I'd have become a normal artist, not a rebellious inventor.'[28]

In this interview Petit describes his relationship with his high wire as involving listening to the equipment and being responsive to it, in a process similar to a dialogue, and he identifies this relationship as the key to making art instead of just performing technique.

★★★★★

Philippe Petit

We have read that you still train three hours a day. Is that right?
Philippe Petit: Yes, except on Sunday, when I don't.

So what is it about this continued training that is important to you and your sense of self?
Philippe Petit: You know, it's a strange thing but I never ask myself that question. It's something that's so automatic, so natural in my life, that I have to think a second before being able to answer. I think basically it's that the arts that I practice – juggling, magic, high wire – are so ingrained in me because I didn't go to any schools, I learned them by myself. And anything that you learn by yourself, you have to fight for. And when you fight for something, that thing is going to stay inside you, very powerfully for the rest of your life. So I think I have no choice. I have all this magic, and juggling, and wire inside me and I have to cultivate it. That's one part of my answer. The other part is that I am a perfectionist at heart. Of course we don't find perfection often on earth, rarely in human beings. But a quest for perfection is enough for me, and so I do that. So that's another reason for practicing every day, it allows you to get closer to perfection.

And it's a dialogue with my passion, with what I love to do. If I don't practice, I don't have this marriage, this dialogue. But when I practice it, I revisit it every day. Because of this special way that I do my practice I'm able to revisit my passion, and that's the basic reason why I practice. I love the circus, I love the circus so much. It was one of my first loves. It is because of going to the circus and going to circus rehearsals that I became the artist I am, one of the reasons. So I love circus so much that I am rarely satisfied when I go to see a circus. Either a modern circus, that claims to reinvent everything, or in an old-fashioned circus, a small one, or a three-ring circus, whatever, I am rarely satisfied with what I see. Maybe it is because I love it so much that I want it to always be more.

I think if I'd been born into a Traditional Circus family, I'd have become a normal artist, not a rebellious inventor.

What sort of body-mind preparation do you go through to ready yourself for extreme wire walks?
Philippe Petit: My preparation, either to practice on the high wire on a daily basis, or to practice for a specific big walk I am going to perform, is probably very different from what you see wire-walkers do in the circus. How can I start to explain it? There are so many, so many things that are different. I pay attention to small details and I pay attention to enormously important points.

I will give you a small detail. Very often, no not very often, all the time in the circus, the wire-walkers don't work very high. They have a little platform, usually a disc of wood or metal at the top of an X, on both sides of their practice wire, or performing wire. And then they stand on that platform and then they put their feet down on the wire because the wire is hooked underneath the platform. And I don't like that at all. I think it's a wrong poetic thing to climb down onto a wire. I think you have to climb up. So, on all my platforms, and you see that sometimes on a high wire, very high, with many people and pyramids, the wire is above the platform. So, you are standing on the platform, and when you want to start walking you climb up onto the wire, which to me is much more interesting, it has a subliminal feeling of elevation, which is what a wire-walker is – a wire-walker should become a bird. That's one thing.

I also do not believe in silly, mechanical repetition. If you are a juggler or magician, or here in this instance we are talking about the high wire, and if you believe that you should do the same movement 2,000 times, you are an imbecile. You will not progress. But if you do the same movement a few times, not with the feeling of a robot, but instead with the feeling of a poet, and of an inventor, and of a creator, if you do a few moves, a few times in a row with the feeling of an explorer, you are going to achieve a lot, you are going to make a lot of progress. You are going to make a lot of discoveries that repeating the same moves thousands of times will not give you. So that's another difference.

Another thing is that I take my practice session very seriously and since it's not the cold repetition scenario, it has a climbing line of drama and of difficulty and of tension and of work.

So, I will give you an example, I have created, nobody else does this, I have created a series of walks from very simple to very complex. And I practice those walks one after the other. There are so many I actually made a list, and that list is attached, it's posted on my departure platform when I practice and I look, 'okay, I have done this, so now I am going on to the next one.' I just read through them so I can just concentrate on the walk and not concentrate on remembering the order. And I do those walks once usually and if I am satisfied,

FIGURE 1.1 Philippe Petit, Eiffel Tower Arrival. Photo: Michel Kerstgens/Collection Philippe Petit.

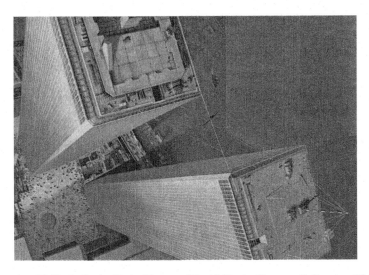

FIGURE 1.2   Philippe Petit, Twin Towers, World Trade Center. Collection Philippe
Petit.

I go to the next one. If I am not satisfied with what I have done, I do it again
until I am satisfied. So, you see, it's not a cold repetition, it's a satisfying process.
That's how I do it. At the end of my list are very complex walks that nobody
else in the world does, only me.

Also, my practice is quite different because of the passion and poetry I put
into my work. For example, before I start practicing on the wire, really, I have
a few little walks that I do, which I call 'les mis-en-fil' which means 'putting
myself into the wire.' So they are not really exercises, they are simple little
walks that I do for my feet to meet the wire, because my feet need to meet the
wire before I'm going to really walk. So there are simple little walks with the
variations of looking, variations of speed, and variations of gliding my foot
onto the wire, before I put my weight on one leg. Those things would probably
make a circus wire-walker laugh, because they would think, 'What is he doing?
This is ridiculous.'

So anyway, I will give you another example, with the juggling, before I start
practicing juggling, I say 'hello' in a child-like and poetic way to my props. I
don't take a club and start juggling like you would see in all circus schools in the
world. I greet them and it's something that I invented, I call it 'salut à l'objet' and
the translation could be 'greeting the props.' Before taking a prop and putting it
into action you need to say hello to the props, you need to gently wake yourself
up to the props and wake up the props to you. And so I have invented for all of
my props, a little like the 'mis-en-fil,' like putting myself on the wire, a little
'salut à l'objet,' a little greeting of the props before I start practicing with them.
So, these are just two or three examples but, I have 200, I could write a book.
Actually, I wrote a chapter of a book on how I practice.[29]

That's how it's very different than seeing acrobats in the circus, you know, 'practicing,' and very rarely do they actually practice. What they do is they 'rehearse,' they rehearse the show that they are going to do.

That is fascinating because so much of the traditional training is framed as being all about the mastery of the object, and what you're talking about is not only how you affect the wire, but also how the wire affects you, and it's a circular process.
Philippe Petit: Absolutely, and without that circular process, without that marriage, without that dialogue, there is no art, there is only a technique. I mean if you read 'Le Funambule' by Jean Genet you would see he describes a young acrobat, who he says is asked to fall in love with the wire.[30]

In India there is the traditional rope called Mallakhamb which is considered to be sacred, and before anyone can climb it they have to perform a special greeting to the rope.[31] The rope is sacred to Hanuman, the Hindu Monkey God. So, the climber approaches the rope with respect because they believe it is powerful, and can kill them, and can flick them off with one move of its tail.
Philippe Petit: Absolutely, and also this chemistry you could just relate to its essence. It's basically, it's very cold and uninteresting to just practice technique. What you have to do is just to work with your body and your soul. Without that marriage, one is nothing, and there is no art.

So, do you feel in a sense that it's a kind of spiritual connection that you have with the wire?
Philippe Petit: Oh yes, absolutely. First, in those little walks to meet the wire before I really practice, I always start barefoot, because barefoot is more difficult, the feet don't really glide easily. But, also barefoot I get the temperature of the cable. And the real temperature, 'Is it cold? Is it warm? Is it too hot?' Sometimes it burns my feet. Yes, I really have to converse with the wire and there are many ways to do that.

And do you feel that the way you practice enables you to reach spiritual parts of yourself that you can't reach in any other way?
Philippe Petit: Absolutely, and it's so surprising and amazing to me that when I practice in that special way which is always my way, I make a lot of unusual progress and unique discoveries, to the point that I am so amazed that after 50 years of working on the wire or more, I still discover things and I still make progress. I actually have this journal, this practice journal, which you can find out about in my book Creativity: The Perfect Crime. And in those journals which I have for juggling, for the wire, for all my art, I write the day, and I write the weather, and I write any observations, and anything that's happening. And it's amazing, it amazes me to see that each time I practice there is something new, unheard of, amazing things happening, and that's why I write it down.

And it's an incredible thing when you have a kind of spiritual pathway even though it may look like simple repetition from outside, inside you're feeling different things and it feels like a real journey.

Philippe Petit: Yes, and that's exactly what I was describing a second ago, when I practice, it's an adventure, it's a journey and an adventure; a journey is never a repetition. Even though I repeat things, it's never repetition. It's an adventure.

So, we did read that you've also created works that are plays and operas for the high wire, are you still doing that?

Philippe Petit: Actually, most of my work on the wire was never just a walk. It was to present, as I like to describe it, a piece of theatre and I'm probably the only wire-walker who does that. Any other wire-walker, they put a wire between two spires of a cathedral, they walk from one side to the other, maybe they walk again, and that's it. And then they come down, and say, 'I walked.'

Although I use the phrase, 'I walked,' it's always a performance with costume, with music, sometimes even with actors and a script. I have done some opera on the high wire. And very rarely in my life I just walk. I can give you the biggest example, well, besides walking the Twin Towers, which was a very strange kind of performance.

Legally, I did an immense walk of 700 yards inclined from the ground, over the River Seine to the second story of the Eiffel Tower. It was a show for the Bicentennial of France with [Jacques] Chiraq on the other side, and I was bringing him a historic document via the air.[32] So that show had seven types of music that I was directing from the wire. It had three different costumes that I changed into while I was on the wire, and it had chapters like in a book and you could follow my theatre work from the programme. So, that's an example. I mean, when you are doing such an immense walk with the wind and with the difficulty of being in the air like that, nobody would think of theatre. And actually, that's the only thing I am interested in.

In the history of funambulists, they often walked in coronations and important events like that, and they were considered to be messengers from the gods who brought good fortune if the walk was successful.

Philippe Petit: Oh yes. There is no serious and accurate history of high wire-walking in print. They are all full of mistakes and most of them are written by amateurs and not by historians of the wire. One day I would like to write a definitive history, but I'm not that old yet!

Anyway, many of those historical accounts show, if you rely on engravings and stories printed in the old days, yes, that wire-walking was mostly in the seventeenth and eighteenth century, and that very often the walks were taken as a celebration for the coronation of a king or queen or sometimes a messenger would bring something to somebody. So, yes, it had meaning and it had in a way a little bit of theatre to it.

That idea of connection with the gods as well, and divination, was a sort of spiritual connection, too.

Philippe Petit: Yes. The connection to the gods is an interesting aspect. When I was talking about climbing up on to the wire, if you pushed that metaphor higher, pun intended, then when the wire-walker does an inclined walk sometimes the wire-walker comes from the top of the church steeple and goes all the way down to earth, and I find that ridiculous and anti-poetic, because the wire-walker is as close to a bird as a human being can ever get. And what is beautiful about a wire-walker is to see the tiny man or woman walking very high up in the sky. So, when I do an incline, I always go from the earth, like almost saying 'bye-bye' to the audience and to my terrestrial world, and I disappear into the sky, so to speak, I climb up to meet the gods. And actually, one day I did exactly that because, it was in Israel, and at the end of the incline, I had a helicopter picking me up and we disappeared into the sky and some people thought it was like a vision of God.[33]

In terms of balance and maintaining balance on the wire, do you see any metaphorical aspects to that for you?

Philippe Petit: Absolutely, and I always react very negatively to people who want to explain balance, like in the circus schools, people who say, 'Put your hands like this, and then do this, do that.' Balance is a miracle and balance is a sense, and balance is another worldly continent, and you cannot experience and experiment with balance without, again, your body and soul. So it is not by putting the student's arms in a certain position that you are going to have them understand balance and make progress in balance. Balance has to do with your appetite for victory, of being able to walk on a wire. And balance has to do with a certain presentation of yourself on the wire, a certain spirit, a certain mood. You must not be sheepish, or timid. You have to be victorious. You have to be beautiful. You have to be proud of trying to balance, which is such an impossible thing. And the minute you have that feeling, the minute you take it so seriously, with that naive poetry that I'm trying to describe, that moment you are going to make immense progress because to walk on a wire you have to be majestic. You have to be proud and beautiful to look at.

'It's a miracle, it's a sense, it's another worldly continent.' That is such a great image of balance.

Philippe Petit: Yes, and you know talking about the miracle of balance, I can tell you something very strange is that I am my own witness to the miracle of balance. I consider, sometimes I consider, walking on the wire is the easiest thing on earth to do, much easier than walking on the ground where a bus might kill you. But on the wire nobody can touch you. When I walk on the wire, when I practice, sometimes I feel the miracle of each step. How incredible that I'm able to, or rather the body knows after all those repetitions, how to put each foot exactly at the centre of the wire and glide perfectly, and move in unison with the wire.

So, I realise the miracle of it, and then what actually I am amazed about is that I'm able to create that miracle, every step, every second. So, that also is a poetic statement, that you have to be ready to be impressed by your being the magician, being the miracle creator. With a certain humility, of course.

Could you speak about your way of rehearsing?

Philippe Petit: It has to do with the spatial chemistry. Let's imagine I am travelling and I go to a circus school and they invite me to put a little wire between two Xs or we use some of the equipment that is there. I have found out that most people never think of the space, the relationship of your body to the space.

So, let's say if I'm in a room that is not a circular room, if it's a square or a rectangle, and it has door and windows, I will never put my wire or I will never agree to practice on a wire that is set in a diagonal, or in an askew way, or close to a door so that when you are on the wire, when you look at the target at the end with the wire attached, on the right you have for example a white wall with no distraction and on the left you have a window and a door with people passing. Well, that's a nonsense. You should, before practicing, you should be the architect of your practice, you should decide. So I place myself or I choose a place that is, of course, as symmetrical as possible and never in a diagonal way, never where on the left and on the right, I don't have the same field not only to look at but even to feel. So, that's something that I have never seen anybody talk about or even understand, or think of.

Discussions about the body in space are often missing from circus, don't you think?

Philippe Petit: Yes. I find the placement of the body in a performance space is so important. People don't think of it, but it has a subliminal power.

For example, if I have a wire-walker student that I am working with, and we're rehearsing an actual performance, an eight-minute circus show or a theatre performance and the wire is set and I say, 'Okay and we'll go backstage and then come in.' Well, I would have a lot of things to say about the entrance of the performer, before the performer even climbs onto the wire. For example, 'Are you coming from stage left or stage right? Are you coming from backstage centre? Are you coming by the shortest way from backstage to the wire, or are you coming with the detour that you create?' You are the architect of your body movement, and all those things, actually, right there before you even start walking on the wire, say a lot, and this is part of the performance.

The minute the curtain opens or the minute the person enters and is seen by the audience, right there is your performance. If you don't pay attention to your position of your body in space, and, much more than the position, the speed, the timing, the volume of air that you move, then you are just a technician, you are not an artist or a performer in my view. So right there is what I'm talking about – the body in space and the body in performance.

★★★★★

From Philippe Petit's discussion of how he has moved beyond a relationship of mastery over the apparatus to a relationship of interchange and dialogue, the next conversation is with a circus artist also known for the way she extends and develops possible interrelationships with apparatus.

Shana Carroll, Co-Founder and Co-Director of The 7 Fingers in Montreal, originally intended to work in theatre, but, while working in the office at The Pickle Family Circus in San Francisco, she caught sight of a trapeze artist training and felt such a strong emotional connection that she decided to start training on trapeze herself.[34] She went on to study trapeze at the National Circus School in Montreal, and then worked with Cirque du Soleil, performing the trapeze solo in *Saltimbanco*.

In the following extract Shana Carroll talks about her interaction with traditional apparatus, and the ways in which when she is creating new work she aims to uncover the poetic and emotional resonances in the relationship between the performer and the apparatus.[35]

★★★★★

Shana Carroll

Would you say that there is anything distinctive about particular types of equipment that leads to specific metaphors? Is there a different metaphorical potential within for example, trapeze, to tissu (silks), or Chinese pole?
Shana Carroll: I used to feel incredibly strongly about that, especially when I was younger. It would frustrate me because there's an inherent metaphor in each of these circus disciplines, and there's various stories that are linked to being told on that apparatus, and I would get frustrated if people would just ignore it and treat it like it was the floor. Like you were on the trapeze and you just were doing what you would do on the floor in a way, not acknowledging that you are suspended between earth and sky, and that on the one hand you have flight, on the other hand you're trapped on this apparatus, and that there's so many compatible stories that go with this apparatus.

It was a big part of my inspiration, specially towards the beginning, especially as a trapeze artist, trying to find what images were really linked to the apparatus. When I would teach directing and choreographing, I would do that with my students, where I would make them talk about everything that the apparatus symbolised to them. In fact, I even had an improv exercise where I would make them write down verbs that they associated with their apparatus. If it was 'to float,' 'to burn,' 'to fly,' 'to fear,' then as they improvised I'd read those words back at them and then it would influence the way they would move. So already they would have a movement vocabulary on their apparatus that was automatically connected to something very deep in their own motivation and in their apparatus.

Now, because circus is just a mode of expression, and in a way you can say anything with anything, I feel less like, 'Oh you have to be really super loyal to what each apparatus has to say.' Now I find it more interesting to say, 'Well let's see if we can tell this story on this apparatus that wouldn't normally be used in that way, and figure out where that intersection is and why.'

FIGURE 1.3   Shana Caroll in The 7 Fingers' *Loft*. Photo: Christian Tremblay.

I still feel like it needs to feel essential. In a way I could compare it to a musical. If they break out in song and dance it has to feel like they have to break out in song and dance – that it is something that just can't be told in words and so you never feel like, 'Why are they singing?' You feel like it just explodes out of them. I feel like, similarly with circus, you want to feel like if we're telling this through acrobatics, if we're telling this on a trapeze, we need to get the sense that it has to be told with that apparatus or acrobatically. Sometimes I think it doesn't have to be quite so logical as analysing the symbolism of the apparatus and all of that. Sometimes the intersection is a little bit more visceral or image-oriented.

The Chinese pole act in *Psy* felt so essential, and so connected with that particular apparatus.[36] It was as though no other apparatus would work in that context. The movement on the pole gave that particular feeling when you are falling asleep, and you experience a falling sensation, or a drifting weightlessness.
Shana Carroll: That actually applies to the thing I was saying earlier, because the other reason I had the idea for that act was because Héloïse [Bourgeois], who I had already worked with for quite a number of years on *Traces*, she has this very

languid quality of movement, and I thought of the thing of her being sort of sleepwalking.[37] I just felt it worked very well with what she naturally fell into. So it's a combination of something that I feel worked with that artist and with the apparatus, so that's interesting.

For instance, I'll just give the example of Matias [Plaul][38] in *Cuisine and Confessions*. He's Argentinian. His father, when he was a baby, when he was eight months old, his father was a revolutionary, and he was kidnapped, and brought to a concentration camp, and tortured, and eventually murdered in Argentina. Matias was just a baby. He tells this story of his father. He will tell a piece of the story and then go on to the pole and kind of physicalise it, and then tell another piece of the story. And back and forth, and there are four of these back-and-forth sections in that way. And you see in this case that the pole is really interesting. In one moment when he is talking about the kidnapping, it's a very aggressive piece with the other guy going to get him, and it's saultos, and it's jumping, and it's swinging around. You feel like the pole is this tool for chasing and escaping. And then he's telling the part about wishing he could make a toast with his father, and thinking how his father would have liked to have his last meal. Then he's using the airiness of the pole and floating and doing these positions, flags, and things like that, and taking that quality of it. In a way you see the four sections like that, and you see the potential that it can be used to tell anything, and yet each time it's using an essential element of the pole as well as the story.

Are you interested in developing new circus apparatus?
Shana Carroll: I think it is always exciting when new apparatus are being developed and it helps the form to evolve.[39] Myself, it's not so much my interest. I am glad it is being done. I'd rather take a known apparatus and really spend my time and creativity on how to use it, than if you spend your time and creativity on figuring what the apparatus is, and how to move on it, you don't have a lot of time and creativity then left to create something.

I mean that's what I find even with circus school students who have decided to create new apparatus and you see there is so much research that needs to be done just with the physical aspect, that those particular students often don't get on top of it to develop anything very theatrical. I guess that's my own feeling though I'm glad new apparatus are being developed.

★★★★★

Shana Carroll's approach of exploring the metaphorical and narrative potential in the relationship between the performer and the apparatus, is also a central concern of the circus artists Charlotte Mooney and Tina Koch, Co-Founders and Artistic Directors of the UK-based circus company Ockham's Razor.[40] However, instead of working with pre-existing traditional apparatus these artists explore these ideas through investigating performer interactions with new bespoke apparatus which they design and create with the company's other Co-Director and Co-Founder, Alex Harvey. All three artists studied together at Circomedia, Centre for Contemporary Circus and Physical Theatre in Bristol, UK, before setting up Ockham's

Razor in 2004. The company has gone on to create numerous shows including *Memento Mori* (2004), *The Mill* (2010), and *Tipping Point* (2016) all of which have featured unique new pieces of apparatus designed and created by the group.

Here Charlotte Mooney and Tina Koch talk about how they create their shows by starting with the designing and making of a major new piece of apparatus for each work. The physical material and the themes of the new show then emerge out of the performers' interplay with this new apparatus.

*****

Charlotte Mooney and Tina Koch

When was the first time you developed new apparatus and how did that come about?

Charlotte Mooney: The first time we used new apparatus was in the show *Memento Mori* [2004] where it was myself and Alex, one of the other Co-Founders of Ockham's Razor. We were creating a work on a doubles trapeze and a lot of the movement that we came up with seemed to relate to images of rest and struggle, and from that it reminded us of the Hans Holbein woodcuts which are about the Dance of Death, and we wanted to create choreography that was about someone's struggle with death.

FIGURE 1.4 Ockham's Razor, *Memento Mori*. Photo: Nik Mackey.

We had two main reasons for doing away with the doubles trapeze. Initially it was to remove all of the associations that you have with a doubles trapeze. When you walk on stage and you see a doubles trapeze, it's such a loaded object in its own right. It has associations, and what we wanted to do was to create a piece of equipment that also worked like a set, so it was open and had its own associations. The other thing was from a very technical point of view by removing the ropes, what we replaced them with was just a very simple rectangular piece of metal, and because this metal was stiff, it gave a whole new ability to move on it. Choreographically it was incredibly interesting because there were ways you could move around the sides, and it took away that constant wobble that you have on doubles trapeze, so it gave you a stillness. The other thing was it had a top and a bottom so you could be above it and below it. So by transforming the equipment it opened things up choreographically, it opened up associations. We also turned it sideways on so what the audience saw was just a thin line and then the bodies around it. That meant you were able to see the bodies framed in space and because that piece is about someone wrestling with death, and in a theatre set-up or in a big top set-up where it has been performed you'd have a black void behind it and just this one single line, you saw the image of the body completely in space.

From there, with each of our shows we've used different pieces of equipment, very sculpturally. As pieces of sculpture they thematically suggest things and open up narratives and images, but they also, each of them, have allowed the body to move in new ways, so it has created new circus choreography.

Also there's something that we've discovered along the way about creating space around the body. That once you take the body into the air, and you try to create these pieces of equipment that don't overcrowd the space and leave air and space around the body, there's something about seeing the body in space which creates vulnerability, and a lot of the work that we do looks at the humanity of the circus performer. Rather than being superhuman we're trying to show the vulnerability and the humanity of the performers, and we do a lot with the relationships between performers, and a lot of that comes out of the reliance and trust that comes from being in the air. Part of that visually is about having the space around the body in the air.

Listening to the sort of language you use to discuss these ideas it sounds as though you have a background in visual arts.
Charlotte Mooney: We've got a strange mix. So Alex [Harvey] has a degree in fine arts. My background is actually English literature and dance, and Tina … do you want to talk a bit about yours?

Tina Koch: I think it certainly is that me and Alex come from fine arts backgrounds. We kind of see things in that way, but I think Charlotte as well, even though you say you are from a literature background, as a company we work very visually, and actually use the object as a starting point for all our creations, and that's a really important element. I think sometimes maybe we're even not that aware how much that training influences our decisions in the rehearsal room.

Is this development of the use of the apparatus in terms of its metaphorical qualities something that is an integral part of your process?
Charlotte Mooney: It's the starting point, and I think the thing that we've learnt over a long period of time is some of that is fairly intuitive. We do have a very similar eye, so often when we start working with an object there will be metaphors that will be working upon us, each of us in the room, and we may not even necessarily be openly articulating them to each other at the time, but we'll see certain things and go, 'Yes that's right, I'm not even necessarily sure why that's right but that's feeding the same story.'

We've allowed a lot more time as we've got more confident to not necessarily pin down what is metaphorically being said but know it's part of the same terrain. So initially we'll create a piece of equipment, and we'll have the performers in the room improvising and creating movement, and we'll be drawing pictures and looking at what sort of clusters seem to go together, and then very late on in the process will we actually articulate, 'Ok what are the narratives that are actually in this, what are the stories, what are the worlds,' and verbalise what they are.

So to give you another example, there's a show we made with a wheel that's like a wooden hamster wheel with performers inside it, and they are linked across stage by rope to a system, and they are essentially trapped within a system; and a lot of the images are about toil and being trapped within a system, and revolution, and being tied in and struggling against that.[41] Then the logical conclusion for us to that was that the system should at some point break apart and explode, and we never overtly had a conversation, that this is a show about revolution or the system, until quite late on when it was very apparent that that's what it was about, and it was about struggling against something and whether you can rebuild. Because it was inherent in the object. The other thing is that same piece of equipment at some point functions like a Ferris wheel, and it's very joyful. I think because we kept things open we found all this material that was joyful Ferris wheel kind of firework material as well from a movement perspective, which then later on made a lot of sense in that, 'Ok you subvert the system and it becomes something joyful and what would happen narratively to make that happen?' I think the fact that we kept it open until quite late enabled us to find that movement material which may not have necessarily fitted with the idea if we'd started from a narrative perspective.

And so that sense of play is really part of the development process?
Tina Koch: Obviously when we design a piece of equipment there are metaphors in the back of our minds, but once we've made it, and we go into the rehearsal room it's very important for us to put that all aside, and just have an interaction between the object and the bodies in space without any preconceived ideas. We choose an object usually that promotes movement and almost has a reaction to the body, so there can be a certain dialogue happening, and we usually have some improvisations.

FIGURE 1.5 Ockham's Razor, *The Mill*. Photo: Graham McGrath.

We sometimes just play when we put some music on, sometimes we have led improvisations, and sometimes we just look at the equipment in the space, and draw pictures in our minds and then stage that. It's very important for us to keep things very open. Then, only once we've found things that touch us, will we draw a picture, and then once we have lots of pictures, we'll see what the object actually says. What's the story? What's the metaphor? What is the hidden thing that's actually inherent in the communication between the body and the equipment once we put them together? So we don't come with a narrative and then kind of try and jam it in, because over the years we've learnt that you have to start from the movement and what's possible, in order to really have a gelling of the narrative or the metaphors with the circus, so that you don't end up with a story where the circus is sort of plonked inside it.

What are the difficulties with trying to come to grips with a whole new piece of equipment? Does that stretch out your development periods?
Tina Koch: Yes. It's obviously time. We need a lot more time, and we need a lot more money to be able to do that. There is this very strange thing that you have to come up with a whole new vocabulary, and train it, and get good at it, but you don't know what to train yet because you don't know what it's about, but obviously the earlier you hone down what you need to train, what goes in the show, the better the show will be, and only once you've trained certain things can you see whether they actually work.

That balance between actually getting good at things, and being able to play and to be safe, makes it quite a slow process in some ways, especially if the equipment we use is very different from our training. For instance, with the wheel there was all this going around. It has a bar like on a trapeze, but the movements we came up with were very new to our bodies; while *Tipping Point*, uses a pole,

FIGURE 1.6 Ockham's Razor, Tower and Pole image by Marleen Hiels.

so we could draw on all the knowledge of all the performers knowing how to feel on a Chinese pole which made it a lot faster.[42]

Charlotte Mooney: But even so because the poles aren't anchored and they swing, a lot of the pole people were like [demonstrates being disoriented], even a minor thing would make it function differently. I think some of them found it quite frustrating they couldn't necessarily use all of their training.

The apparatus you have in *Arc* tips like it is a frame, so you're using some of the discipline of duo trapeze or trapeze, but there's an added element in that the centre of gravity as it moves is tipping the whole apparatus, so someone up the other end of the apparatus is tipping up at the same time. That must have taken a great deal of time to adapt your traditional physical skills to this new apparatus, as it seems to almost have a life of its own.
Tina Koch: There's a lot of dealing with fear involved because in a lot of circus equipment you're controlling it yourself, and even in doubles [trapeze] there's certain moves where you're in constant communication with the one person that's holding you, or the person you are holding. You're very connected. Whereas with this piece of equipment we sometimes find ourselves in different places and there are three performers. So you can sense the other two, but as soon as there's one more person it becomes more demanding on your concentration, plus the apparatus is so sensitive I think you have to really learn to know that everything you do, even if you move a leg, has an effect on everybody else. And to trust a lot more that the others are constantly aware of you whilst they're also performing. The element that was quite hard was the mechanics or the physics of it. We catapulted Alex off once because we decided to go through a different bar. We said, 'Oh why don't we go through here. That will be great,' and we ended up shooting Alex into the air!

With apparatus that has got this unpredictable element, it almost has a life of its own. Does this make it easier to keep the immediacy in the live performance as opposed to a more traditional apparatus?

Charlotte Mooney: I think that's really interesting. I've never thought about it that way before, but that's very true. I think especially it's to do with what Tina was saying, it's the negotiation between the three people on stage and the equipment, because when it does do something odd you don't know, you're like, 'Is it because someone else did something, or is it the equipment.' And you do click into each other so there is a whole raft of communication that's happening between you.

We performed that piece recently. It's quite an old piece actually but it's still getting performed and the apparatus has started doing something really odd and none of us can figure out why after ten years of performing it. Towards the end when it flips, it's getting this swing. For the life of us none of us know why it's started happening. There is this seam of communication that's happening during the piece between us looking at each other trying things each time to make it stop happening.

I think in terms of staying present, obviously there's a world of things that you do. That's part of being a performer, is learning how to do that, how to keep present and to keep things different each time, and we work very hard to make the shows constantly evolve so that people are keeping that communication and that presence. I think that the rogue element of the equipment probably does help.

When you were saying about just moving one tiny part of your anatomy and it affects everybody else, it's a really interesting metaphor for how every aspect of your behaviour affects people around you, isn't it?

Tina Koch: There's a whole thing that we make about that in *Every Action*. The piece has twenty-five metres of rope and the rope goes over one pulley and then over another pulley, and then down to the ground and based on Newton's Law – every action has an opposite and equal reaction – that is literally anything you do will affect someone on the other side.

Charlotte Mooney: And one of the reasons we first thought of making that show was that with a lot of circus you'll end up when you're interacting with someone where it's these really close interactions, either with doubles trapeze or with hand-to-hand, and you get a lot of tales about love or about fighting because you're in these very close extreme physical positions and that's what an audience sees, especially people that are not used to seeing bodies so close to each other.[43]

So one of the benefits we had with the rope in *Every Action*, which was the first piece we made after *Memento Mori*, was that we wanted to be able to effectively put people at a distance from each other, so that you could have a different relationship that wasn't necessarily one that was so close. That piece is light clowning, almost a Comedy of Manners piece about one-upmanship and status, and trying to get the upper hand. I think it was able to play out because you can either screw someone up or help them over this distance, so the style of it, and the story of it, was enabled by this fact of distance. We wanted people to have quite extreme reactions but over space.

★★★★★

From Charlotte Mooney and Tina Koch's discussion of their approaches to creative exploration with their bespoke apparatus, we move to Elizabeth Streb, Artistic Director of STREB Extreme Action Company in New York, who also develops unique new apparatus for her shows.[44]

Streb problematises traditional understandings of the function of apparatus as a means of displaying the performer's mastery of the apparatus by creating innovative equipment with new functionalities that provoke specific explorations of space, rate, speed, physical forces, and unpredictability.

Here Elizabeth Streb, in this short extract, discusses how exploration of space is the key starting point for her when she is imagining possible new apparatus.

★★★★★

Elizabeth Streb

How do you go about designing your pieces of apparatus?
Elizabeth Streb: I think the main idea is 'Where in space have I not gone?' and 'What situation could provoke turbulence and speed?' The body goes so slowly in modern dance, back and forth, and they realise that they're going to get to the other side of the stage so they slow down even more, and then they turn and come back without fully examining that a big part of physical theatricality is rate, and motion.

If you think of how investigative the field of music has been – they have names for every sound, and octave, and keys, and tones. So what we try to figure out is what about if you could name every spot in space, give it a name, an accurate lexicon, nomenclature, so people will notice that it matters where you are. So the apparatus is really like a musical instrument for me, and the action cannot survive without the equipment. Movement has only done that I think in circus.

Anyway, I'm right now struggling with, 'What's the next piece of equipment?' and I work with my technical directors. That's really who's ever in the room next to me. It could be an eight-year-old, 'Why haven't you done this?' 'What do you mean why haven't I done this? Who do you think you are talking to?' and then I go, 'What a good question!'

The real part of my job now is figuring out how to understand where we haven't gone in terms of our exploration of space, time, and forces, and to design a machine that can provoke those explorations.

★★★★★

FIGURE 1.7 STREB Extreme Action in Breckenridge. Photo: Joe Kusumoto.

The notion of creating a unique piece of apparatus that instigates new movement and also sets in place different understandings of space is central to the work of Elizabeth Streb. The French artist Johann Le Guillerm also creates new forms of apparatus in order to investigate space.

Le Guillerm is the Founder of Cirque Ici in France. His work combines circus, sculpture, installation, and performance art. In this next conversation he speaks about the unique sculptural creations that he designs and creates, and then includes in his performances, using them as forms of apparatus. Le Guillerm describes his creations, not as objects that the performer is required to master, but rather as extensions of the human body that allow interrogations of the elements of balance, movement, and three-dimensionality.[45]

*****

Johann Le Guillerm

How would you define apparatus?
Johann Le Guillerm: Apparatus? Well, it's a prosthesis, a human prosthesis. I see it as a tool, an extension of the human being. An extension. A growth.

And so how did you come to your current practice of creating personal apparatus?
Johann Le Guillerm: Well, in my second show, which was called *Secret*, and then in *Secret II* even more so, I removed everything that might be associated with Traditional Circus practices. Tight wire-walking, all my practices that might be identified as a Traditional Circus practice I removed so I could produce more personal practices, moving from the traditional to the personal,

with the creation of personal objects, so I could find out whether, if by doing only these Non-Traditional Circus practices, I would still be identified as being a circus artist, and whether my background would function in the same way as before when I was performing traditional acts in a ring. I realised that, yes, it worked just as well. And so the technique didn't have limits, well, the practice didn't have limits. It was just a matter of inventing things that weren't being done.

Could you talk a little more about the objects that you created for _Secret_, and for _Secret II_? How were they different from traditional apparatus?
Johann Le Guillerm: Well, I invent objects that don't exist and that do not serve any other purpose than what I do with them. That said, some of these objects could have afterlives.

By inspiring other artists?
Johann Le Guillerm: There are some that have inspired others, yes, that's for sure.

When you create these objects do you create them in relation to particular human limits that you are looking to test?
Johann Le Guillerm: Around 2000, I started a lab around the theme of 'le pas grand chose' ['the nothing much']. Since then this research has resulted in a form of knowledge that's not a normal part of our culture.

Generally, I choose a few of these ideas and start a research laboratory and begin to realise these ideas through the production of maquettes.[46] Some of my imaginings come to nothing, because these ideas do not always work in practice. However, even so, something else will become evident from the imaginings or fantasies, and the actual material the object is made out of, and the way they come together in the realisation.

Could you describe what happens in these laboratories?
Johann Le Guillerm: So, the first step is that whenever I have an idea, at whatever hour of the day or of the night, I write it down – even if it's just some little thing, but if I feel there is something there, I set it aside and organise it into a folder. From time to time I go through these folders and I take out what I think is interesting. Often I find the same ideas at different periods in different forms, and at some point or other, when I decide to work with these ideas, I start a laboratory.

Often I deal with several ideas at the same time, during the same period. I take four different ideas, I have four different tables, and I work on one thing. As soon as I get stuck, I move onto another thing. I am always moving onto other things. Because it's important, I think, and life is like this as well, on some level of cognitive awareness, thinking about one thing always leads to thoughts on something else. So, I always have several things going, in progress. So then I develop things very quickly. I try to develop maquettes quickly, using Scotch tape, paper, whatever materials can show me whether the ideas are going to work very quickly. Even if it only hangs together for five minutes, as Scotch-taped things aren't that stable, it's just enough for the maquette to show me whether it's possible to make the object.

FIGURE 1.8 L'Observatoire, Johann Le Guillerm. Photo: © Philippe Cibille.

Once I have working prototypes, I work with a construction crew to build things often on a 1:1 scale. At this point, I'm always present during the construction process. The slightest shift, the slightest idea, absolutely everything, it's always important that I be there, because if there is one thing that's decided without me, I always realise at some point that it's a problem because it doesn't have a place. It's not part of my construction. It's always important that I decide everything. Because even if I tell myself, 'Well, they did this. I wasn't there. I won't say anything. Right?' Two days later, we need to remove it because I tell myself, 'This cannot work.' It's often like that.

And why doesn't it work?
Johann Le Guillerm: In the end, because during construction there are always things to add. And I don't know why, but in nature, everything has a function. I've often worked with things like this, making extremely simple things, and in this simplicity, each thing serves several functions. Everything must work so that there are the minimum of things that are superfluous. No flourishes, and everything has a function. So the object is very minimalist, and there is coherence in the whole. Often in nature, there are things like this. For me, it is the building of these things that interests me, without sophistry.

Is there a difference between the objects that you exhibit in installations and the apparatus that you use on the stage?
Johann Le Guillerm: For me, it's the same thing. I realise my thoughts in a concrete way in these objects. But afterwards it is people who use these objects. So often there are things tied to movement in my work, there are a lot of objects that I build on stage.

There are also things that I build outside which are fixed – certain objects that I have called 'architextures' that are between texture and architecture, but with movement in the combination of force-lines in these objects. These are architextures, structures that hold together without ties, or nails. They are put together using pieces of wood.

Constructed without nails?
Johann Le Guillerm: Yes.

And do you feel that these objects that are handled by the public are showing people how to interact with the world differently?
Johann Le Guillerm: Well, to see things in another way. In *Imaginographes*, in a number of my installations, there is a demonstration of these tools and the public can handle them.[47] There are always little videos that serve as instructions for the tools. And these tools offer each person the opportunity to look at the things they see in relation to their own culture.

Each one of the spectators perceives what I call their own 'mental circus.' If they interact with the object, they will perceive a mental circus that stems from their own eyes, from their own culture. And each person will see things differently in relation to their culture. For my part, I offer nothing, they are the ones who see. I offer them something similar to a lens, and they will see for themselves what their own culture sees using this tool.

When the audience handles the objects you create, what sort of experiences do they have?
Johann Le Guillerm: A lot of people are astonished to realise that they have something in front of their eyes that they have never seen before. But what really interests me in my work is to create disturbance. To bring about disturbance by introducing new horizons to established landmarks.

I think that a work of art exists to disturb the world. Not to be pretty. If it's fixed to a wall and it's pretty, alright yes, but what else? Art must disturb people, move them, set their world into movement.

And this brings me to balance. Balance is about movement. It's not a fixed thing. Often, we think to ourselves: Balance, finding balance, it's about informing oneself constantly, until one day – there we go, we have it, we are in balance. We can wait like that until death. But, I think that to be in balance is to be in a state of continual motion. If we pay attention to balance we can never reach the point of being fixed in position. Balance is a permanent fight because the world is moving. And if we stop, if we tell ourselves, 'we've got it!' the world will still continue moving and we will need to readapt our balance again to a world in the process of moving.

So balancing involves imbalance?
Johann Le Guillerm: That's it.

FIGURE 1.9 *Secret (temps 2)*, Creation 2012, Johann Le Guillerm. Photo: © David Dubost.

Momentarily?

Johann Le Guillerm: Permanently.

★★★★★

Johanne Le Guillerm's idea that a work of art exists 'to disturb the world' is also an essential component in the work of Phia Ménard, the French transgender performer and creator. Ménard originally trained with the French juggler Jérôme Thomas, and performed with Thomas' company for several years, before forming her[48] own company, Compagnie Non Nova.[49] Her notion of 'unjugglability' radically destabilises the notion of mastery over the apparatus, allowing her to explore a range of other relationships.

Ménard was born into the body of a boy in 1971, and was known as Philippe until she announced her transition as a transgender woman in 2008, the same year that she premiered the show *P.P.P. (Position Parralèle au Plancher)*, a work investigating the use of ice as an apparatus.[50]

In the next conversation Phia Ménard discusses her group of works called 'ICE' ('*Injonglabilité Complémentaire des Éléments*') and speaks about her relationship with apparatus. She describes herself as 'a juggler who does not master matter, but rather who follows matter.'[51]

★★★★★

Phia Ménard

We would like ask you about your concept of 'unjugglability' and where that comes from.
Phia Ménard: You are starting with the monster! The concept of 'unjugglability' emerges in opposition to the notion of jugglability. Which means that for me, having learned to juggle at the age of 18, I am now 47, I realised years ago, because it's now more than ten years since I worked out this concept, that from the viewer's point of view when they are watching a juggler in performance, they are waiting for the juggler to fail. This is the general rule.

Then in my case I was supposedly a virtuoso at juggling. So I managed to master what we call the 'trajectory,' what we call the 'rhythm,' and what we call the 'gesture,' as a whole. And this notion of virtuosity created the situation in which, with each demonstration of my art, I was always questioned about my capacity to do more, to achieve more mind-boggling tricks.

At the time I was only juggling with white juggling balls, silicone balls, bouncing balls, and at that point, the more I worked on this specific form, the more people would associate my name with being one of a virtuoso. And that's what, for me, poses real problems – I feel that juggling is a cosmic act, that juggling round balls, is playing with the cosmos. The juggler is someone who defies the laws of gravity, and therefore someone who is in direct relationship with the most human relationship one can have with the cosmos – I'm talking about balance, equilibrium, the fact of standing up, and this notion is much more important than just virtuosity.

When in the two trajectories, this journey, the question of my identity at the time and the question of virtuosity, I got to a moment in my life where I understood that the more we look at the virtuosity of the man I was at the time, the more I understood that I was destroying myself.

And so I made a break. That break was unjugglability. That break consisted in not choosing objects that allow me to be virtuoso, but instead taking things that would contradict my virtuosity. And the first thing I took to juggle was a cactus.

It was, to put the question simply, it was this. As a spectator you will not wait for my virtuosity, you will instead be afraid for the juggler. You will not be in a state of admiration, you will be in a state of empathy.

And, above all, unjugglability is about changing the viewer's perspective. I think that the important thing is to succeed in bringing the onlooker back to the possibility of the artist not being worshipped or admired, but rather being understood as being human.

Could you speak about the different elements that you have chosen to juggle with, for example ice, water, and air, and the metaphors inherent for you in this work?

Phia Ménard: If I work today with so-called natural elements (water, air), it is simply because all these elements are what connects me to other human beings – the 'Other' knows these elements. And from that point on, a relationship emerges in which the onlooker has their own experience, they bring their own experience into play, and can compare it to my own. They can put themself in my shoes because they have their own experiences to draw on. From there, I give them the opportunity to project themself into the body of the circus artist, and more so to experience something (an action, a situation) that they wouldn't dare to experience themself and I offer them this possibility.

Perhaps the most beautiful example of this is in *P.P.P. (Parallel Position to the Floor)* where being a body in amongst the ice makes the onlooker feel their own body. For example, I lie on a bed filled with ice, and automatically, the audience goes, 'brrr!' (she shivers), simply because they feel the cold by projecting themselves into my body. So they are imagining their own body. That's an important form. The natural elements, from there, will ultimately be the vector for a dialogue between the onlooker and myself or the performer, simply through the body, and no longer through admiration or the intellect. It is a body-to-body relationship through projection.

Paradoxically, the juggler usually masters the object, but I am a juggler who does not master matter, but rather who follows matter. By this I mean that I must comply with the laws of matter. It's a sort of combat. So it's not important whether you win the fight, but rather that it will be a beautiful battle. This is a battle where we well know that I will lose. But on the other hand, the spectators immerse themselves in the fight hoping it will be a good one.

★★★★★

From Phia Ménard's description of how she uses natural elements such as ice to connect to the audience through the idea of a shared bodily experience, we move to a conversation with David Clarkson who talks about some of the virtual apparatus he is working with and how they offer opportunities to generate shared imaginative states between audience members and the performer.

Clarkson originally began as a physical performer, often performing on the streets as a stilt walker. He co-founded Stalker in New Zealand in 1985 with Emily McCormick and Rachael Swain, before the company moved its base to Sydney, Australia. Clarkson has created and directed numerous Stalker shows including *Encoded* (2012), *Pixel Mountain* (2013), *Phosphori* (2013), *Compartmentalized* (2014), *Creature* – the Installation and the Performance (2016), and *Frameshift* (2016).[52]

He has been working with interactive technology for several decades, and here he discusses how interactive environments can allow audience members to move

FIGURE 1.10 Compagnie Non Nova, Phia Ménard in *P.P.P.* Photo: © Jean-Luc Beaujault.

beyond being passive spectators, and instead become active participants in the performance through direct interaction through virtual imaginative play spaces.

★★★★★

David Clarkson

How would you characterise working on the cutting edge of immersive circus/theatre performance?
David Clarkson: It's high tech, it's high problems, it's high problem-solving. But at the same time it enables a particular type of body-centred learning, engagement, and body-centred participation.

Everyone is talking about interactivity, it's awful! It's the new marketing, everything is the 'human/computer interface.' But if that interface can be imaginative, if it can be body-centred and physicalized, not just screen-based, then for a physical theatre artist it opens up possibilities.

Computers – in some ways they're limiting what's happening with humanity and in some ways they're opening it up. The United Nations has been holding a series of annual conferences *Technology for Good* about using social media technology in positive ways for example to go into a Syrian refugee camp or to experience an Ebola crisis centre. The ability of this technology to generate empathy, to generate imaginative states, to expand the potential of what it is to be human, and also to learn, I think is fantastic, and if I can harvest that in a theatrical sense I've got a whole new type of play space.

Do you think that conventional proscenium arch theatres are the best kind of space for interactive performance?
David Clarkson: No, I am redesigning a performance space right now. I'm looking at a 21 metre dome, a geodesic 21 metre dome. You have to buy them ready-made mainly because the camera positioning is so precise, all the math has to be figured out.

How do you think it changes everything and how do you see your performances evolving in response to this?
David Clarkson: Look, I don't know. I want six months playing with this to be able to answer that question! Each time I present the *Creature* play space I develop it a bit more so I can learn to answer that question.[53] But it's potentially no longer the audience/performer divide. Both become participants in an experience – one has prior knowledge, one doesn't. What then become the rules of engagement? I'm not sure. I know they're different. I know I'll be able to work with them because I know how to respond in a live situation, but it's kind of like flying by the seat of your pants which you always do in live performance. Unless you're kind of going, 'Ok what the hell's going on here?' you're not really creating.

I see it as the new playground and in that way I see it as profound. It's the whole thing of the role of live performance in the wider world and it's often down-played, but I think it has a crucial role in the development of the human imagination and what is possible with that human imagination. And I think these new types of performance spaces will open it up. Will it be live performance as we know it? Will it be the end of live performance? Was film the end of live performance? It's just another version of that question coming around for 2020. It's the old question reframed.

If we were to ask you to just dream or imagine how new technologies could work in a circus context – are there any kind of dreamings that you have, that you could project into a possible future?
David Clarkson: It's very simply being able to know at any time where any limb or any atom, if you want to get really subtle, of a performer is in a 3D space and so then you have the ability to craft an interactive system that is fully responding to the performer. And whether that is then 20 metres up, lying flat on the floor, doing a backflip, wherever they are you have their position. So that in some ways is the logical outcome. And really what you would want is then a projection system that could use that data anywhere within that environment in 3D and that's probably the logical extension of that.

So at the moment everything is not quite there. We are just working in true 3D so If I wave my hand, butterflies come and fly on it. You see it. I see it. That's

FIGURE 1.11 Stalker, *Frameshift*, City of Sydney, 2018. Photo: Katherine Griffiths.

3D interactivity. That butterfly isn't projected against the wall on a screen it is happening in the field around us.

So that is the dream?
David Clarkson: No, we're doing that now, you have to wear 3D goggles, but it is happening.

How do you see that interacting with a spectator that enters into the performance space?
David Clarkson: This is where it is no longer a performance space, which is kind of interesting because it takes me back to the beginning of my career which was street theatre. The thing I loved about street theatre, was street theatre isn't owned in the way that a traditional theatre space is owned. The three-dimensional play space is in some ways a hi-tech version of street theatre because it's a more democratic space.

What is the overall goal for the audience in terms of their experience? When we watch traditional circus performance there is a kinaesthetic experience. Is the goal of performance with immersive technology to heighten that kinaesthetic experience?
David Clarkson: It's kinaesthetic. It's empathetic. I guess I'd like to think it takes you back to your fundamentals of what is at the heart of performance. And this

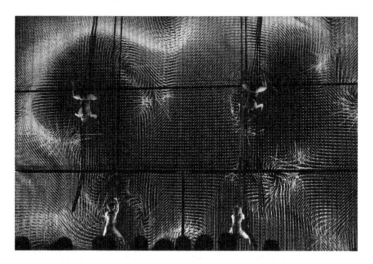

FIGURE 1.12 Stalker, *Pixel Mountain*. Photo: Aaron Walker.

again takes me back to [my] street theatre days. Taking a street theatre piece into the heart of Serbia during the war, or taking a street theatre piece into a barrio in Medellin at the height of the drug wars. There, what are you doing? You are somehow stripping back the performance experience to not be consumer-based or led, or necessarily entertainment, but it's something about the fundamental right of humans to engage imaginatively in space, to play. It's the birthright of us all to play. We need to create space and moments of play in life otherwise we're drones.

★★★★★

The final conversation in this chapter is with another creator working with new and emerging forms of apparatus, Adrien Mondot, Co-Founder and Co-Director of the performance company, Compagnie Adrien M & Claire B, based in France.[54]

Mondot graduated from the National Institute of Computer Science in Grenoble in 2004, and in that same year founded Compagnie Adrien M and presented his first show *Convergence 1.0*. The show combined juggling with the software he had developed called eMotion which tracks movement in space. In 2011, Mondot went on to co-found the company Compagnie Adrien M & Claire B with visual artist and scenographer Claire Bardainne.

In this conversation, Mondot talks about the interactive environments he creates with Claire Bardainne and how they act as apparatus.

★★★★★

Adrien Mondot

So, how would you define 'apparatus' in your work?

Adrien Mondot: It's the structure of play with forces. Apparatus is what allows us to act on forces. For me, that's what makes my performance circus, it's this discussion of pleasure through apparatus. It can be with juggling balls, but now it is our digital workspace that will determine the rules by which we define this game with forces. So that's what apparatus is for me.

Do you still regularly practice juggling?

Adrien Mondot: No. I think that the last time I was on stage was more than six months ago, so it's starting to be a little while ago now. That said, it's not out of the question that sometime in the next few years I might go back to juggling projects. I feel that you do need to leave room for younger generations who juggle. Also I have the distinct impression that I've said all that I have to say about juggling. I've basically already said it. So if I stop juggling completely, I know that I won't have any regrets about things I haven't done.

Has juggling changed much since when you first started juggling?

Adrien Mondot: There has been such an increase in the level of juggling in the last few years. Since the advent of internet videos. Since YouTube around 2005–2006, really. I feel that the mental barriers to levels of difficulty are hugely different now.

I started juggling in 1998. At that time it was considered fairly complicated to juggle with five juggling balls. You needed a year of work before managing five balls. And because juggling five balls was considered complicated, that meant we approached the task telling ourselves it would be complicated because we didn't know that it could be easy. Today people who are starting to learn to juggle watch plenty of videos on the internet of people juggling five balls and they tell themselves that it's normal, and they learn to juggle with five balls in three months. In three and a half months, they get it. And yet it's still as difficult as it was. It's just that in the collective imagination it's perceived as being easier, more normal.

And as a result there is a sort of levelling of progression, that happens very quickly, but then we've always found this. Also there's a difference between an amateur and a professional practice, in the sense that amateurs have the time to work on the practice and the professionals only maintain their skill between shows. Most often they have a lot more work to do elsewhere. I don't feel like continuing to present things that could be seen as dated in juggling.

How did you come to turn towards this kind of virtual juggling?

Adrien Mondot: Claire [Bardainne] often says, 'The real does what it can, and the virtual what it wants,' and we both find that this idea really resonates with us. I felt the limits of juggling. This notion of invested time in a subject where, if we look at it mathematically, is an asymptote. We spend more and more time to refine juggling further and further or to maintain a technical ability. Because technical ability is important in circus. And as a result we felt this limitation, and I asked myself, 'What would happen if we replaced the real juggling balls with virtual juggling balls? I would be able to do something else.'

The impression that I had was that we could transform reality with circus. Circus can do that, transform reality. In circus, we look at doing things that we all think are impossible. There is a history of revolution in contemporary arts that started with dance, and since the '80s, in an aesthetic explosion this revolution has spread to other disciplines. From the middle of the '90s it spread to circus, with people like Jérôme Thomas, people who question the essence of their disciplines. I have a friend, Yoann Bourgeois, who I think has a very beautiful definition of circus, who talks of it as a balance of forces.[55]

As a person myself who works through movement ideas modelling mathematically how physical forces add to each other to create interesting situations, Yoann's definition really speaks to me. As a result, in fact, the actual apparatus always seemed to me like a pretext – you could say a working aide to approaching movement. 'How can we push the form of juggling further?' 'What's left of juggling when we take away the juggling balls?' and 'What is it that in essence juggling really is?' Well, it's the revolution within each discipline that began asking questions such as these. Our working tool is actually forces, for all circus artists – we create with forces. Gravitational forces, but also muscular forces, the axes of rotations that permit us to do things. The forces that we have in play. So that is our focus. For me in the beginning my focus was the juggling balls, but in fact I am more interested in it being these forces. For instance, when making one of my pieces I asked myself, 'Can I juggle with time? ... Can I juggle with abstractions? How do you do that?'

What does that look like? To juggle with time?
Adrien Mondot: Well, there's a piece called *reTime* that was created in 2006.[56] That was a more formal experiment, but that's one of the questions that interests us.

Could you talk about your collaboration with Claire Bardainne? How does that work?
Adrien Mondot: So, Claire is a visual artist and scenographer, a graphic artist, and she likes to conceptualise spaces through using visual, or digital scenery on stage. She likes to conceptualise spaces in a symbolic way. How does our collaboration work? Well, she explores the universe of video projections, of light, and of movement, and how we put different elements in motion. Conversely, in my first profession as a computer science researcher I developed drawing software for graphic artists, and as a juggler I brought my knowledge to bear on the movement of things. And working with Claire, a visual artist, and scenographer, she brought the tools necessary for serious artistic creation. As a computer scientist, I'm more concerned with the actual construction of an artistic project.

So that's how we work. We each bring the things that are essential to our common identity, but we had these abilities and interests with us when we first met up, the movement and the light for me, the graphic construction and scenography for her.

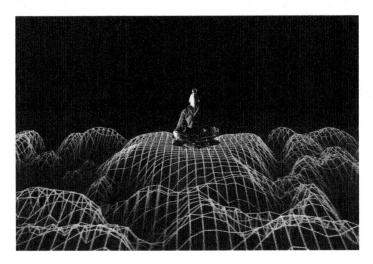

FIGURE 1.13 Cinématique – Novembre 2009 – Les Subsistances © Adrien Mondot – 1.

How does the body fit into this?

Adrien Mondot: So, the body is what gives life to the image. It's what allows the image to exist. Without a body inside it, the image remains just an image. But when it is inhabited by performers, dancers, circus artists, jugglers, inhabited by people, it becomes transformed. It becomes a territory inhabited by a partner in play. It becomes a sort of status. And the scenographic work seamlessly integrates the body with the image. A projection on the ground, for example, will allow the body to be evident in the image. I've worked with projections on tiles, projections on scrim, projections on transparent surfaces that allow one to be in the image also, that allow the image to be in front of the body, to be in a position that we aren't really used to.

So the entire show is actually staged behind the scrim?

Adrien Mondot: Yes. If we project on a screen behind the body, we are in a false relationship with the image. That is to say that the performers do not see the image, and they are more ensconced in something that is cinematic. We are used to an image in a frame. That's the cinema. And what is very important is that we build our pieces on a basis of improvisation. So we always have this dialogue between the person on stage, the performers or circus artists, and the system that places images in movement, because everything we do is done live.

And are you and Claire Bardianne there every night?

Adrien Mondot: Not necessarily, no. It could be people to whom we've taught the roles. These are written parts, of intention, of movement. In fact, we manipulate images like juggling balls, it's really with our hands that we do this. It can be activated with motion capture in the space, so we place things in motion. So for all the whole gamut of creation, and the conceptualisation of the show, it's Claire and I who manipulate it, until after the first week or the first month or so when we try to pass it on and see how long it will take to teach it to the performer. They in fact have a written part that is minutely detailed. However, there is room for their personal responses. They have to use their own eyes as they make decisions.

The interactive system is a tool, a musical instrument. In the same way that a violin is a responsive apparatus and we continue to have different interpretations with a violin that can be done in different ways, that's exactly the same process when we have a score and work with an interactive system.

How do the performers describe their experience of working with these systems?

Adrien Mondot: People on stage always find it surprising that the sensation is essentially visual. It is not embodied. In effect, it's just light. So, then it gives the impression of a presence that's not really there. And so it's this paradox that's at work here.

Another thing that is very important for us, that we explain when we begin a collaboration with someone who dances or who juggles, is that overall we need them to be able to transmit their imagination for the images to actually exist. For example, where we have a sort of field that flows over the stage, that is an amorphous projection. That is to say, the public sees holes, mountains, and peaks, and the performers move through this landscape, and it's the physical fact that they through their movement cross over this terrain that makes us believe that the field exists. If they as performers don't believe in it, it destroys the illusion that the field exists. So their imagination is a pre-requisite for the illusion, in fact.

So if they think that they really will fall into a hole, then we believe as spectators in the feeling that this hole exists. If they just go through the movements, and if they don't believe in the hole and think that they are just avoiding a shape, well we as spectators won't believe there is actually a hole there. When the performers do believe, and they do succeed in transmitting their imaginations, then they give us as members of the audience permission to create stories for ourselves.

What do you give as a primary directive to performers at the beginning of the process?

Adrien Mondot: We give them a narrative which is like a support during the construction of the show. Then ultimately we often remove it. Sometimes we look, later, to remove the overly figurative to keep the form of abstraction that allows the spectator to tell themselves more stories. The stories that we, as spectators, want to tell ourselves. It's this liberty of the spectator that interests us. We find that it is more interesting than a story that is heavily guided.

Do you think that the working in this virtual environment fundamentally affects the quality of the artists' movements?

Adrien Mondot: There comes a moment in the work where we are advanced enough in the construction of the actual final spectacle that we do a run-through, in full without the images to remind ourselves of the body. Generally, we will have built an entire universe in dialogue with the terrain, and then at one moment we remove the virtual universe, and we try to see how we can rework the body. Because in fact, if we are able to re-energise this part, we can reinvigorate the whole of the show.

It's interesting to take each of the parts, the images, the music, the voices, the body, the costumes and to question them without the other elements and see whether each element stands on its own. I find it an interesting process to see them one by one to and then stitch them all together afterwards.

Do the performers talk about their experiences working with these technologies?

Adrien Mondot: Yes, there are often several phases in a work. At the beginning there is a fascination with the game. People are like, 'Ah! This is amazing! Anything is possible!' Then, it's, 'Ah! But this is awful! Everything is possible! It's difficult because we have to choose!' Really what we do when everything is possible is the real question.

And then, there are all these real constraints in the work. It's not common to work with props that are made of light and are digital. I also find that sometimes it doesn't work very well because it's a question of a different sense of time involved when working with the body. You think, 'Wait a second, I just need to fix this bug for two minutes,' and then there's a glitch extends to an hour. The performers' bodies get cold and then it's really hard for them to get back into running the piece.

How does your creative partner Claire Bardainne contribute to the development of the work?

Adrien Mondot: So with the speed of changes in the field, we are in a fairly peculiar position given that we are forging the tools that allow us to build our creations. We are building the brushes, and the pigments, and more than that, we are also building the canvas and the frame. We're building everything. Everything that will make the final painting. And in this way we are looking to master everything from A to Z. To see someone [like Claire] who has an artistic vision, and a vision for technical and digital tools and who is able to make those digital tools evolve in the areas where we want to go, it's hyper-interesting. Also Claire is more than an end user, she assists in the conceptualisation of the software. And she knows, by necessity, how to program. We often have conversations like, 'Ah, well, if we change this functionality it will do this and we will be able to work in this way.'

And you have made your own instruments and environments to enable you to create your work?

Adrien Mondot: Yes! We have created instruments as we've gone along. That is something that will stay in the DNA of our artistic projects. To try to push and to conceive projects from A to Z and to not let ourselves be swayed by the available tools.

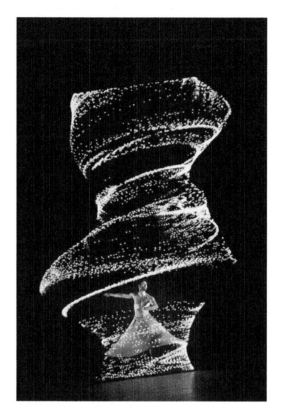

FIGURE 1.14 Le mouvement de l'air by Adrien M & Claire B. Photo: © Romain Etienne.

What does the future hold?

Adrien Mondot: I don't know. There's a whole area of experimentation. We are touring with a show that's really exciting for us. It's a series of installations.[57] A conceptual project that should be finished in the fall. Right now, it's still being worked on. An imaginary that is superimposed on the real. We perceive windows of reality. We stand in it and we see the real standing perfectly behind the imaginary, including the bodies of the people who are there. So it's a question of a little, simple dramaturgy. The dramaturgical effects retain elements of natural forces.

How is the body of the spectator placed in these shows?

Adrien Mondot: At the moment we are in a process of creating the work with half of the show still to be created. In the next half, the space will be darker with more interactive elements.

So that puts the body of the spectator into play with the projections. And so we as the spectators are ...?

Adrien Mondot: We are both the subject and the object.

Notes

1 See the Introduction, p. 6n1 for definitions of the terms 'Traditional Circus,' 'Modern Circus,' 'New Circus,' and 'Contemporary Circus' as used in this book.

2 Throughout this book the term 'to contest' is used in the sense of 'to call into question' as discussed in the Introduction, pp. 1–6; p. 6n1.

3 Giorgio Agamben (2009). *'What is an apparatus?' and other essays* (D. Kishik and S. Pedatella, Trans.). Standford, CA: Stanford University Press, p. 14.

4 Michel Foucault (1980). *Power/Knowledge: Selected interviews and other writings, 1972–1977* (C. Gordon Ed.). New York, NY: Pantheon Books, pp. 194–96.

5 Giorgio Agamben (2009). *'What is an apparatus?'* p. 14.

6 Ibid., p. 15. See also Bauke Lievens (2018). First open letter to the circus: The need to redefine. *Sideshow Circus Magazine.* http://sideshow-circusmagazine.com/being-imaging/letter-redefine

7 André Lepecki (2018). Variations on things. *Esferas: NYU Dept. of Spanish and Portuguese Undergraduate Journal,* (8). https://wp.nyu.edu/esferas/current-issue/9-variations-on-things/

8 Andy Clark and David Chalmers (1998). The extended mind. *Analysis, 58* (1), p. 18.

9 Michael Lynch, cited in Kevin Lincoln (2018). Where is the boundary between your phone and your mind? *The Guardian,* (Guardian Selects, Technology). https://www.theguardian.com/us-news/2018/dec/09/tech-mind-body-boundary-facebook-google. See also Marshall McLuhan (1994). *Understanding media: The extensions of man.* Massachusetts, MA: MIT Press (Original work published 1964).

10 Ibid.

11 Michael Lynch (2016, February 20). Leave my iPhone alone: Why our smartphones are extensions of ourselves. *The Guardian.* https://www.theguardian.com/technology/2016/feb/19/iphone-apple-privacy-smartphones-extension-of-ourselves, see also Michael Lynch (2016). *The internet of us: Knowing more and understanding less in the age of big data.* New York, NY and London: Liveright.

12 Jessica Hamzelou (2009). Learning to juggle grows brain networks for good. *New Scientist* (11 Oct). n.p. https://www.newscientist.com/article/dn17957-learning-to-juggle-grows-brain-networks-for-good/; See also, Jan Scholz, Miriam C Klein, Timothy E J Behrens, and Heidi Johansen-Berg (2009). Training induces changes in white-matter architecture. *Nature Neuroscience, 12,* pp. 1370–1371. https://www.nature.com/articles/nn.2412

13 Ibid. This change was monitored over a period of only six weeks, and this research focused only on jugglers. Data is not yet readily available to measure the scale of changes to body and brain that occur after intense interaction over a longer period of time, or the changes that may occur with other forms of apparatus.

14 See Tony Lofaro (2013). A travelling family. *Ottawa Citizen.* https://www.pressreader.com/canada/ottawa-citizen/20130713/283699772106416

15 See FEDEC. (2018). Russian bar, basic circus arts instruction manual: Chapter 10. http://www.fedec.eu/en/articles/416-russian-bar

16 There are reports of aerialists experimenting with fabric as an apparatus from the late 1950s. However, silks became a widely recognised apparatus from the mid-1990s. While André Simard was developing silks in Montreal for Isabelle Chassée, Gérard Fasoli (now Director of CNAC in France) was also developing what was called for a time 'les cordes Fasoli' for his student Isabelle Vaudelle who presented her act in 1995 at the Festival Mondial de Cirque de Demain. See Magali Sizorn (2019). Les Tissus. http://cirque-cnac.bnf.fr/fr/acrobatie/aeriens/les-tissus

17 Although there are records of people using a similar apparatus from the 1950s onwards in sports, this piece of circus equipment is widely credited as having been developed by Daniel Cyr.

18 See Cirque Éloize (2018). Daniel Cyr, designer of the Cyr wheel and its technique. https://www.cirque-eloize.com/en/about/

19 Sean Gandini (personal communication with Katie Lavers and Jon Burtt, July, 2018).

20 Phia Ménard, p. 12.

21 Shana Carroll (personal communication with Katie Lavers and Jon Burtt, December, 2017).

22 See discussion about Ménard in Katie Lavers (2014). The political body in new circus and contemporary circus arts: Embodied protest, materiality, and active spectatorship. *Platform: Theatre Politics, 8* (2), pp. 55–68.

23 See Jimmy-Gonzalez (2018) D'Argile – Jimmy Gonzalez – Clay juggling. [Video file]. https://vimeo.com/137182637

24 See Mercat de les Flors (2016) CIE. NON NOVA – L'après-midi d'un foehn. [Video file]. https://vimeo.com/175823718

25 Adrien Mondot, p. 14.

26 For video links to Philippe Petit's high wire performances and other documentary footage, see Philippe Petit – Topic. (2019). https://www.youtube.com/channel/UCLczgJc_VokuACXvK8gK2gQ

27 See Katie Lavers (2014). The political body in new circus and contemporary circus arts, pp. 55–68.

28 Philippe Petit, p. 15.

29 See Chapter 5, 'Criminal Practice' in Philippe Petit (2014). *Creativity, the perfect crime.* New York, NY: Riverhead Books.

30 Jean Genet (1910–1986) was a French poet, writer, playwright, and political activist. His poem 'The Tightrope Walker' ('Le Funambule') is included in a collection of his poems entitled, *Fragments et autres textes,* and explores the sensual, almost erotic, nature of the relationship between the funambulist and the wire. See Jean Genet (2003). *Fragments et autres textes/Fragments of the artwork / Jean Genet* (C. Mandell, Trans.). Stanford, CA: Stanford University Press (Original work published 1954).

31 Mallakhamb is an Indian rope form dating back to the 11th century. Originally used as a training apparatus by wrestlers to build grappling strength, the form has evolved into a rope technique combining aerial acrobatics and yoga postures. See Jon Burtt (2010). Mallakhamb: An investigation into the Indian physical practice of rope and pole Mallakhamb. *International Journal of the Arts in Society, 5* (3), pp. 29–38.

32 Jacques Chirac was the French Prime Minister from 1974–1976, French President from 1995–2007, and Mayor of Paris from 1977–1995. In 1989, Petit staged an inclined high wire performance, before an audience of 250,000 from the Palais de Chaillot to the second storey of the Eiffel Tower, to commemorate the French Bicentennial and anniversary of the Declaration of the Rights of the Man and of the Citizen of 1789.

33 *Walking the Harp/A Bridge for Peace* (1987) in Jerusalem, Israel, was a high wire performance by Philippe Petit on an inclined cable bridging the Jewish and Arab quarters for the opening of the Israel Festival.

34 Shana Carroll, p. 116.

35 For video links to Shana Carroll's work with The 7 Fingers, see http://7fingers.com/shows/; for links to her work with Cirque du Soleil, see https://www.cirquedusoleil.com/about-us/our-shows

36 For Chinese Pole act in *Psy* see Les 7 doigts de la main (2013, June 10). CORPO MAT CHINOIS PSY. [Video file]. https://www.youtube.com/watch?v=FbeSDIXzMds&list=PLm64B5dLfVe3QUVWS1Oske6gNt-kCEYj2

37 Héloïse Bourgeois is a French acrobat, and a specialist in hand-to-hand (see note x) and a Chinese pole performer. She has performed with The 7 Fingers, perhaps most notably as one of the original cast members of *Traces*, and is now a member of Compagnie Entre Nous, a Chinese pole collective.

38 Matias Plaul is an Argentinian-born acrobat, director, and specialist in Chinese pole. Plaul also performed with Cirque du Soleil, at the time when Shana Carroll was there as a performer.

39 The 7 Fingers, along with Cirque du Soleil, Cirque Eloize, Moment Factory, and other industrial and academic partners (Concordia University, Université de Montréal and its Polytechnic School) are working alongside the state-funded Canada Industrial Chair in Circus Arts and the social innovation research centre at the National Circus School, and pooling resources to attract some of the top creators and researchers in the circus arts, in fields such as acrobatic and apparatus design as well as multimedia and dramaturgy, to research and develop new apparatus.

40 For video links to Tina Koch and Charlotte Mooney's work with Ockham's Razor see https://www.ockhamsrazor.co.uk/shows

41 *The Mill* (2010) involves an aerial performance featuring a large suspended wheel operated by a system of ropes and drums controlled by the performers.

42 *Tipping Point* (2015) is a full-length work featuring five-metre metal poles which are transformed from the traditional Chinese pole to also function as a moving sculptural environment, and are also used in new ways choreographically.

43 Hand-to-hand is a form of acrobatic partnering involving a base and a flyer and featuring balances, release-and-catches, and other acrobatic moves. See Sébastien Soldevila and Mimi Bonnavaud's hand-to-hand performance, choreographed by Shana Carroll, at the Festival Mondial du Cirque de Demain. Les 7 doigts de la main (2008, February 1). Les 7 doigts de la main – Seb et Mimi – Main à main médaille Or Cirque de demain. [Video file]. https://www.youtube.com/watch?v=ISFmWpexS5g

44 For video links to Elizabeth Streb's work with STREB Extreme Action Company see https://www.youtube.com/user/strebvideo

45 For video links to extracts of Johann Le Guillerm's work with Cirque Ici see, for instance, Théâtre Sénart (2017, June 26). SECRET (TEMPS 2) // Johann Le Guillerm. [Video file]. https://www.youtube.com/watch?v=Eqd6f_KrEUM

46 A maquette is a preliminary temporary model often used by sculptors.

47 *Les Imaginographes* are a series of ongoing interactive installations which form part of Johann Le Guillerm's ongoing *Attraction* project. These installations explore Guillerm's art objects which are created out of his research programmes. They are presented in museums, art galleries, theatres, and public spaces. See http://www.johannleguillerm.com/les-imaginographes/

48 The pronoun 'her' is Phia Ménard's pronoun of choice.

49 Jérôme Thomas is a highly influential French director, juggler, actor, and dancer whose work pushes the boundaries of contemporary juggling. He founded ARMO (Association for Research in the Manipulation of Objects) and Compagnie Jérôme Thomas in 1992 in Burgundy, France. See http://www.jerome-thomas.fr

50 For video links to Phia Ménard's work with Compagnie Non Nova see http://www.cienonnova.com/#/en

51 Phia Ménard, p. 38.

52 For video links to David Clarkson's work with Stalker see https://www.stalker.com.au

53 *Creature* (2016-present) a multidisciplinary installation and performance work directed by David Clarkson for Stalker Theatre, combines immersive interactive video technology created through a research partnership with the Creativity & Cognition Studios at the University of Technology, Sydney. The original production included aerial choreography, songs, music, and dance. There is a recent iteration of the show in the form of an interactive 3D installation for young people. See https://www.stalker.com.au/creature/

54 For video links to Adrien Mondot's work with Compagnie Adrien M & Claire B see https://www.am-cb.net/projets/

55 Yoann Bourgeois is a French contemporary acrobat, juggler, and choreographer whose work explores what he terms 'the suspension of the point' using object manipulation, trampoline, acrobatics, and dance. Since 2012, Yoann Bourgeois has been associate artist of the MC2: Grenoble Maison de la Culture. He founded his own company Compagnie Yoann Bourgeois in 2010.

56 *reTime*, created by Adrien Mondot in 2006, was a short experimental piece that explored the introduction of interactive augmented reality software eMotion into juggling and movement-based performance.

57 See Adrien M & Claire B (2018). Mirages et miracles – trailer. [Video file]. https:// vimeo.com/248983439

References

Adrien M & Claire B. (2018). Mirages et miracles – trailer. [Video file]. Retrieved from https://vimeo.com/248983439

Adrien M & Claire B. (2019). Projects. Retrieved from https://www.am-cb.net/en/ projets

Agamben, G. (2009). *'What is an apparatus?' and other essays* (D. Kishik and S. Pedatella, Trans.). Stanford, CA: Stanford University Press.

Burtt, J. (2010). Mallakhamb: An investigation into the Indian physical practice of rope and pole Mallakhamb. *International Journal of the Arts in Society, 5*(3), 29–38.

Compagnie Non Nova. (2019). Cie Non Nova. Retrieved from http://www.cienonnova. com/#/en

Cirque du Soleil. (2019). Our shows. Retrieved from https://www.cirquedusoleil.com/ about-us/our-shows

Cirque Éloize (2018). Daniel Cyr, designer of the Cyr wheel and its technique. Retrieved from https://www.cirque-eloize.com/en/about/

Clark, A. & Chalmers, D. (1998). The extended mind. *Analysis, 58*(1), 7–19.

FEDEC (European Federation of Professional Circus Schools). (2018). Russian bar, basic circus arts instruction manual: Chapter 10. Retrieved from http://www.fedec.eu/en/ articles/416-russian-bar

Foucault, M. (1980). *Power/Knowledge: Selected interviews and other writings, 1972–1977* (C. Gordon Ed.). New York, NY: Pantheon Books.

Genet, J. (2003). *Fragments et autres textes/Fragments of the artwork / Jean Genet* (C. Mandell, Trans.). Stanford, CA: Stanford University Press. (Original work published 1954).

Hamzelou, J. (2009). Learning to juggle grows brain networks for good. *New Scientist* (11 Oct). n.p. Retrieved from https://www.newscientist.com/article/dn17957-learning-to- juggle-grows-brain-networks-for-good/

Jerome Thomas (2019). Armo – Compagnie Jerome Thomas. Retrieved from http:// www.jerome-thomas.fr

Johann Le Guillerm (2019). Les Imaginographes. Retrieved from http://www.johannleguillerm. com/les-imaginographes/

Jimmy-Gonzalez (2018). D'Argile – Jimmy Gonzalez – Clay juggling. [Video file]. Retrieved from https://vimeo.com/137182637

Lavers, K. (2014). The political body in New Circus and Contemporary Circus arts: Embodied protest, materiality, and active spectatorship. *Platform: Theatre Politics, 8*(2), 55–68.

Lepecki, A. (2018). Variations on things. *Esferas: NYU Dept. of Spanish and Portuguese Undergraduate Journal,* (8), n.p. Retrieved from https://wp.nyu.edu/esferas/current-issue/9-variations-on-things/

Les 7 doigts de la main (2008, February 1). Les 7 doigts de la main – Seb et Mimi – Main à main médaille or Cirque de Demain. [Video file]. Retrieved from https://www.youtube.com/watch?v=ISFmWpexS5g

Les 7 doigts de la main (2013, June 10). Corpo mat Chinois Psy. [Video file]. Retrieved from https://www.youtube.com/watch?v=FbeSDIXzMds&list=PLm64B5dLfVe3QUVW-S1Oske6gNt-kCEYj2

Lievens, B. (2018). First open letter to the circus: The need to redefine. *Sideshow Circus Magazine.* Retrieved from http://sideshow-circusmagazine.com/being-imaging/letter-redefine

Lincoln, K. (2018). Where is the boundary between your phone and your mind? *The Guardian,* (Guardian Selects, Technology). Retrieved from https://www.theguardian.com/us-news/2018/dec/09/tech-mind-body-boundary-facebook-google

Lofaro, T. (2013). A travelling family. *Ottawa Citizen.* Retrieved from https://www.pressreader.com/canada/ottawa-citizen/20130713/283699772106416

Lynch, M. (2016). *The internet of us: Knowing more and understanding less in the age of big data.* New York and London: Liveright.

Ockham's Razor. (2019). Ockham's Razor shows. Retrieved from https://www.ockhamsrazor.co.uk/shows

Petit, P. (2014). *Creativity, the perfect crime.* New York, NY: Riverhead Books.

Philippe Petit – Topic. (2019). [Video files]. Retrieved from https://www.youtube.com/channel/UCLczgJc_VokuACXvK8gK2gQ

Scholz, J., Klein, M. C., Behrens, T. E. J., & Johansen-Berg, H. (2009). Training induces changes in white-matter architecture. *Nature Neuroscience, 12,* 1370–1371. Retrieved from https://www.nature.com/articles/nn.2412

Sizorn, M. (2019). Les tissus. Retrieved from http://cirque-cnac.bnf.fr/fr/acrobatie/aeriens/les-tissus

Stalker. (2019). Immersive physical theatre. Retrieved from https://www.stalker.com.au

strebvideo. (2019). [Video files]. Retrieved from https://www.youtube.com/user/strebvideo

The 7 Fingers (2019). Shows. Retrieved from http://7fingers.com/shows/

Théâtre Sénart. (2017, June 26). Secret (Temps 2) // Johann Le Guillerm. [Video file]. Retrieved from https://www.youtube.com/watch?v=Eqd6f_KrEUM

Further Reading

Banks, G. L. (1862). *Blondin, his life and performances.* London & New York, NY: Routledge, Warne & Routledge.

Blondeau, C., Cibille, P., & Quentin, A. (2009). *Johann Le Guillerm à 360°.* Arles, France: Actes Sud.

FEDEC. (2019). Resources. Retrieved from http://www.fedec.eu/en/articles/?c=216

Freixe, G. (Ed.) (2017). *Le corps, ses dimensions cachées. Pratiques scéniques.* coll. A la croisée des arts. Montpellier, France: Deuxième époque.

Mondot, A., Bardainne, C., Bardiot, C., Derobert, L., Farcet, C., Godon, N., Guillois, P., & Rossi-Batôt, C. (2016). *La neige n'a pas de sens.* Valenciennes, France: Éditions Subjectile.

Petit, P. (1997). *Traité du funambulisme*. Arles, France: Actes Sud.

Petit, P. (2002). *To reach the clouds: My high wire walk between the Twin Towers*. New York, NY: North Point Press.

Shapiro, D. (1989). *Blondin*. St Catherines, Ontario: Vanwell Publishing.

Quentin, A. (2007). *Johann Le Guillerm*. Paris: Magellan & Cie.

Tait, P. (2005). *Circus bodies: Cultural identity in aerial performance*. Abingdon, Oxon: Routledge.

2

POLITICS IN CONTEMPORARY CIRCUS

Politics in Contemporary Circus – contesting the normate

Many of the politically driven works in Contemporary Circus can be seen as emerging out of the desire to contest, or to problematise the 'normate,'[1] a term which Rosemarie Garland-Thomson, the Disabilities Studies scholar, coined in her 1997 book *Extraordinary Bodies: Figuring Physical Disability in American Culture and Literature*.[2] Garland-Thomson writes that the term has since been widely adopted, especially in Disability Studies, because 'it answers the need to name with just one word something previously unnamed.'[3]

The word 'normate' describes the internalised and hidden social figure that is the constructed image of one who, because of their bodily appearance and the cultural capital that it gives them, can step into a position of authority and wield the power it grants them. The boundaries of this constructed figure become visible by studying 'the array of deviant others whose marked bodies shore up the normate's boundaries.'[4]

In her book *Extraordinary Bodies*, Garland-Thomson writes that if one attempts to glimpse the normate by peeling away the 'deviant others' who mark out its boundaries, at this current moment in time what 'emerges is a very narrow profile that describes only a minority of actual people.'[5] She points to Erving Goffman's comment which she sees as the logical conclusion of this process. Goffman writes that this figure is 'a young, married, white, urban, northern, heterosexual, Protestant father of college education, fully employed, of good complexion, weight and height, and a recent record in sport.'[6] As Garland-Thomson notes, in this portrait of the normate there is no mention of femaleness.

This idea of a socially constructed and internalised cultural 'normate' that directly relates to external bodily appearance is of intrinsic importance in Circus Studies, as in many ways it can be seen as emerging, becoming embodied, and being promulgated through the developments in American circus after 1871 – the year that P. T. Barnum came into circus at the age of 61.

Barnum brought with him into circus the surviving contents of his burnt-out American Museum in New York, including dioramas and waxworks, his extensive menagerie, and his notorious freak shows, which, under his management, had become a new, commercialised form of mass entertainment. In his freak shows, Barnum presented a diverse range of performers with bodies that were out of the ordinary, including,

> some of the most renowned 'human curiosities' of his time, including the conjoined twins Chang and Eng, the diminutive Tom Thumb; the diminutive Lavinia Warren and Commodore Nutt; William Henry Johnson, the 'What is it?'; the giants Anna Swan and Colonel Routh Goshen; Maximo and Bartola, the Aztec children; and Charles Tripp, the no-armed boy.[7]

Barnum, on coming into circus, originally presented the 'human curiosities' in the big top as part of the main show, but soon moved them into separate tents away from the big top.

Ascribing a metaphorical reading to performance spaces, Performance Studies scholar Richard Schechner observes that,

> Theater [or performance] places are maps of the cultures where they exist. That is theater is analogical not only in the literary sense – the stories dramas tell, the convention of explicating action by staging it – but also in the architectonic sense [...] Thus, for example, the Athenian theater of the fifth BCE had as its center the altar of Dionysus.[8]

When Barnum moved the freak show out of the big top into separate closed-off tents in the sideshow annexe it could be said that his decision, in an architectonic sense, not only mapped the increasing segregation of people with 'extraordinary' bodies that was emerging at the end of the nineteenth century, but also began to map out an emerging normate, a normate with its boundaries formed by the 'deviant others,' that is the performers excluded from the big top.

Inside the sideshow annexe alongside the animals in the menageries, were a diverse range of performers variously described as hermaphrodites, fakirs, bearded ladies, living skeletons, wild men of Borneo, cannibals, the armless wonders, albinos, fat ladies, Siamese twins, midget triplets, and snake charmers; 'a "human menagerie" (a term popularised by P. T. Barnum) of racial diversity, gender difference [and] bodily variety.'[9]

In 1874, the German animal dealer and zoo owner, Carl Hagenbeck, began to trade in people he imported and featured alongside the animals he displayed. The first group of people he exhibited was a family of Lapps imported to make the display of reindeer more intriguing and 'most picturesque.'[10] Ethnographic displays went on to become a regular part of sideshows in circus, and First Nations people were often situated in the sideshows alongside the freaks and the animals.

Although in the first few decades after 1768 when Traditional Circus, or Modern Circus, as it is sometimes called, was founded, there were a number of performers of colour in the big top, by the late nineteenth century in Barnum's circus, and in most major American circuses of the period, it would appear that the only performers that performed in the big top were either white or those who could pass as white, or those who were Middle Eastern or Asian in appearance.

Many circus performers and musicians of colour performed in Barnum's circus, they performed however in the sideshow annexe. The musicologists Doug Seroff and Lynn Abbott, researching the origins of jazz, searched the archives of *The Indianapolis Freeman*, an African American weekly publication reporting on African American arts at the end of the nineteenth century. They discovered that there was 'a far greater involvement of African American performers in circus than has previously been acknowledged or documented.'[11] Noting that very little is written about this topic elsewhere, they write that African American performers appeared in every large touring circus at the end of the nineteenth century but that they performed in the sideshow annexe that housed the menagerie, and 'the freaks.'[12]

The architectonic separation between the big top and the sideshow annex, makes clear the essential boundaries of the normate which were metaphorically delineated by the displays of 'deviant others,' those excluded from the big top and situated in the sideshow. This normate remains relevant largely because it was embodied and presented by the nineteenth century American circus, and assimilated and internalised by the large audiences of spectators that came to see Barnum's circus.

It could be argued that this internalised normate, embodied and physicalised in Barnum's separation of the circus into these two parts, the big top and the sideshow annexe, is still perpetuated in Contemporary Circus. Although the actual sideshow annexe has for the most part been abandoned, the boundaries of the normate are still clearly visible in Contemporary Circus by the almost total exclusion of performers of colour, First Nations performers, performers with adaptive or extraordinary bodies, queer performers, sexually ambiguous performers, transgender performers, and increasingly of female performers.

The increasing lack of women in Contemporary Circus performances can be seen as the flow-on effect of the gender imbalance in the circus training institutions. Circus Scholar, Alisan Funk, noting the gender imbalance in French circus training institutions, writes,

> Researchers found that both the student and staff populations of preparatory and professional circus schools in France were 70 percent male [...] Unsurprisingly, analysis of working circus artists in France showed 70 percent male representation and a negligible number of women in creative, production, and artistic direction roles.[13]

Susie Williams, Managing Director of Acrobat Conundrum in Seattle, describing her experience at the 2016 Montréal Complètement Cirque Festival writes that, although she admires the festival and would never miss it, she noted a significant preponderance of male performers,

> Out of nine ticketed productions only one had more than one woman in it. [...] I want to see more women. I want to see women who look different from each other. I want to see so many women that no single woman has to stand as a symbol for what all women can be.[14]

Much of the politically driven Contemporary Circus work currently being created can be read as actively contesting the boundaries of this heteronormative, able-bodied, white male normate.

The emergence of New Circus and the ethos of contestation

The political thrust of much Contemporary Circus work continues the ethos of contestation, embodied in New Circus, after the widespread unrest of May 1968.[15]

The first New Circus companies were set up in the mid-1970s. French Circus Studies scholar Martine Maleval points to various possible origins of New Circus in France, including in 1973 when Christian Taguet founded the company Les Puits aux images which went on to become Cirque Baroque in 1987, or 1975 when Paul Rouleau and Pierric Pillot (who later took the name Pierrot Bidon) started touring shows around France in caravans as Cirque Bidon. Another departure point involved the brothers Kudlak who were playing in a brass band in 1975 and then went on to found Cirque Plume in 1983.[16]

English-speaking Circus Studies scholars often point to the San Francisco-based Pickle Family Circus, which was set up in 1974, as being the first New Circus Company, while Australian scholars often cite Circus Oz as the first. Circus Oz was formed in late 1977 with the merger of two Australian theatre companies – New Circus, an Adelaide-based company set up in 1974 (which continued as New Ensemble Circus), and the Melbourne-based Soapbox Circus which had been set up in 1976 by the Australian Performing Group. The two groups merged in late December 1977 to form Circus Australia which soon became known as Circus Oz.

New Circus companies contested all the iconic elements identified with Traditional Circus shows. Perhaps the most radical element that they contested, and eventually for the most part rejected, was the inclusion of any animals other than humans in circus shows. Even horses were almost entirely excluded. As Traditional Circus had originated with Philip Astley's spectacular equestrian acts in London in 1768, and as horse-riding acts had remained a key element of circus shows, the exclusion of these acts signalled a fundamental change.

Although various reasons are cited for this jettisoning of animals acts by New Circus, for example, 'happenstance,'[17] and 'economic reasons,'[18] in the climate of heated political debate about animal rights emerging in the 1960s, this action can be seen as profoundly significant, reflecting in no uncertain way increasing social concern about the rights of animals.

The period leading up to the development of New Circus in the 1970s was a key point in the emergence of debate about the relationship between humans and other animals. An array of new books and writing led this debate. In 1962, *Silent Spring*, by marine biologist and author Rachael Carson, detailed the disastrous impact of modern farming and the use of pesticides on insects and birdlife.[19] In 1964, activist Ruth Harrison published *Animal Machines*, her exposé of factory farming, and novelist Brigid Brophy followed with *The Rights of Animals* in 1965, with an article of the same name making the front page of *The Times* newspaper and leading to intense public debate around the issue.[20]

In 1970, psychologist Richard Ryder's pamphlet 'Specieism' was printed, 'Ryder coined its title word on the analogy of racism and sexism to show at a glance that the moral revolution of the 1960s, unfinished as it obviously was, had still another ancient orthodoxy to undo.'[21] This pamphlet has proved to be 'the founding text of the modern animal rights movements.'[22] In 1975, Peter Singer's landmark book *Animal Liberation* was published. John Berger's influential essay, 'Why Look at Animals?' followed in 1977 and was the first in an array of works on the subject of the 'symbolic uses of animals in popular culture and art, zoological displays of animals and animal performances, and the literal place of animals in contemporary life, which now constitute the emergent interdisciplinary field of animals studies.'[23]

Within the arts, performance artist Joseph Beuys, in his 1974 performance *I like America and America likes me*, shared a space in the René Block Gallery in New York with a wild coyote over a period of three days. Beuys viewed the coyote as a symbol of the human impact on the environment and animals in America, and saw this performance as touching on a point of trauma in American history, 'You could say that a reckoning has to be made with the coyote, and only then can this trauma be lifted.'[24]

In New Circus, in 1979, the Director Hilary Westlake reimagined the Traditional Circus Liberty Horse Act, creating a new act with a 'female trainer in dominatrix attire who was controlling eight men, harnessed like circus horses, who were made to cavort round the ring and mimic whatever circus horses do.'[25] Aside from its obvious sado-masochistic overtones, this image can be read as a New Circus act intended to provoke questioning around the issue of the rights of animals.

In this climate of intense debate, animal acts were for the most part jettisoned from New Circus. As Pierrot Bidon pronounced about his all-human New Circus company Archaos, 'We are the animals [...] It's our mission to shock society. I'm here to shoot society in the head.'[26]

In addition to contesting the inclusion of animals in circus, New Circus also contested the idea that the transmission of circus skills should only take place through the feudal lines of the Traditional Circus families. Circus workshops soon began to be opened, and circus schools were set up, and 'Circus for Everybody' became a catchcry, 'No one here was born in a circus,' Bidon said talking about the performers in Archaos. 'we all grew up in the street.'[27]

Other iconic elements of Traditional Circus were also contested by New Circus. Many New Circus companies abandoned the big top and the circus ring. Creators and directors coming into New Circus from different disciplines such as theatre and dance, wanted to work with projections and other visual elements in their productions, and often saw the proscenium arch theatre as a more easily controllable space than a big top and a circus ring. Other companies wanted to reposition circus as an artform on an equal footing with theatre and dance and, as part of that, claimed the right to perform circus in proscenium arch theatres.[28]

The ringmaster as a single voice of authority presiding over the circus show was also contested, with some circuses abandoning this central figure of control altogether. Mike Finch, Artistic Director of Circus Oz from 1998 to 2015, in an email to the authors in 2018, writes that when a speaking voice was required,

> in line with the company's political ethos, the idea of the power being vested in a white, straight, male ringmaster was challenged and the company would often use a number of speakers to host the show. If a single 'host' was used to guide the audience through the shows, the role [was] generally played by female performers, and in more recent years by performers of colour, and also a genderqueer performer.[29]

Other New Circus companies contested the sequinned costumes of Traditional Circus shows, choosing instead to present performers in everyday clothes with no conspicuous make up, in order to emphasise the normality and the ordinariness of the performers.

Alongside this ethos of 'contestation,' one of the most significant effects of the events of 1968, as historian Ingrid Gilcher-Holtey points out, was that 'the 68 movements broadened [...] the horizon of the political. They detached "politics" and "the political" from the state and its apparatus, and so they created a culture where personal politics as well as countercultural communities became central.'[30] These ideas of personal politics and countercultural communities became, alongside the ethos of contestation, some of the major informing ideas in the political development of New Circus.

Jon Hawkes, one of the founders of Circus Oz, proposes that the idea of a countercultural community and the possibility of pursuing a radical alternative lifestyle were some of the main elements that attracted many people into New Circus.[31] The circus as an alternative family consisting of outsiders that worked, lived, and performed together became a strong countercultural image promoted through the way the circuses functioned. Scholar Jane Mullet, also a co-founder of Circus Oz, proposes that these alternative families of New Circus were not only lived experience but were also performed. When Circus Oz was on tour and arrived in a new town, the performance of the alternative family began, with the normal divisions of labour broken down so that everybody did everything – women could be seen rigging tents, setting up their own aerial equipment and driving trucks and the men could be seen cooking and washing up.[32]

The San Francisco-based Pickle Family Circus, whose name was an ironic take on the family-based Traditional Circuses, was a company that also celebrated and performed the idea of an alternative family, as can be seen in the Terry Lorant photographs of the time. One of her documentary photographs of the Pickle Family Circus features a group of pregnant women standing together with their tops pulled up exposing their bellies. At that point in time, the bodies of pregnant women were taboo, and they would normally hide their bodies beneath large tent-shaped dresses, so this photo of an alternative kind of family group could be seen as being intended to shock and contest the social norms of the time.[33]

The French circus Archaos, founded by Pierrot Bidon, also had the appeal of an alternative family, 'Archaos was a family and Bidon its patriarch. Members of the troupe came from all walks of life and he exuded an abundance of warmth that encompassed them all.'[34]

The opening up of circus training to anyone interested in learning it brought in new people from outside the Traditional Circus families. Artists and creators came into New Circus from diverse fields such as theatre, music, the visual arts, and dance, often looking for an artform with the potential to reach out to large audiences. They brought with them new ideas which profoundly changed the form propelling forwards the creation of innovative and exciting new work as circus began hybridising with these new diverse disciplines.

A countercultural commitment to the idea of 'the group' often led to the attempt to erase hierarchies, the widespread abolition of the Traditional Circus idea of the 'circus star,' and the development of innovative group acts.

With Feminism an important driving force in much New Circus, many female performers saw their performance as a manifestation of their personal politics and an embodiment of their feminist beliefs. They often rejected Traditional Circus ideas relating to the embodied performance of femininity, contesting the need to shave their armpits, to wear sequins and feathers, and the highly sexualised costumes of Traditional Circus.

The Wimmin's Circus, which operated in Melbourne between 1980 and 1981, would seem to be the first women's circus in the world and it used the gender confusion around the image of 'strong women' in circus to 'present images of women that challenged stereotypes.'[35] Many New Circuses contested the traditional roles of women as flyers in the acrobatic and flying acts, and developed female performers that could act as bases, the weight-bearing role usually reserved for males in partnering. They also began to take on the roles of clowns or ringmasters, and to perform juggling, traditionally male preserves.[36]

The contesting of heteronormative sexualities was also another important element of New Circus, not only through the tacit acceptance of alternative sexualities, but also the active performance of them. Archaos was one company that actively performed alternative sexual mores,

> causing a stir with their naked trapeze artists and men dancing together, and being banned by some of the London councils and even being banished to the outskirts of town in Canada. In one performance at Dunkirk in 1990, two men are described as lying on stage smooching, while another scene showed male courtiers trying to win the affections of a Roman senator who was wearing green lipstick and a see-through skirt.[37]

Archaos also contested the pastoral aesthetic of much Traditional Circus, introducing instead a new ethos of industrialisation, "'The welding torch, when it is used at night," said Bidon, "is a very beautiful thing, is it not? Why not use it in a circus?'"[38] Bidon revolutionised circus. He gave his performers 'oxy-acetylene torches, motorbikes and semtex, and clad his performers in boiler suits and corrugated iron. Crash helmets replaced red noses; [...] trapeze artists swung from forklift trucks and huge cranes.'[39]

With the emergence of New Circus, the whole notion of what circus is, and what it could be in the future, have fundamentally changed, and many of these changes within the genre can be read as being largely brought about by the embracing of this notion of 'contestation' or 'calling into question' existing orthodoxies.

In Contemporary Circus the spirit of contestation can still be seen to be a driving force. Many politically driven Contemporary Circus companies now contest the normate, promulgated through Barnum's circus which still is an active presence in the genre with implications for training, casting, presentation, and content of work.

English Contemporary Circus company Extraordinary Bodies contests the exclusion of disabled artists from circus. The company takes as its motto 'Circus for Every Body,' a play on the New Circus catchcry. They describe themselves as creating 'integrated' circus combining exceptional performers who are deaf, with disabled and non-disabled artists.[40]

New companies are now being set up by performers of colour to contest the whiteness of much Contemporary Circus. In Australia, Kim 'Busty Beatz' Bowers, along with Co-Founder Lisa Fa'alafi, set up the all-women of colour company Hot Brown Honey to contest sexism and racism in particular within the performing arts. Other companies are initiating training programmes to create new pathways to enable performers of colour to transition into existing Contemporary Circus companies. BLAKflip, an initiative that Artistic Director, Mike Finch helped to set up at Circus Oz, is a training programme for Aboriginal performers that aims to increase the numbers of Indigenous performers in Australian circus. One of its recent successes is *Chasing Smoke*, a show directed by Natano Faanana for a BLAKflip workshop, which has now been taken into the repertoire of the Australian Contemporary Circus company, Casus.[41]

Tilde Björfors, Director of Cirkus Cirkör in Stockholm, with her trilogy of works *Borders*, *Limits*, and *Movements*, has contested the exclusion of refugees from Europe, and her work *Epifónima*, with a cast of seven female performers, contests the increasing exclusion of female performers from many Contemporary Circus shows.

As can be seen in the conversations in the *Voices* section of this chapter, other creators are contesting the normate by rejecting the narrowing range of acceptable body types in Contemporary Circus choosing to work with performers of differing shapes, sizes, and training, while others are creating work which calls into question the social processes of gender assignment.

Part 2 of this chapter, the *Voices* section, includes conversations with eight creators whose politically engaged work can be seen to directly contest the normate in Contemporary Circus: Mike Finch (Circus Oz), Jennifer Miller (Circus Amok), Tilde Björfors (Circus Cirkör), Kim 'Busty Beatz' Bowers (Hot Brown Honey), Phia Ménard (Compagnie Non Nova), Jo Lancaster and Simon Yates (Acrobat), and Fez Faanana (Briefs).

Politics in Contemporary Circus – voices

The first conversation in this *Voices* section is with Mike Finch who was Artistic Director of Circus Oz, from 1998 to 2015.[42] He came into the role at the age of 27 and, with 17 years in the position, is the longest serving Artistic Director of the company.

From its very beginning as a New Circus company, Circus Oz's performance has always been overtly political, taking on a wide range of issues from Aboriginal land rights to the banning of uranium mining.

Here Finch talks about how the decision-making processes involved in creating work for the company and running it as an organisation can all be seen as 'political' work, from maintaining the gender balance policy that has been in place since Circus Oz began in 1977, to creating specific targeted programmes like Strong Women, which focuses on the development of female circus artists and their representation in the circus industry in Australia, to BLAKflip, a programme providing pathways into circus for Indigenous Australian circus artists.

We started by asking Mike Finch about the way the bodies of the performers are presented in Circus Oz performances.

★★★★★

Mike Finch

Would you describe the use of the body in Circus Oz as political?
Mike Finch: Yes, part of my pre-Circus Oz background was making shows that were overtly political, that had some sort of inherent thread or message in it that I would consider political. As my work continued on in Circus Oz it was

simply, for example, the gender balance of the company that becomes a political statement, or the choice of which performer gets to speak to the audience, or the choice of the way the audience is arranged around the performer. All of those are political decisions.

In terms of the study of power, I think probably the biggest sustained political action that Circus Oz has taken is the gender balance policy, the quota of female-identifying bodies on the stage. So it's a rigorous 50/50 gender balance that's been there for the entire life of the company. With occasional slight variations, in the ensemble of 12 performers for example, sometimes for a few months it might be seven and five, but for 95% of the time it is a six/six ensemble of men and women.

Was Strong Women a programme that you initiated?
Mike Finch: Yes, along with Antonella Casella, I was part of initiating Strong Women.[43] It was a programme that Circus Oz initiated that actually came after our BLAKflip programme. BLAKflip was about developing capacity in the Indigenous community to bring more Australian Indigenous performers through into the company as circus performers.[44]

There is obviously an amazing culture of dance, music, even comedy, and a growing culture of Western style theatre made by Australian Indigenous artists, but, for some bizarre reason that I still don't completely understand, there are very few Australian Indigenous performers that would identify as circus performers in spite of the huge potential for crossover from the dance culture, the sports culture, the AFL players, the actors, and the comedians.[45]

So, once Josh Bond joined the company, we set up a programme called BLAKflip that is a training programme that runs once a year bringing in Indigenous performers from other traditions, whether dance or comedy or sport, and teaching them circus skills.[46] It was incredibly successful, and has started to lead to some real change, and, as a result of BLAKflip, we then went on to set up the Strong Women programme.

Strong Women had slightly different aims because Circus Oz has always had a really strong representation of women, but the programme was established to set up some training, run by women, encouraging younger, emerging women performers to explore their full potential. So not always literally physically 'strong,' although we were definitely encouraging the notion of female bases and female under-standers, but also strong female characters, really loud, brassy clowns and ballsy character performers. So the Strong Women programme was half-modelled on the BLAKflip programme, and then the company went on to another programme of disability circus. So Circus Oz was gradually working its way through a set of different marginalised areas that we felt were really under-represented.

What are your thoughts on diversity in Australian circus currently?
Mike Finch: As soon as you scratch the surface of it, you think, 'Oh my God, the number of people of colour represented in Australian circus is terrible!' Asian

FIGURE 2.1 Circus Oz. Photo: Ponche Hawkes.

faces on Australian circus stages – they're there because there's this great connection with Chinese circus – but they're very under-represented in terms of reflecting the general population. So all of that feels like it directly speaks to the politics. You could make an all-round entertaining family circus show with real diversity represented, and I believe that, in a way, would be a deeply subversive act in contemporary Australia.

Can you talk about the context for the BLAKflip programme within Circus Oz as an organisation?

Mike Finch: Circus Oz within itself is a very white organisation, and its DNA goes back to middle-class white people in the 1970s doing what they thought was subversive, but actually now needs to move a lot further. So I think Circus Oz needs to work towards people of colour at every level of the organisation, from governance level right through to the artists.

It's very hard to move forward politically in an organisation. There's the internal politics, the external politics, overt politics, covert politics, the politics inherent in the way you make the show, the politics expressed on stage in the way you make the show, the way that the marketing is set up, and the type of audiences you are speaking to. So it's relatively easy for a white organisation to market to a white audience, but how do you get an audience that actually reflects diversity in Australia?

How do you get an Asian audience into the tent, or people of colour into the tent? It goes through into every level, so the challenges are huge.

In the last Circus Oz show the ringmaster was Indigenous, could you tell us a bit about him. Did he come into Circus Oz through BLAKflip?
Mike Finch: Dale Woodbridge-Brown was part of the first intake of BLAKflip.[47] He'd come through AACPA, the Australian Aboriginal Centre for Performing Arts in Queensland, and Josh Bond contacted them via our advisory group and asked, 'Who are some of your students who might be interested in circus?' They were like, 'Well, Dale could be interested in circus.'

So then we invited him into BLAKflip [in 2012] and we actually offered him a job in the Circus Oz ensemble at the end of the training. By 2016, he was the Ringmaster.

How did you go about the casting process – how did you choose the performers for the Circus Oz shows?
Mike Finch: There's been a lot of talk inside the circus community about recent circus shows with the classic token women in the red dress with all the men with their shirts off. Six guys all doing teeterboard together and there's the female hetero love interest who wafts through the middle.

People are so used to seeing those kinds of shows that they would see Circus Oz and go, 'It's all women! It's like the whole show is full of women!' We've actually simply got 50/50 women/men. But in their heads people are so used to seeing shows that are so different to that gender balance. So the way we would approach it at Circus Oz, and I inherited it, I take no credit for the policy, but I do feel really proud of having upheld it for my whole 17 years, there's just no discussions about the policy, it's a rule: 50/50.

You've got a budget to support twelve performers on stage so you are going to have to find six men and six women. It's not a matter of, 'Oh this woman's not good enough but we'll give her a job anyway because she's a woman.' It's a role for a woman so you find the best woman. It might be like, 'We need at least one flying trapeze catcher and we need at least one juggler.' So you have a list of the mix you need and I would literally have a chart up on my wall that was like six blank spots on one column (women) and six blank spots on the other (men).

It depends on criteria, because the definition of excellence in circus is not strictly quantifiable. It's not like we're looking for 100 metre sprinters where you can just go, they either run in under ten seconds or they don't. Circus is a mix of clowning, comedy, strength, flexibility, lyricism, art, and the ability to fit with the group. So you might have relatively few women jugglers, but we found one, Hazel Bock, an amazing foot juggler.[48] There's relatively few lithe male flyers but we found one, Paul O'Keeffe.[49]

So you are constantly hunting to break the gender stereotypes. Always look-ing for strong female bases. My aesthetic is that it is a truly great thing for young girls in particular to see a strong woman on the bottom of a pyramid lifting up two or three other people, and so we would be always looking out for strong female bases that you could have in the show. Strong female clowns, comediennes, who could be brassy, bold, rude, and cheeky because the cliché is that the blokes get to do all the talking, and the blokes get to do all the naughty stuff, and the women get to look beautiful up in the air on the ropes or whatever. So you are constantly trying to subvert it, but essentially it's just like there's six spots for men, six spots for women, our job is to fill them.

So does the policy of 50 percent women in Circus Oz apply through the whole company or just to the performers?
Mike Finch: Over time what would happen is that there were these incredibly strong women who were integral to the politics. In the way that I would love to see Circus Oz have representation of Indigenous people at every level, for decades Circus Oz already has had women represented at every level. For example, the Board of Directors has always had a gender balance of women including, for my entire time at Circus Oz, a female Chair of the Board. Then the executive committee, which was three of us, there was Linda Mickleborough, and now Lou Oppenheim. Both General Managers – women, so there's a gender balance there.

The ensemble was always 50/50, but there is also a really strong tradition of female technicians, so a history of female lighting operators, female riggers, female stage managers, very hands-on physical, visible, onstage stage managers. So that what you get is a constant set of checks and balances against sexism right through. In a positive way, I completely affirm all of those politics, but there would also be women, and women in positions of equal or senior power to me, looking over my shoulder, all the time, at every level. There are women in the casting committee, there are women in the ensemble. If you do that for long enough it stops feeling like a quota at all.

Then we would be looking for interesting diversity in bodies, and it was kind of sometimes awkward because you're dealing with gender identity and body issues, and all of the politics that go with it. You'd sometimes go to a performer and typically women are much more oppressed by body policing – but in casting or devising you go to a female performer and say, 'We really like how chunky you are and how strong you are, and you've got really strong thighs and you're in the show. We want to make costumes that celebrate your body type and we don't want you to be embarrassed by who you are at all.'

Mel Fyfe, who was our strong woman for many years, would go out into the foyer, like a lot of our performers do, and talk to people after the show.[50] Mostly it's just audience members wanting to say 'Hi' and thank performers for the show, take a photo, that kind of thing. But one thing would happen to Mel regularly, every few shows. Typically, a woman would come up with a daughter and say, 'Oh I was so glad my daughter got to see you because she's struggling a bit with her weight, and it was so good to see such a competent woman who was sort of heavy. You walked on stage and I saw you and I was thinking, "She's a bit fat, she's not going to be able to do anything at all, and then you did all that incredible tumbling and you lifted all those people and it was so great!'" They were actually trying to be really complimentary, and to be totally clear, Mel is definitely not 'fat,' she is simply strong and not the shape of the women that mainstream entertainment generally puts onstage.

For the mother and the daughter, this may well be life or death. For a girl who's got bulimia or a kid who has been bullied, or has been struggling with self-image, to see someone like Mel on stage, and she's doing this incredible stuff, and then to meet her in person can literally be life-changing. Mel would come back to the dressing rooms going, 'Oh, someone just came up and told me I looked really fat!' and of course it's challenging. But Mel is incredible and would always keep a smile on with the public, and always be like, 'I'm so glad you enjoyed the show!' and talk to the girl, and encourage her, and probably change her life. But it was serious emotional labour for Mel. Political labour.

So it was conscious and we would talk about it. We would be designing a pyramid for example, and it'd be like you could make a pyramid that obviously had all the big blokes at the bottom and the littlest woman at the top in terms of the sort of averages of body types, but we'd be like, 'Mmm ... that's a bit boring.'

So we would be constantly trying to find the three-high with the woman at the bottom. There's a huge amount of pride at the moment in the current Circus Oz ensemble because they've managed to nail that with Freja Edney at the bottom of an all-female three-high.[51] And also three-highs with women on the bottom and men up the top. And women on the very bottom of a four-high pyramid.

So all those things were an overt part of the aesthetic conversation openly discussed in the rehearsal room, like going, 'Oh boring! Men on the bottom!' You'd make jokes about that sort of stuff.

What about the ballet aesthetic that's so strong in much of the Montreal circus, the aesthetic of balletic lines in the movement, how does that relate to Circus Oz?

Mike Finch: Yeah, that's fascinating too, seeing that rising up through, obviously Cirque du Soleil were playing with a lot of that. But when The 7 Fingers arrived with *Loft*, their first show with all seven of them in it, and so much of the underlying thread was this very lyrical dance-based movement that flowed through it.[52] So there'd be particular dance-trained acrobats who went into Cirque du Soleil as part of the house troupe, that ended up using that as their informing vocabulary.

With Circus Oz, the DNA came from subversive theatre – agit-prop theatre, political theatre, a combination of rock and roll and comedy, Brecht, Dario Fo, Augusto Boal – that tradition. So Circus Oz was an off-shoot of the Pram Factory that was really a bunch of activist theatre makers, and dance was not part of it.[53]

It was almost as if there was a kind of toughness about the 1970s in Melbourne, the political theatre scene particularly around the Pram Factory which was like,

'We're doing the tough stuff.' It was maybe a bit macho, or at least 'guerrilla' in a way. Lots of women involved, but lots of women who went on to have no kids, and really had to fight hard to survive inside that tough counterculture culture.

So the tradition wasn't abstract choreography, non-linear. It was more like, 'We've got a message to tell and we're going to talk it and we're going to sing it and ...' Like some of the early acts, there's some great footage of the 23rd Tractor Brigade satirising Chinese propaganda, with the flags and they're all riding group-bicycle, all dressed as Chinese peasants but sort of sending it up. There was a lot of satire, like satirical send-up, but also sometimes almost a homage.

The notion of getting the whole ensemble together to all move together in synchronisation was the antithesis of the individuality of that Circus Oz culture. That DNA flowed right through and just continued on. You get a 7 Fingers show and a Circus Oz show and it's like, 'well they're all doing this lyrical dancing, and we're all doing fart jokes!'

★★★★★

Mike Finch's discussion of how Circus Oz engages with its political ideals in its shows through its commitment to gender equity and its representation of gender, leads us to a conversation with Jennifer Miller, Artistic Director and Founder of Circus Amok.[54]

As Juggler, Bearded Lady, Ringmistress, Founder and Director of Circus Amok, Miller tours city parks in New York City with the company performing circus shows each summer that combine large-scale puppets, street theatre, acrobatics, and postmodern dance movement, and also address local social justice issues.

We started our discussion by asking Jennifer Miller about the ways the bodies of the performers are presented in Circus Amok shows.

★★★★★

Jennifer Miller

How does the way the body of the performer is presented in Circus Amok performances differ from Traditional Circus performances?
Jennifer Miller: Well of course the most obvious way is the genderqueer body. From our early days we have had the woman with the beard (me) as the ringmaster, not in the sideshow. That sets it up right there. The queer body is the interlocutor, the welcoming presence. It's a circus of extraordinary bodies, beautiful bodies, but there are no so-called normal bodies that they are all seen in relation to. Our bodies of many genders are displayed in clothes of many genres. Sometimes what you see is drag and sometimes it's a gentleman wearing a dress. The gender binary doesn't exist in our world, our performance of gender in general has always been a destabilised kind of place. We always made it a little off-kilter just by being who we were.

FIGURE 2.2 Circus Amok, Jennifer Miller. Photo: Rahav Segev.

We also have non-traditional kinds of circus bodies in terms of strength and build. In the same way that Circus Oz has, we have women who are strong, who are buff, and who are basing partner tricks. That's still somewhat uncommon. I guess it takes a consciously feminist circus to do that. We use bigger people, fatter people than are traditionally in circus, not just for clowning, but for tumbling and vaulting, the whole thing. We also work with people with disabilities. We have an incredible performer, Cathy Weiss, who has multiple sclerosis and so moves in her own particular, slow, completely compelling way.

So I guess there's many ways, but those are maybe the four or five ways that I feel like we've used a kind of non-traditional circus body.

Do you see that different way of presenting the body as offering a challenge to Traditional Circus?
Jennifer Miller: Well, I see it as 'other' than Traditional Circus.[55] I don't feel like I'm in that much of an active dialogue with 'circus' but I suppose I am. And maybe it is a challenge to circus, but it's also a challenge to our audiences and that's what I'm really interested in. Or actually not a 'challenge.' It's not what they are used to but I think it's actually quite welcome.

Part of what we do is to present a world that is wider than the kind of hemmed-in heteronormative world that audiences are used to seeing and being in. In the same way that we often talk about real-life material concerns in the show, we want to put real bodies, and really exceptional bodies on the stage, populating our queer world. We do it because that's who we are.

I worked with a couple of circuses when I was very young that asked me to get rid of my beard. Circuses were the predominant employer that asked me to get rid of my beard. When I was teaching in after-school programmes they didn't ask me to get rid of it. You would think that circus was the place where I wouldn't be asked to do that!

I just wanted to not have to bother with all that and to make circus shows.

There's a strange irony there, isn't there?
Jennifer Miller: Yes. North American circus has always been intertwined with the sideshow and based on a fetishising and exoticising of a particular other.

In the previous Circus Amok shows there's been a lot of referencing of traditional sideshows. Does this reflect your time performing at Coney Island?
Jennifer Miller: Well I started Circus Amok before I worked at the sideshow, but over the years sideshow has influenced Amok quite a bit. You find that in the banner design, the verbal rhythms, and the punk factor. I spent a lot of time in the sideshow. I worked at Coney Island Sideshow for several years and it really toughened me up. The performance persona that I developed there is at play in the streets with Amok. One has to be strong in both of those places.

Do the sideshows still exist on Coney Island?[56]
Jennifer Miller: Yes, there is still a sideshow at Coney Island. There aren't any what we would call 'born acts' in the show anymore. There's just 'made' acts and 'skill' acts, sword swallowers, fire-eaters.[57] Actually, that's not true. They do get some 'born' acts coming through now and then, but they're all doing the kind of postmodern cyclical wrap around investigation that I was doing.

You know Mat Fraser, the incredible performer who's now playing Richard III in London, and was on *American Horror Story*? He comes and goes through the sideshow world.[58] He's a Disability Studies scholar, burlesque performer, musician, and actor. He brings a very smart and very entertaining act. Velvet Crayon is another wonderful disabled performer working at Coney Island. He's a great musician and storyteller.[59] Actually, there have been a couple of waves of sideshow revival in the past 20 years and now there are more born freaks working the show than at the beginning of the revival in the nineties.

How did you find performing in the sideshow at Coney Island?
Jennifer Miller: It's a love/hate relationship. The act that I developed while working there is the most well-honed five to ten minutes of material I have. I do a feminist act in which I talk about the choice to wear the beard, life on the street as a bearded woman, there's joke, joke, joke, and then I pull out my knives. A lot of

fake dropping ensues. I get caught up in the mic stand – I could practice that physical comedy for ever, it gives me such joy … and then 'di di di di dum boom!' [gestures precise knife throwing]. Sideshow's an incredible training ground. You do ten to twelve shows a day. That act is my secret weapon, honed and ready.

In the sideshow and with Circus Amok I am making theatre in non-traditional spaces. In the sideshow I get to do this very feminist vaudeville act for all kinds of people, not just the ones that choose to go see downtown theatre. The same is true for Circus Amok.

Does the audience have an opportunity to dialogue with you in that situation?
Jennifer Miller: Only when they yell out, 'Hey you! Prove it!' Though that doesn't really happen so much anymore. The audiences have become much more polite now that the show closes at 7:00 pm and not midnight. I often dialogue with people in-between shows. In Circus Amok most of the dialoguing with the audience happens as we are setting up and striking the show.[60]

And is that an important part of it for you?
Jennifer Miller: Yes. That's rich territory. That's where a lot the questions about gender and sexuality will come up. Kids in particular will come up and ask us if we're gay, or 'Are you a man or a woman?' all of that. We do have a fairly long set-up and strike. Usually we get the sex and gender questions as we're setting up, and by the time the show is over they are unconcerned with sexuality and gender and they are asking us about juggling and 'Where's the lion, where's that paper mache lion?'

And the puppetry elements with the lion and all the other animals seem to reference Bread and Puppet Theatre, is that part of your background?
Jennifer Miller: I was influenced by Bread and Puppet Theatre.[61] Several of my early collaborators have worked with Bread and Puppet. It's a circus, so we're going to have animals, but they need to be fabric or paper mache. We've had some beautiful animals – tall, gorgeous giraffes on stilts. We've had zebras, and we've had elephants, black panthers, condors, and of course the classic circus animal – the lion. With puppet animals we can have the lion training the trainer!

Sometimes you have placed a performer in the audience, like a hetero–redneck heckler.
Jennifer Miller: Yes, I love the audience plant.

So how do you use the audience plant?
Jennifer Miller: We often use the plant to open up a topic, to actually stage a conversation. For example, we will be in the middle of an act about immigration, the audience plant gets up and starts to argue with us, and then another audience plant gets up and argues with the first plant. It's an opportunity to tear into the ideas. At the same time it activates the audience. It encourages them to think about the possibility that they might talk back. It breaks the fourth wall. It has us

reach out across that divide. Then there is the magic of the reveal, when the audience realises those folks were audience plants. The stagecraft gets the same kind of appreciation a good juggling trick does.

We use the plant in another way in our juggling act where we do the old traditional 'get a member out of the audience' bit. This is when we are playing our old, sexist, Fratelli Brothers jugglers. When I was first coming up, the street performance world was all male. I had to work to figure out how to claim space in the streets, how to own space. I'm thinking way back. A certain machismo was often used to build a crowd, 'Come see what I can do.' Not a valued feminine behaviour. So we made a juggling act modelled on a fusion of a Vegas and a street juggler act, The Fratellis.

We'd get a woman [plant] out of the audience to put her in the middle of the passing pattern. We, of course, tried to get her to smile and wave to her boyfriend, take a cute pose – all the awful sexist things male jugglers are wont to do. I'd play a horribly sexist drag king. We would put the lady in the middle of the pattern and then push her one step too far, one too many pats on the butt – and off she goes into a fabulous raging feminist rant, after which she starts walking through the pattern and stealing and replacing the clubs. It's then revealed that she's one of us. She becomes a feminist hero. There is relief in the audience who had been wondering what the fuck we were doing!

What sort of relationship does Circus Amok's body representation on stage have with drag?
Jennifer Miller: Well there's a complex relationship. I have learned so much from drag queens who, of course, learned so much from the great female divas before them. The world of drag and high camp was very influential for me as a performer in terms of elevated performance styles, and fabulousness, and resistance through fabulousness. This kind of gay, sassy, in-your-face glamour as a strategy, is a glamour that is rooted in pain and anger and says, 'Fuck you, outa my face, and I'm going to take my space and take it with panache. And I am gonna take it so hard and with so much fabulousness you are going to wish you were me.'

We are very careful about our use of the traditional drag queen on stage, as we are with all our representations. Look, male to female drag can be misogynist. And sometimes not. Sometimes it has nothing to do with representing women. At its best it is its own gender.

We also use female drag queens. I might think of myself that way, that is, in Circus Amok I play both drag queens and drag kings. Whatever gender I'm doing, if it's of a certain elevated style, it's drag in whatever direction.

Many drag kings seem in some ways to be missing a developed language, whereas there is a such a developed, fabulous language for drag queens.
Jennifer Miller: Yes. There was a real evolution in drag kinging in New York in the '90s. A lot of putting on drag is acquiring the power that one sees in the other. It's dangerous, we mentioned before – is it exoticising? Fetishising the colonised subject? Race, gender, class – is it minstrelsy?

When I first started seeing drag kings I was often seeing women give themselves the space to be kind of nasty and oppressive, whereas men who were drag queens were enacting the powers they hadn't been allowed – to be glamorous, and fabulousness. Seemingly the powers that women hadn't been allowed, were to be bossy and horrible.

As drag kinging evolved, performers started picking characters with a bit more flair and with an eye towards entertainment, as the queens had been doing.

Does a drag aesthetic inform Circus Amok shows?
Jennifer Miller: It's funny because I really resisted drag at first. I was more interested in expanding the performance of gender. Still am. In the very first circus, Scotty [Heron] was wearing a dress.[62] A fabulous dress and he wore it fabulously – not a hippy man in a dress, let me say! But he wasn't in drag. Men can wear dresses. Women can wear whatever and I was very invested in that aesthetic and ideology. So we have a man in a dress and it isn't drag, and in another moment we have a man in dress and it is drag. We do both things, but they're very different things, and they both exist in the show.

Is there a different audience response to a man that's just wearing a dress and a man in a dress doing drag?
Jennifer Miller: It's hard to pin down. The drag queen is much more familiar and comes with a familiar type of comedy and elevated style of performance. The other might be a costume in an acrobatics act that is just quietly expanding our notions of how gender is constructed or performed. We don't do drag queens very often at all because it can be a problematic territory, can tend toward the misogynistic. It's true that often when I first think of casting a fabulous female character I think of giving it to a man in the company to do in drag – to make it big and fierce. I have to take myself to school – give that to a woman – she can do it! We had a show a couple of years ago where Carol Channing played a big part, and the guy who played Carol Channing really did it up, he was the best singer in the company. It was great drag but then we all put on those blond Carol wigs and she was joined by six other Carol Channings!

Looking at Circus Amok performances and seeing such ethnically diverse performers it becomes very apparent how rarely performers of colour are part of contemporary circus. Is it a deliberate choice to include more performers of colour?
Jennifer Miller: Yes, it's very conscious, yes. There aren't a lot of people of colour working in the New Circus world. We have to do outreach – we can't just work with people that come to us through word of mouth.

So how do you interact and find performers of colour, or do they find you?
Jennifer Miller: Some find us. We also put the word out that we are looking for new performers in Black, Latinx, and Asian communities. Some of our

performers of colour come from circus, and some from theatre and some from activism, as is true with the whole company. Victor Vauban, who worked with us for the last several years, is a black Brazilian circus performer and Michelle Matlock, who, since she left us, has been starring in Cirque du Soleil as the Ladybug in *Ovo*.[63] We had the great Osmany Tellez who came from dance but was an acrobat as a child.[64] Most of us are drawing on old childhood skill sets.

It's hard to find someone, anyone, who is willing to be underpaid! Because it's such hard work our performers generally have to have some alliance with the politics in order to stick with the project. For many Amok performers this is the place where they can bring my politics and their art practice together – envisioning a queer utopia, demanding free health care of all, and play in a hot band, and dance on stilts.

Over the years we have trained actors and activists in circus skills, and acrobats in politics and sass.

So you're prepared to put the time into training people?
Jennifer Miller: We must. The training never stops. Some years we just try to hit the bare minimum skills-wise, no new tricks, we just brush off the old stuff. And some years we have time – which means we have money – to practice and train. When we started we would have what we called Circus Sundays once a week at my loft. A bunch of friends who were performers in other fields would come over, we'd have coffee and pastries and I taught people to walk rope, and to juggle. They were performance artists or dancers or actors. We've always had a very mixed skill level. We'll have a couple of good flippers, and a few good jugglers and then a few people who just have a great physical presence, and politics, and wit, and attitude. The flippers will learn from the dancer/actor/activists, and the activists will learn some tumbling from the acrobats – a couple of cartwheels, a two-high and some basic juggling, and you are good to go!

★★★★★

From Jennifer Miller's work with Circus Amok which opens up new spaces for performers with a diverse range of bodies, sexualities, gender identities, and ethnicities, the next conversation is with Tilde Björfors, Artistic Director of the Swedish Contemporary Circus company Circus Cirkör, who is gaining international attention for her politically engaged circus work. In her trilogy of works, *Borders* (2015), *Limits* (2016), and *Movements* (2017), she explores the issue of refugees in Europe, and in her 2018 show, *Epifónima*, a work created for seven female performers, she contests the growing prevalence of male performers in Contemporary Circus.[65]

Tilde Björfors begins by discussing her political circus work on the issue of refugees.

★★★★★

Tilde Björfors

Could you talk a bit about the works you have created on the theme of refugees?
Tilde Björfors: Well, it's a trilogy, one show is called *Borders*, then *Limits*, and then *Movements*.

What were your reasons for exploring the issue of refugees through circus?
Tilde Björfors: Circus is always a study of physical movement material, but for me it's also an investigation into questions about life and death, and also boundaries or borders. For me it was very much connected to the reason why I choose circus as my artform. It goes back to the existential idea that you are choosing possibilities instead of risk. For me circus is all about transcending boundaries and limitations, and circus shows us that we as human beings can do so much more than we think we can, if we work hard and train. Contemporary Circus is not only about transcending physical limitations, it's also about crossing different artforms, and it's also about how we've all often worked internationally, toured internationally, and we often have casts that are international.

I have been working with these ideas with Cirkus Cirkör for 20 years now, exploring the idea of boundaries and limits, through circus. We have learned so much from this exploration. I have seen artists start training here when they were wild kids that didn't fit into school and now they're fantastic artists touring the world. I have seen so many great benefits of transcending boundaries and limitations, and then to find out that the borders around Europe are closing, the borders are opening between European countries but closing tightly around them, and people are dying in hundreds, thousands, every day.

So I felt that we at Cirkus Cirkör couldn't be silent with all the knowledge that we had gained about the benefits of risk-taking and of crossing limits and borders. That is why we chose to speak out and let society and people know what we have learned from circus, that the benefits of risk-taking can far outweigh its drawbacks. Of course, it's a big risk letting new people from another culture come into your country. It's not an easy undertaking. But in circus, the artists have specialised training in transcending risk, and boundaries and limitations.

We know that it takes a lot of discipline, and it's a lot of hard work, but you always have to choose opportunity and possibility instead of focusing only on the risk. One of the main things with taking a risk is to break it down into small steps, so that instead of focusing on the one big, dramatic risk – the new idea or the difficult challenge you want to succeed in – instead of focusing on the impossibility of reaching that level, you break it down into small steps and then you can focus on the possibility of achieving each small step. Then suddenly you are there and before you know it you have succeeded in making the impossible possible.

FIGURE 2.3 Cirkus Cirkör, *Limits*. Photo: Einar Kling Odencrants.

So this was the idea – the idea of sharing the knowledge we have gained about risk-taking in circus, and using it to inspire society and people to believe in possibilities and opportunities, instead of only seeing the risk factor. If your mind is focused solely on the risk even that which is possible will seem impossible, instead of the other way around. So that was the underlying idea.

We did *Borders* first, but we finished *Borders* in May or June 2015. Then in July and August 2015 a lot of refugees started to come into Sweden – 2,000 a day began arriving. During the creation of *Limits* in 2016 many of us volunteered at a refugee transit centre that opened at our location. The centre was in operation at the same time as we were working on our performances. Then in *Movements* in 2017, I felt that now was the time for the next stage and that we also needed to give space to the newcomers. How can we let them into our space if we don't give them space on the stage? So, in the last show I also had artists and dancers and actors in it who were newcomers and had newly arrived in Sweden. The performances *Borders, Limits,* and *Movements* became a trilogy about this experience.

What are you working on currently?
Tilde Björfors: I'm just about to have workshops for my new Cirkus Cirkör performance which consists of only female artists. It's about the qualities of being female and the low status women generally have in our society. Looking back through history you can find movements all the way back to 2000 BC, with Ishtar and Inara, up to the present, in which women were leaders.[66] The leadership style of Hildegard von Bingen can be described as being on the same level – the same eye level.[67] Instead of thinking of a leader as being at the top of a pyramid, she saw leadership as an army where the leader is in the centre and everyone is on the same eye level with each other, and this is true for most of the

early women's movements in the thirteenth century. You can see how women organised themselves, how they described leadership in that way in different women's movements. So that's what we are working on right now.

Is that work with the network, Nordic Women in Circus,[68] or is it a separate thing?

Tilde Björfors: It's a separate thing, but at the same time it's not completely separate because I think we are a link in a long chain. I think the reason I started to work with this issue is that it evolved from working with ideas of boundaries, borders, and immigration for several years. I believe that the solution lies with women. We have tried this structure of war and power, and we haven't succeeded in making the world a better place. I think we need new ways of doing things. In recent years, within the circus movement itself, there have been a lot of female companies creating shows.

In Scandinavia?

Tilde Björfors: In Europe and maybe also in Australia, female companies have a hard time with the buyers. The programmers of theatres and festivals are not buying the shows. Despite circus being a young artform, we are already falling into the same power structures as there are in society.

Would you say that there seems to be an increasing number of circus festivals choosing to present companies where most of the performers are male?

Tilde Björfors: It's totally a trend in Contemporary Circus, and it's not because there are no female companies, or companies that are a group of women with one male – it's because the programmers are just not buying them. It's not about the quality of the shows.

FIGURE 2.4 Cirkus Cirkör, *Epifónima*. Photo: Maryam Barari.

We are in quite a powerful position here because the Cirkus Cirkör company is well known and programmers will book our shows – even a show with only female artists. Our plan is to tour with this show, but also to communicate with the programmers and the festivals, and to put the question to them, 'Why are you only presenting companies with a predominantly male cast?'

What is the topic of the show?
Tilde Björfors: We're trying to look at the issue of power structures in the actual creative process, in the way we are making the show. We have changed the structure of how we are creating it, and we're taking inspiration from different historical women's movements, and I don't know where it will end up.

We are in the process of doing this research, and when we work, when we read and collect information, we are looking at how we organise ourselves in order to see if we can change the power dynamics or hierarchy in the structure of the creative process and in the workshopping. We are looking to see if we can be influenced by the female way of organising, and then seeing if this is something we could implement in the future.

FIGURE 2.5 Cirkus Cirkör, *Epifónima*. Photo: Maryam Barari.

You can say that when the #MeToo movement started it came from the inside and worked its way out. The focus is the same in this work. Now we are working with the office staff and the leadership in the company and looking into all the structures we have, trying to see it with new eyes. There is a wave of change occurring across the whole world and it's very interesting to be in the middle of it.

What is the work called?
Tilde Björfors: *Epifónima*. It's a Greek word used to express an outcry, or an emotion or feeling. In the Greek it is also the word for the exclamation mark.

★★★★★

Tilde Björfors' insights into her work and how it contests the male normate in Contemporary Circus leads us into this next discussion with Kim 'Busty Beatz' Bowers, Co-Founder, Co-Writer, and Musical Director of Hot Brown Honey, the Australian company whose performers are all women of colour.[69]

Hot Brown Honey is an overtly political company both in its physical performance material, and in its spoken text which references feminist writers of colour, including Angela Davis, Lilla Watson, Audre Lorde, and Chimanda Ngozi Adichie. Hot Brown Honey has created a new space for female performers of colour in the performing arts industry in Australia, which is predominantly white, with white males in most of the power positions. Kim 'Busty Beatz' Bowers, together with her sister, performer Candy Bowers, are founders of the production company Black Honey.

Kim 'Busty Beatz' Bowers starts this conversation by talking about the origins of Hot Brown Honey.

★★★★★

Kim 'Busty Beatz' Bowers

How did Hot Brown Honey start?
Kim 'Busty Beatz' Bowers: Lisa Fa'alafi, who's the Director and Co-Writer of Hot Brown Honey, well ... we'd had enough actually.[70] We'd been working in this world for over 20 years and we'd been working together for 15 years. It was also the fact that we just weren't represented.

In everything we did we just felt like we were very qualified to make work, and we just weren't getting the gigs.

First of all, Hot Brown Honey was a side project. Because of Lisa's movement base, and I'm very much on the sound trip, we came together to create some funny pieces of work that we could laugh at ourselves. We actually went 'What could we make where we didn't have the normal boundaries?'

We were always sitting on the fringes. So that was really interesting because on the fringes, that's where all this amazing art lies – all these artists that aren't

FIGURE 2.6 Hot Brown Honey, Kim 'Busty Beatz' Bowers as The Queen Bee. Image by Dylan Evans.

really centre stage but should be centre stage. We were all working in these different areas, and because we love to mix things up as well, all different types of forms and disciplines, that's also seen as not being of the mainstream. So with Hot Brown Honey we were actually going 'It's really our time. We really want to represent ourselves in our own way.'

Hot Brown Honey has got this incredible spectrum of First Nations performers – Australian, South African, Indonesian, Islander – an all-female troupe and all women of colour. The work has been really well received in Australia. How has it gone in different countries?
Kim 'Busty Beatz' Bowers: Well it's been quite amazing actually. We knew that we didn't care anymore about where the gates were, where the gatekeepers were. We developed the work in Australia. Hot Brown Honey is like our friends and family, this is how we have to operate in a land like Australia, where we are on stolen land. How do we make art in that space?

Did you expect the show to translate and work for international audiences?
Kim 'Busty Beatz' Bowers: We really kind of went 'Let's see! This is so unique to us and our situation here, would this work overseas?' And what we've found is that some of the truths are universal. The way that we've been able to craft it is universal and especially using a discipline such as circus and movement, there's a way of cutting through language barriers, cutting through cultural barriers.

How has the show gone at the Edinburgh Festival Fringe?
Kim 'Busty Beatz' Bowers: It was crazy. This was our third year. The first year was quite full on because we were a bit tentative actually. We were like 'We're not sure how this will roll. We're not really sure if will people get it. We're coming from the other side of the world,' and what we found is that people really got it. They really understood. Our audiences really understood and they were actually willing to go on that journey with us.

Before Edinburgh we played at the Southbank Centre in London. We played in the Queen Elizabeth Hall, and from there we went on to Edinburgh, so it has been quite an experience. We actually won an award the first year we were there called the Total Theatre Award, and that was for 'Innovation, Experimentation and Playing with Form.' It's amazing to win an award – it felt like, yes, this is what we do and this is recognised in other parts of the world.

You've been to the Edinburgh Fringe for three years, have you changed the show at all or has it been the same show?
Kim 'Busty Beatz' Bowers: The show is constantly morphing, in the fact that we constantly have to talk about what's happening now. So the first year we went, we were talking a lot about Brexit. Also the Black Lives Matter movement, we talked about that as well because I suppose in the world that we live in, the work, especially the social commentary part of it has to change, and even though it's a play in the sense of we've got a script, we feel what's going on at the time. The last time much of the movement was around Me Too and what was happening in the world at this point.

So we play with the acts, within the acts of the show and within the narrative. Some stuff we say is classic. We're not going to change that, because classic is universal and they are like the pinnacle points of the show.

FIGURE 2.7 Hot Brown Honey. Image by Dylan Evans.

The act with Ghenoa Gela wrapping herself in the Australian flag was extraordinary.[71]
Kim 'Busty Beatz' Bowers: We've had different First Nations artists come in and do that role and do that piece, and it morphs every time with the different artists.

Can you talk about the straps act about domestic violence.[72]
Kim 'Busty Beatz' Bowers: With that piece, Lisa [Fa'alafi] and I came up with that concept and then Crystal Stacey, who's our aerialist and hoops artist, really connected and actually brought the whole piece to life.[73] Just in the knowledge that as women, we look around and we go, 'Wow!' All of us knew of, or had some experience of, domestic violence. Then when you look at the statistics, it's like one in three women.

Is that across Australia or internationally?
Kim 'Busty Beatz' Bowers: That's Australia and the UK. This is just something that you talk about in hushed voices. This is actually an epidemic, and how do we actually bring that to a place where we can talk about it? And that's the whole point of Hot Brown Honey. We want people to have conversations well after the show.

It was interesting that you came into the performance space asking for donations to help with childcare.
Kim 'Busty Beatz' Bowers: Well in the arts we've found there's nothing in place. Is the expectation that parents can no longer work? What's the deal? I've still got to work. We have to do this. No venue or presenter is actually going to go, 'Oh no, here's the amount you need for your children to come, and for a teacher, and the nanny to come as well.'

Do you actually tour with kids or is it just making a political point?
Kim 'Busty Beatz' Bowers: With my daughter, Lily May, and Hope [Materharere 'Hope One' Haami], the beatboxer, with her son. It's real.[74]

It's interesting when circus is ideas-driven and the apparatus has to work with the idea, rather than the other way round.
Kim 'Busty Beatz' Bowers: Yeah, definitely. I suppose for myself, and for Lisa as well, we always talk about that because we see a lot of work. We go and watch a lot of work, and for us that is the thing with circus work, we're always like, 'Come on. We want a narrative. It doesn't have to be spoken.' It's like the skill is amazing. Skill is amazing at any given level but actually what we want is the story. What makes these apparatuses become a part of the picture? I suppose the other really big thing with Hot Brown Honey and talking about circus is we're all clowns. We're really into what makes us laugh.

With Hot Brown Honey, the way everybody in the company relates to each other, and supports each other looks really strong.
Kim 'Busty Beatz' Bowers: We say it all the time. We say, 'decolonise and moisturise.' We actually do have to really look after each other on stage as well

because of that whole experience of being on stage and telling truths. Sometimes in daily life you just don't want to think about those truths. You just want to have a life and go, 'Oh my gosh, I just can't deal with that today and I'm not going to,' but on stage, night after night, you have to confront them.

Have you ever had any hostile reactions?
Kim 'Busty Beatz' Bowers: Yeah, and they've been quite full on. People are having a lot of feelings and that's what happens. The show is a rollercoaster ride and there are a lot of feelings involved for audience as well as for us.

We try and make it really clear, even at the beginning when we're collecting for childcare, this is our space and we will hold this space for you as an audience member. As well at the end, wherever we can, we will try and be outside when audiences leave to say, 'Thank you,' because that's part of safe space. There's something called the 'third place mentality' that we have going on for lots of things, which is where we can meet safely, and artists can meet in a safe place.[75] Some theatre companies have put that into a policy and we try and be very aware of that too, because we are also inviting people in, people who look like us and there's a lot of vulnerabilities in the show too, so we need to make sure that everyone's held while we can hold them.

It's really quite confronting when people are really full on. They've always been Australians too. When we were in Manchester … this Australian woman was just like … she really felt she just had to say it at the end of the show. We were trying to say goodbye to everyone and shaking people's hands and she was like, 'That is not okay what you just did.' Yeah, it was quite full on. We were like, 'We can give you only so much right now. We just did a whole show and at this point you need to actually let go, get some love, and you're going to have to unpack that.'

★★★★★

Kim 'Busty Beatz' Bowers' conversation about how Hot Brown Honey challenges the patriarchal and racially biased performing arts in Australia leads us to a conversation with Phia Ménard, the transgender female circus artist and creator, who founded her[76] own company Compagnie Non Nova in France in 1998.[77] Talking about the change in her lived experience with her transition from male to female, Ménard says, 'I lived on the side of power for 30 years. I was invisible then: I could walk into any street at night, and the chances that something would happen to me were very slim. Now it's absolutely impossible. I've lost the right to invisibility. It's a reminder that suddenly, I no longer own space – I'm just a tenant.'[78]

Here Ménard talks about how her experiences as a transgender woman inform her work, and how her works directly contest the process of gender assignment, and challenge audiences to rethink gender and to see it as a political and social construct.

★★★★★

Phia Ménard

We're interested in the metaphorical resonances in your work and how the transformation involved in your journey from the body of a man to the body of a woman relates to the material transformation of the ice to the water in your show _P.P.P._ Could you speak to that?

Phia Ménard: Sure, if you have a long time! We all are in constant transformation. All the time. At every moment we are in transformation. We are young, we become old. We live. We die. It's a relationship to the cosmic. It's the notion of very limited time. From there, when I decided, although I didn't really have a choice, to go from a man's body in which I never felt comfortable, to that of a woman, and through that process becoming a 47-year-old teenager, I was faced with one of the most obvious questions – what is gender attribution? And this is the topic that speaks to me the most – what is gender attribution one-way or the other? And to raise once again the questions of power in relation to that.

You are born a man, and you are told, 'being a man means that you have to be like this.' Since you have this body, you are framed, and the same goes for a woman. So that's what the notion of gender attribution refers to – it is an attribution given from the start. It's the assigning of a role.

So today, in the work I create, I ask again the question of how to step away from these assigned roles. Since I have been taught to be a man, and since today I am a woman but haven't forgotten what I've been taught, I now know the codes of the male, while today I am in the process of discovering the codes of the female.

But the most important issue in that regard points to how it is only my body that has changed. I'm still the same person, but my rights have changed. I no longer have the freedom I once had.

In _Dry Season_, the group piece, _Saison sèche_, is that what you're talking about in that piece?

Phia Ménard: In the process I'm in today, I'm questioning how we can free ourselves from this patriarchal power dynamic. How can we change the situation? How can we invite reflection on the fact that these gender attributions constrain both women and men, that they are only roles, and that they aren't sustainable anymore.

It's an old model. It is a model based on a story of misunderstandings, perpetuated by the perpetuation of fears. Many anthropologists (Francoise Héritier for example) have to be reread in order to notice that the basis, perhaps even the heart, of a bad dialogue, is linked to a mere bodily notion.[79]

I'm going to take a very simple example which for me constitutes a strong analysis of this. When I was in the skin of a boy, when I had a little injury or I was a little sick, I would make a scene out of it, exaggerate my pain to make it seem like I was on the verge of death.

Today, in the body of a woman, with its form of bodily cycle, my body calls my awareness back. It reminds me that I am not on the verge of death, it's just that the body calls my attention back.

This is what makes me say that the calendar is different in our society for men and women in the following way – for a man, a year contains 365 days, interspersed with times where he is in pain, where he is hurt, and so on. And on the female side of things, it's not 365 days; it's 28 days plus 5, 28 days plus 5. Which means that the real calendar for a woman is not the same real calendar for a man.

From this point on a society is created with a difference in the perception of time, and therefore in the perception of the body's state, of the body's transformation. That's why as a woman, the relationship we have to our own body is one where our body reminds us of its existence and calls us back to ourselves. And each time, on a regular basis and within less than a month, the perception we have of our body and of space shifts. And that's what a patriarchal society forbids, forbidding us to show it, to express it. Above all else, we are told to hide it and be ashamed of it.

How do you go about tackling the question of gender assignment in your work?
Phia Ménard: Whether we are talking about solo pieces, or group pieces, all of them are pieces that use symbols and codes. I'm using the symbols to reclaim the question of how gender was constructed, how role attribution was created, and also to ask, 'Are we still there?' We must rebuild, reconstruct.

I work with Paul B. Preciado, the philosopher, and we discuss these issues using our personal paths as lenses.[80] He went from the body of a woman to the body of a man, while I went from the body of a man to the body of a woman. And we ask each other the question of what space is. And for me to discover the deprivation of freedom, and at the same time for him to discover the reality of gaining full freedom.

And what do these notions of freedom and space mean today? How do we look at them? How was architecture created in order to maintain patriarchal power? We look at all of these elements, and it's from that dialogue that I build the future of my performances. And to continuously raise the question of how this attribution works and how we can break the cycle, a cycle which is ultimately doomed to disappear because it creates destruction. And I think that today, we ask ourselves this question in the Anthropocene, our current era, about what we want to make of this planet. And all these questions are in fact very interrelated; they are completely intertwined.

So are you still working with Paul B. Preciado?
Phia Ménard: It's an ongoing collaboration we have been involved in since last year's *Documenta* in Kassel which I was invited to attend.[81] We have been pursuing the collaboration since then.

So, in relation to the political metaphors and resonances in your work, what are the sorts of metaphors you are talking about in your work *Vortex*?
Phia Ménard: When I created *Vortex*, there was a basic question pertaining to the question of role attribution, and it was … if we looked back on the path we've

walked since childhood, since the moment we left our mother's womb, would we be able to identify who we really are – considering how society, from that moment onwards and on a regular basis, took us in hand and we adapted.

We have transformed in order to fit in with situations around us and social moments. In order to be socialised, we have practiced resembling others. And this resembling means it's a copy, it's not the original.

★★★★★

Phia Ménard's discussion of how her work questions patriarchal power leads us into the conversation with the Contemporary Circus artists Jo Lancaster and Simon Yates, Co-Founders and Co-Directors of the Australian company Acrobat which they set up in 1995. Acrobat's work is highly political in its rejection of capitalism and consumerism and is filled with an anarchic sense of contestation.

In this short extract Lancaster and Yates talk about how their works *smaller poorer cheaper*; *Propaganda*; and *It's Not for Everyone* contest the commodification of the body, and also of the arts, in consumerist society.[82]

★★★★★

Jo Lancaster and Simon Yates

Acrobat often includes nudity in its performances – why is that?

Jo Lancaster: In *smaller poorer cheaper* each of us made very personal kind of content for the show and for me it just felt like it was best expressed that way.[83] I feel like I don't want to be denied that kind of space. I want to be able to own that space.

Simon Yates: Often the clothes you wear are making some kind of statement about who you are, or what kind of power you have.

We're animals. There's a lot of masking of that fact. Often the things that we use for that masking, the symbols or things that we use for that, hold a particular meaning.

The other thing about nudity and bodies in general is that as circus performers, with the physicality of what we are doing, we're often in very intimate contact with other people in a way that not everybody would be accustomed to. I find it interesting because, at least within our culture, a lot of that kind of intimacy with bodies is read as being sexual, and I think the same thing goes for nudity.

At some point in our evolution, it's become a convention that you must wear clothes when you're in public, and if you're not wearing clothes it's automatically seen as being a sexual thing. Usually in our performances when there has been nudity, it has not been in order to elicit some kind of sexual response. We've made a point of going, 'It's a body. We all have bodies.' People in our society are very self-conscious about their bodies because the only time you see bodies there have been decisions made about which bodies are good ones to see. There's a whole lot of complexity to do with bodies, when in fact we are animals.

I think as humans we often like to take ourselves out of the rest of the animal kingdom, finding as many ways as possible not to see ourselves as being biological entities in the same way that other living beings are.

Acrobat's shows have some very unusual titles – how do you go about naming your shows?
Simon Yates: Originally, we didn't want to name our performances. We had this idea that we would just use 'Acrobat' and the date. The shows would evolve and shift and change gradually but the idea that you stop and you go to rehearsal and make some different thing, I was going 'Well, that's a construct that we don't have to own.'

Now each time, when we've done a whole different show, it's been because there was a disturbance in our trajectory. We're going along, and then we have a break because of injury, or pregnancy, or breakdown.

Jo Lancaster: Circus people want to make you out to be bigger and better and greater and more, and so with *smaller poorer cheaper* it's going in the opposite direction. In a way we are interested in finding a title that should scare some people off, and *It's Not for Everyone,* that's going to scare a few people off too![84]

It sounds like an anti-marketing stance, is it?
Jo Lancaster: Yes. I hate all that, 'Awesome company that's been around for a zillion years doing all sorts of stuff everywhere, overseas, getting awards.' It's tiresome.

FIGURE 2.8 Acrobat, *It's Not for Everyone.* Photo: Karen Donnelly.

Simon Yates: And it means nothing because it's what everybody says. It's hollow. The performing arts funnel more and more of what money they generate to the corporate world through marketing.

★★★★★

From Jo Lancaster and Simon Yates' contestation of the commodification of the body and of the arts in consumerist society, the next conversation is with Fez Faanana, performer, and Co-Founder and Co-Director of the 'boylesque' company Briefs in Brisbane, Australia.[85] Briefs has had worldwide success with its two shows to date, *The Second Coming* and *Close Encounters*. Both shows are introduced by the character created and played by Faanana, the fabulous Shivannah, who is fierce, funny, sassy, and also highly political. These shows have toured widely internationally, with *Close Encounters* recently performing an eight-week season in London's West End (2018–2019).

Through the shows he has developed with Briefs, Faanana is claiming new space for a wider range of performers, in particular racially diverse non-heteronormative performers, and performers with a diversity of body shapes and sizes. We start by asking Faanana how his character Shivannah, the Bearded Ringmistress, came into being.

★★★★★

Fez Faanana

How did your fabulous character Shivannah develop?
Fez Faanana: I feel like it was my traditional side as a Samoan, and an upbringing in performance that comes from an oral tradition, and then this other side that was this little punk, with the self-important art school *Club Kids* connection.[86] Those two married together and made this character, a character naturally embedded in politics when it came to gender, when it came to race, when it came to the environment, when it came to habitat, when it came to paying respect and acknowledging the amount of guilt that's in the ground, and in the air in Australia.

I adopted the term 'the love child of the Bearded Lady and the Ringmaster of the circus' because I felt like they were the two parts of circus that I connected to. I felt like I had the spirit of the ringmaster who was an orchestrator, who brought people together, who was the master of ceremonies, but then the other side of that was the bearded lady, who had almost a sexual energy to her, who was also featured in the side tent after the main show. Those two worlds collided nicely in my brain.

Well it's a great mix!
Fez Faanana: I feel like a lot of the theatrics and the balance for Shivannah came out of hindsight, questioning, and having discussions with Mark [Winmill]

FIGURE 2.9 Fez Faanana as Shivannah of Briefs. Image by Sébastien Gracco de Lay.

and with the collective of Briefs.[87] 'How is she allowed to get away with a certain amount of things? Why is she allowed to?' And even moments like me coming off stage really early on in the first incarnations of Briefs, saying, 'Wow, that really didn't work. It didn't go down well. I just came across as a sassy, mouthy, drag queen.' Sometimes in the absence of one part of her, another side came out which didn't read well.

I remember Rudi [Mineur] who was part of the original cast of Briefs, the first incarnation very early on, and a very experienced performer, a little bit older, part of the first collective of Rock'n'Roll Circus, really early on, he schooled me about being articulate and being smart, not just being a trashy, bearded drag queen.[88] He was like, 'The reason why you're funny, and the reason why it reads, is because the punchline is unexpected, and if we don't understand your words, or you just become sassy, or you become that drag queen who just has a mean streak in her and points out everyone's faults in the audience, then you become predictable, and you fall into a mould that doesn't have its point of difference and doesn't have its anarchy, which is what I feel people are interested in.'

What do you think he meant by the word 'anarchy'?

Fez Faanana: I think he meant the protest and rebellion of anarchy, we've just got through this marriage equality situation which was hectic.[89] We were in the UK at that time and I remember saying in one of the interviews about it, 'Of course it's very personal, and this hits home, and it's very connected to me personally, and the company.' I said, 'But this is one of the many things we have on our list. We have a list, we all have lists of things that we need to get through, and there's no pecking order, there's just a bundle of stuff that we need to fix, and at this point this issue is in front of us. Forty years ago we had artists, and collectives, and groups that were protesting to get Aboriginal and Torres Strait Islanders acknowledged as humans and not flora and fauna. There are so many lists for us to get through, so many things to get through.'

For our company there's a strategy, in terms of holistically we want to move forward, and we want everyone to get to a place where we can transcend this kind of ideology of sabotaging one another in order to elevate oneself.

Just having Shivannah, not only in the tent but at the helm of the show, in itself can be daunting for some audience members. Shivannah needs to be the right balance. There needs to be a sense of fierceness, funniness, as well as this welcoming that ringmasters do. They invite, they welcome, they settle, they make everyone feel like the show is specifically for them. Then there's the Bearded Lady who challenges ideas, who challenges imagery, who challenges, 'Yes it's acceptable in this tent but outside of this tent when is it not? When is it something that you allow your kids to laugh at, or when does it become something that you don't accept.'

I think there's this interesting ideology about both those characters, the Ringmaster and the Bearded Lady. When it comes to the idea of the Bearded Lady, obviously I'm not a lady but for me my piece with gender is from being a Samoan who acknowledges how we define the Fa'afafine, the third gender, the two-spirited person in the Pacific, specifically in Samoa, that is what I can speak of.[90]

So with my understanding of the Samoan version of sexuality and gender identities, I like the idea of playing around with stereotypes, obviously I'm not a bearded lady, obviously I'm not a ringmaster, but the suspension of belief, and the idea and the artistry behind those two worlds are something that I connect to. The fact that the Bearded Lady plays with gender, and stirs the stereotype, is something that I feel like I embody and I have utmost respect for.

Sue Hird is a bearded lady from Spaghetti Circus near Mullimbimby, who's been swallowing razor blades and doing trick riding on horses for years.[91] When we first met her, when you meet someone like that you go, 'There are no rules! Circus is amazing!' Circus has a soft canvas, that's why it can always be split and rebuilt. So I feel like in terms of those two roles, they definitely encompass my brain, and my spirit, and my identity.

The politics within circus is also interesting. The freak show, the sideshow, versus the mainstream tent, and what happens when those worlds are together.

FIGURE 2.10 Briefs, *Club Briefs*. Image by John Tsiavis.

I remember working for Flipside Circus and even the politics around gymnastics versus circus was interesting.[92] 'What are they next to each other? What do they mean when they sit next to each other?' I think there's a place for everyone.

It's like Dallas Dellaforce's famous line that I always keep in the back of my brain.[93] Within this mainstream world of drag there's rules now. You're not doing drag if you don't have nails; you're not doing drag if you don't block out your eyebrows; you're not doing drag unless … and that's one type of drag. But Dallas said, 'Drag is such a sophisticated artform, there's enough room for everybody,' and I've always remembered that. Dallas is like, 'Your drag's very different to mine and we don't discredit each other, any more than we do the old school drag queen who's never experienced contouring. They're just part of our massive world, and there is enough room for everyone!'

Briefs is creating new pathways for Aboriginal performers and performers from all different nationalities and ethnicities. Is that a conscious thing or has it just happened organically?
Fez Faanana: We always pride ourselves on our diverse casting. I think it's part of the reason why we started Polytoxic, and why we started Briefs, particularly my brother Natano [Faanana], myself, and Mark [Winmill].[94] For myself I know that I started Polytoxic initially because no one was booking us, because we couldn't get the gigs that we thought we should have been considered for, so we carved our own place in the industry, as opposed to trying to find a place in the industry that had already carved its own pathways. We set that up to be something that carved its own place, and we realised that sometimes people don't know

what they want, or sometimes people don't know what they can digest. I think with Briefs in particular it's really important for us to have a broad demographic of body shapes, of ethnicity, of economic background, and of training.

Notes

1 Rosemary Garland-Thomson (1997). *Extraordinary bodies: Figuring physical disability in American culture and literature*. New York, NY: Columbia University Press.
2 Throughout this book the term 'to contest' is used in the sense of 'to call into question' as discussed in the Introduction, pp. 1–6; p. 6n1. See Introduction p. 6n1 also for definitions of the terms 'Traditional Circus,' 'Modern Circus,' 'New Circus,' and 'Contemporary Circus' as used in this book.
3 Rosemary Garland-Thomson (1997, 2017). Preface to the twentieth century edition. In *Extraordinary bodies: Figuring physical disability in American culture and literature* (pp. vii–xvii). New York, NY: Columbia University Press, p. xii.
4 Rosemary Garland-Thomson (1997, 2017). *Extraordinary bodies: Figuring physical disability in American culture and literature*, p. 8.
5 Ibid., 8.
6 Erving Goffman (1963), cited in Rosemary Garland-Thomson (1997, 2017). *Extraordinary bodies*, p. 8. See also, Erving Goffman (1963). *Stigma: Notes on the management of spoiled identity*. New York, NY and London: Simon and Schuster, p. 128.
7 Rachel Adams (2012). Disability and the circus. In K. Ames (Ed.), *The history of the circus in America* (pp. 419–435). New Haven, CT: Yale University Press, p. 421.
8 Richard Schechner (2004). *Performance theory*. London and New York, NY: Routledge, p. 179.
9 Janet M. Davis (2002). *The circus age: Culture and society under the American big top*. Chapel Hill: The University of North Carolina Press, p. 10.
10 Ibid., p. 118.
11 Lynn Abbott and Doug Seroff (2007). *Ragged but right: Black traveling shows, 'coon songs,' and the dark pathway to blues and jazz*. Jackson: University Press of Mississippi, p. 158.
12 Ibid., p. 158.
13 Alisan Funk (2018). Gender asymmetry and circus education. *Performance Matters, 4* (1–2), p. 23.
14 Susie Williams (2016). Gender in circus – a note from managing director Susie Williams. *Acrobatic Conundrum*. [Blog]. http://www.acrobaticconundrum.com/blog/2016/8/3/gender-in-circus
15 See Introduction, p. 3; p. 6n1.
16 Martine Maleval (2016). An epic of New Circus. In P. Tait & K. Lavers (Eds.), *The Routledge Circus Studies reader* (pp. 50–65). Abingdon, Oxon & New York: Routledge, p. 51.
17 Chantal Côté (2003, January 14). CDS responds to Pierre Parisien's opinion. Public relations letter sent to *Circus News* from Cirque du Soleil, retrieved 16 October 2014. [Letter].
18 Jane Mullett (personal communication with Katie Lavers, April 14, 2011).
19 See Rachael Carson (2002). *Silent spring*. Boston, MA: Houghton Mifflin Harcourt. (Original publication 1962).
20 See Ruth Harrison (2013). *Animal machines*. Wallingford: CABI. (Original publication 1964).
   See Brigid Brophy (1965). *The rights of animals*. London: Animal Defence and Anti-Vivisection Society Ltd.
21 Matthew Simpson (2013). Ruth Harrison and other animals. *Oxford Magazine, 340* (2nd week, Michaelmas Term), pp. 6–7.

22 Ibid.

23 Cynthia Chris (2006). *Watching wildlife*. Minneapolis: University of Minnesota Press, p. xiv.
   See Peter Singer (1990). *Animal liberation*. London: Jonathan Cape.
   See John Berger (1980). Why look at animals. *About Looking* (pp. 3–28). New York: Pantheon.

24 Joseph Beuys (1974), cited in Carin Kuoni (1993). *Joseph Beuys in America/energy plan for the Western man*. New York, NY: Four Walls Eight Windows, p. 141.

25 Paul Bouissac (2006, December 1). Timeless circus in times of change. Paper presented at the Fabulous Risk: Danger in Performance in Circus and Sideshow Conference, University of Wollongong, Australia, p. 66. https://semioticon.com/virtuals/circus/timeless.pdf

26 Pierrot Bidon, cited in Janine Peacock (2010). Vale Pierrot Bidon. *RealTime, 97* (June-July), p. 14.

27 Ibid.

28 See Jane Mullett (2005). *Circus alternatives: The rise of New Circus in Australia, the United States, Canada and France* (Unpublished doctoral thesis). Melbourne, VIC: La Trobe University.

29 Mike Finch (personal communication with Katie Lavers and Jon Burtt, July 13, 2018).

30 Ingrid Gilcher-Holtey (2014). *A revolution of perception? Consequences and echoes of 1968.* New York, NY and Oxford: Bergahn Books, p. 11.

31 See Jon Hawkes (2019). The history of Circus Oz. https://www.circusoz.com/circus-oz/history.html

32 See Jane Mullett (2005). *Circus alternatives: The rise of New Circus in Australia, the United States, Canada and France.*

33 Ibid.

34 Mark Borkowski (2010, March 22). Pierrot Bidon obituary, Archaos founder who reinvented circus as an edgy art form for the industrial world. *The Guardian.* https://www.theguardian.com/stage/2010/mar/21/pierrot-bidon-obituary

35 Jane Mullett (2005). *Circus alternatives*, p. 163.

36 See Peta Tait (2005). *Circus bodies: Cultural identity in aerial performance.* Abingdon, Oxon: Routledge.

37 Ibid., p. 122.

38 Mark Borkowski (2010, March 22). Pierrot Bidon obituary.

39 Ibid.

40 See extraordinary bodies (2019). Circus for every body. http://www.extraordinary bodies.org.uk/

41 Natano Faanana is a Samoan-Australian circus artist and director, who has worked with Polytoxic in Brisbane, and was Co-Creator and a performer in *Briefs: All Male Review*, and is the Co-founder, Creative Director, and a performer with Contemporary Circus company Casus, based in Adelaide, Australia. The BLAKflip programme achieved a milestone with *Chasing Smoke*, originally the programme's 2017 showcase, directed by Natano Faanana, which has now been taken into the repertoire of Casus. See https://www.circusoz.com/sidesault/BLAKflip.html, and http://casus.com.au/portfolio/chasingsmoke/
   See also Katie Lavers and Jon Burtt (2017). BLAKflip and beyond: Aboriginal performers and Contemporary Circus in Australia. *New Theatre Quarterly, 33* (4), pp. 307–319.

42 For video links to Mike Finch's work for Circus Oz see http://archive.circusoz.com/

43 Antonella Casella is a long-time member of Circus Oz, and the current Senior Artistic Associate of the company. She began performing in circus as an acrobat and aerialist, and went on to co-found Rock'n'Roll Circus in 1986 (now renamed as Circa), and Vulcana Women's Circus in 1995 in Brisbane. She has been involved with Circus Oz as a performer and Artistic Associate since 1991.

Strong Women is a programme run by Circus Oz to provide 'a dedicated path for the development and celebration of women within the contemporary circus industry.' See https://www.circusoz.com/sidesault/strong-women.html.

44 BLAKflip is a programme run by Circus Oz to provide 'a pathway for talented Indigenous performers to be identified, mentored, and supported as potential members of the Circus Oz ensemble.' See https://www.circusoz.com/sidesault/BLAKflip.html; and Katie Lavers and Jon Burtt (2017). BLAKflip and beyond: Aboriginal performers and Contemporary Circus in Australia. *New Theatre Quarterly, 33* (4), 307–319.

45 AFL is the acronym for the Australia Football League.

46 Joshua Bond is an Australian performer, director, and producer, and a former Artistic Associate and Indigenous Programmes Coordinator at Circus Oz responsible for helping to set up the BLAKflip programme in 2011. He is also Artistic Director, Executive Producer, General Manager, and Founding Member of Indigenous dance/theatre ensemble DJUKI MALA (The Chooky Dancers), and Creator and Co-Director of Legs On The Wall's *The Man With The Iron Neck* (2018).

47 Dale Woodbridge-Brown, is an Indigenous Australian Kamilaroi man from Mungindi. He first became involved in circus as a child with Circus West, and was also a state gymnast. He attended the Aboriginal Centre for the Performing Arts (ACPA) in Brisbane. He joined Circus Oz in 2012 after taking part in the company's BLAKflip programme for Aboriginal and Torres Strait Islander artists. He went on to join the Australian boylesque company Briefs in 2017. See, On the Couch. (2014, June 16). On the couch with Dale Woodbridge-Brown. *Arts Review.* Retrieved from http://artsreview.com.au/on-the-couch-with-dale-woodbridge-brown/

48 Hazel Bock is an Australian circus artist who performed with Circus Oz from 2010 to 2015.

49 Paul O'Keeffe is an Australian circus artist who has worked with the Australian companies, Circus Oz, Circus Monoxide, Legs on The Wall, and is currently a member of Brisbane-based circus company Circa.

50 Mel Fyfe is a long-time member of Circus Oz, joining in the late 1990s as a performer, and is now Operations and Venue Manager for the company.

51 Freyja Edney-Wild is a circus artist who worked with Circa from 2010–2017, and in 2017, joined Circus OZ.

52 The 7 Fingers' first show *Loft* (2002–2013) has been performed over 900 times to over 300,000 people.

53 The '70s counterculture that Circus Oz came out of was based around The Pram Factory (1967–1981), a theatre venue in Carlton, Melbourne, which formed a key creative hub for the 'New Wave' of Australian theatre of the 1970s, whose members 'shared a goal of revitalising Australia's theatre scene with distinctively Australian and experimental drama,' (Wolf, 2008, p. 32). It was the home of the Australian Performing Group (APG) (1967–1981). See, Tim Robertson (2001). *The Pram Factory: The Australian Performing Group recollected.* Carlton, VIC: Melbourne University Press, and Gabrielle Wolf (2008). *Make it Australian: The Australian Performing Group, the Pram Factory and New Wave theatre.* Sydney, NSW: Currency Press.

54 For a video link to Jennifer Miller's work with Circus Amok see, Jim Moore (2018). Circus Amok – "Enough is Enough" – Video Excerpts. [Video file]. https://www.circusamok.org/circus/

55 For further research around the notion of 'the other' in circus, see Karen Fricker and Haley Rose Malouin (Eds.) (2018). Circus and its others. *Performance Matters, 4* (1–2). This double issue of *Performance Matters* consists of papers from two conferences 'Circus and its Others' in Montreal in 2016 and in Prague in 2018. These conferences explored, amongst other issues: gender and difference in Contemporary Circus, the circus body/bodies, location and mobility, social circus, the freak, and queer circus.

56 Coney Island, on Long Island in New York, is a destination known for its amusement parks, beaches, and hotels, and its first seaside resort was built there in 1868. The first

'freak show' opened in 1880. See Rachel Adams (2001). *Sideshow USA. Freaks and the American cultural imagination.* Chicago, IL: University of Chicago Press.

57 Born Acts are those 'people with real physical anomalies who came by their condition naturally,' Made Acts are those who 'do something to themselves that make them unusual enough to exhibit, such as getting adorned with tattoos or growing their beards or nails exceptionally long,' Robert Bogdan (1988), *Freak shows: Presenting human oddities for amusement and profit,* Chicago, IL: University of Chicago Press, p. 8. See also Elizabeth Stephens (2005). Twenty-First century freak show: Recent transformations in the exhibition of non-normative bodies. *Disability Studies Quarterly, 25* (3), n.p.; Rosemary Garland-Thomson (Ed.) (1996). *Freakery: Cultural spectacles of the extraordinary body.* New York, NY & London: New York University Press.

58 The sideshow or freak show as a form of entertainment was revived in the early 1990s with the advent of the modern sideshow such as the Jim Rose Circus Sideshow (1992–2013) and Mat Fraser's one-man show, 'Sealboy: Freak.' See Carrie Sandahl (2016). The Jim Rose Circus Side Show: Representing the postmodern body in pain, in P. Tait and K. Lavers (Eds.), *The Routledge Circus Studies reader* (pp. 267–277). Abingdon, Oxon & New York, NY: Routledge, and http://www.worldsideshowfestival.com

59 See https://www.facebook.com/velvetcrayon/

60 'Strike' here refers to clearing the set, or 'bumping out' after the show

61 Bread and Puppet Theatre (1962–present), based in Vermont, USA, is a political theatre company that creates public performances using puppetry to help 'women, men and children alike to overcome the established order and the obsessive submission to its politics and consequent brutalities,' Peter Schumann, Director of Bread and Puppet Theatre. It is one of the longest running self-supported theatre companies in America, See http://breadandpuppet.org/

62 Scotty Heron is a founding member of Circus Amok, a juggler, stilt-dancer, tumbler, and slack-rope walker. He still tours regularly with Circus Amok, Cathy Weis Projects, and Deborah Hay. He received a 2003 New York Dance and Theater Award for his body of work as a performer. http://www.scottheron.org/

63 Michelle Matlock is an American professional clown who has performed for Cirque du Soleil, the Big Apple Circus, and Circus Amok. *Ovo* (2009–present) is a Cirque du Soleil touring show, directed by Deborah Colker, taking its inspiration from the world of insects, see https://www.cirquedusoleil.com/ovo

64 Osmany Tellez is an independent dance artist, choreographer, and gymnast, originally from Cuba, who has worked in New York with Cathy Weiss, Jennifer Monson, David Zambrano, and Circus Amok.

65 For video links to Tilde Björfors' work with Cirkus Cirkör see https://www.youtube.com/user/CirkusCirkor/videos

66 Ishtar, a Mesopotamian fertility goddess, is also called *Inanna.*
   Inara, in Hittite–Hurrian mythology, was the goddess of the wild animals of the steppe and daughter of the Storm-god Teshub/Tarhunt.

67 Hildegard von Bingen (1078–1179), also known as Saint Hildegard and Sibyl of the Rhine, was a German Benedictine abbess known for her theological and scientific texts, and writings based on prophetic visions. Her writings explore the reform of the church, the relationship between God and humanity, and redemption. She also wrote treatises on medicine and natural science, composed music, and wrote plays.

68 Nordic Women in Circus Network (2017–present), an organisation focused on building networks between women circus artists, and advocating for the status of women in the circus arts. The Network has members from 23 countries, and organises activities throughout Scandinavia with funding from the Nordic Culture Fund and Nordic Culture Point.

69 For video links to Kim 'Busty Beatz' Bowers' work with Hot Brown Honey see https://www.briefsfactory.com/hot-brown-honey

70 Lisa Fa'alafi is a Samoan-Australian performer and director, who co-founded Poly-toxic, an Australian physical theatre company, in 2000, and co-founded Hot Brown Honey in 2011.

71 Ghenoa Gela is a Koedal and Waumer Torres Straits Islander woman from Rock-hampton, Australia. She is a circus artist, choreographer, dancer, and comedian, who joined Circus Oz in 2012 after taking part in the company's BLAKflip programme. She has worked with the Sydney-based dance theatre company Force Majeure, and currently performs in Hot Brown Honey. She was the winner of 2016 Keir Choreography Award, for *Fragments of Malungoka – Women of the Sea*, which explores her female ancestry in the Western Torres Strait.

72 Straps is an aerial circus act using two fabric straps, which is usually performed by men but this is now being contested by female circus artists such as Crystal Stacey who performs with Hot Brown Honey.

73 Crystal Stacey is a circus artist of Indonesian descent, who has worked as a trainer and co-director for the Sandfly Circus in Broome, in the North West of Australia. She trained with the Flying Fruit Fly Circus in Albury-Wodonga, New South Wales, and worked with physical theatre company Marrugeku, also based in Broome, before joining Hot Brown Honey.

74 Maori performer Materharere Hope 'Hope One' Haami is an internationally recognised beatboxer, and has been with Hot Brown Honey since 2012.

75 The 'third place,' as identified by Ray Oldenburg, is a place where people can gather and interact, outside of home and work, and is sometimes described as the heart of a community's social vitality and the grassroots of democracy. See Ray Oldenburg (1999). *The great good place: Cafes, coffee shops, bookstores, bars, hair salons, and other hangouts at the heart of a community*, New York, NY: Marlowe and Company. (Original publication 1989).

76 The pronoun 'her' is Phia Ménard's pronoun of choice.

77 For video links to extracts of Phia Ménard's work with Compagnie Non Nova see http://www.cienonnova.com/#/en

78 Phia Ménard, cited in Laura Cappelle (2018). A transgender director who defies genres (to France's confusion). *New York Times*. https://www.nytimes.com/2018/07/08/theater/phia-menard-saison-seche-avignon.html

79 Françoise Héritier (1933–2017) was an influential French anthropologist, ethnologist, and feminist. See (2002) *Masculin-Féminin II. Dissoudre la hiérarchie*. Paris: Odile Jacob.

80 Paul B. Preciado (1970-), also known as Beatriz Preciado, is a Spanish-born trans-gender male writer, curator, and philosopher whose work explores gender and sexual politics. See Beatriz Preciado (2013). The pharmaco-pornographic regime: Sex, gender, and subjectivity in the age of punk capitalism. In S. Stryker & A. Z. Aizura (Eds.), *The Transgender Studies Reader 2* (pp. 266–277). New York, NY: Routledge.

81 *Documenta 14* (2017), the fourteenth edition of the *Documenta* art exhibition, took place in Kassel, Germany.

82 For video links to extracts of Jo Lancaster and Simon Yates' work with Acrobat see https://www.acrobat.net.au/current-shows

83 After the larger self-titled works (1996–2003) and a hiatus of three years, Acrobat returned in 2006 with *smaller poorer cheaper* which toured Australia and Europe with three performers Lancaster, Yates, and Mozes, with a sound score from composer Tim Barrass.

84 In 2015 came Acrobat's most recent show, *It's Not for Everyone*, a circus duo performance featuring Jo Lancaster and Simon Yates, and a sound score from long-time collaborator Tim Barrass.

85 The term 'boylesque' refers to all-male burlesque performance. For video links to extracts of Fez Faanana's work with Briefs see https://www.briefsfactory.com

86 Australian performance artist and fashion designer Leigh Bowery was a key 'Club Kid' figure opening clubs including Taboo in London in the mid-1980s. In Brisbane

similar gay clubs were linked to the Club Kid scene like The Beat Megaclub which was founded in 1983.

87 Mark 'Captain Kid' Winmill is Co-Creator and Co-Founder of Briefs Factory, and an original member and performer in Briefs. He was 2011's King of Burlesque in Las Vegas, and is a former performer with Circa.

88 Rudi Mineur is a circus artist and trainer in Australia, who was a founding member of Briefs, and performed with Rock'n'Roll Circus, now renamed Circa, where he is now Head of Circus.

Rock'n'Roll Circus (1987–2004) was a circus collective based in Brisbane, Australia, formed by circus performers Antonella Casella and Derek Ives, which was renamed Circa after Yaron Lifshitz took over as Artistic Director.

89 On 9 December 2017, The Marriage Amendment (Definition and Religious Freedoms) Act 2017 came into law in Australia after a national referendum.

90 Fa'afafine is a recognised gender identity in traditional Samoan culture. Fa'afafine are assigned male at birth, and embody a non-binary gender identity of both male and female.

91 Sue Hird (personal communication with Katie Lavers, April 9, 2018), 'I'm not doing the trick riding now I'm 62. I'm not too fond of putting both feet behind my head for anyone let alone punters … I have a beard I'm quite proud of and I do like that several generations of Spaghetti kids have had me there.'

Spaghetti Circus is a circus school and performing arts company in the Northern Rivers region, in New South Wales, Australia. See http://www.spaghetticircus.com

92 Flipside Circus is a youth circus company and training centre incorporated in 1998 and based in Alderley in Queensland, Australia. See http://www.flipsidecircus.org.au/

93 Dallas Dellaforce is an iconic Australian drag artist and member of Briefs' first show, and the alter ego of performer Daniel Styles Cater.

94 Polytoxic is an Australian physical theatre company formed in 2000, based in Brisbane, Australia, led by Co-Artistic Directors Leah Shelton and Lisa Fa'alafi. See http://www.polytoxiclovesyou.com/about/

References

Abbott, L., & Seroff, D. (2007). *Ragged but right: Black traveling shows, 'coon songs,' and the dark pathway to blues and jazz*. Jackson: University Press of Mississippi.

Acrobat (2019). Acrobat performance research farm, current shows. Retrieved from https://www.acrobat.net.au/current-shows

Adams, R. (2001). *Sideshow USA. Freaks and the American cultural imagination*. Chicago, IL: University of Chicago Press.

Adams, R. (2012). Disability and the circus. In K. Ames (Ed.), *The history of the circus in America* (pp. 419–435). New Haven, CT: Yale University Press.

Berger, J. (1980). Why look at animals. *About looking* (pp. 3–28). New York, NY: Pantheon.

Bogdan, R. (1988). *Freak shows: Presenting human oddities for amusement and profit*. Chicago, IL: University of Chicago Press.

Borkowski, M. (2010, March 22). Pierrot Bidon obituary, Archaos founder who reinvented circus as an edgy art form for the industrial world. *The Guardian*. Retrieved from https://www.theguardian.com/stage/2010/mar/21/pierrot-bidon-obituary

Bouissac, P. (2006, December 1). Timeless circus in times of change. Paper presented at the Fabulous Risk: Danger in Performance in Circus and Sideshow Conference, University of Wollongong, Australia. Retrieved from https://semioticon.com/virtuals/circus/timeless.pdf

Bread + Butter (2019). Retrieved from http://breadandpuppet.org/

Briefs Factory (2019). Hot Brown Honey. Retrieved from https://www.briefsfactory.com/hot-brown-honey

Briefs Factory (2019). Briefs. Retrieved from https://www.briefsfactory.com

Brophy, B. (1965). *The rights of animals.* London: Animal Defence and Anti-Vivisection Society Ltd.

Cappelle, L. (2018). A transgender director who defies genres (to France's confusion). *New York Times.* Retrieved from https://www.nytimes.com/2018/07/08/theater/phia-menard-saison-seche-avignon.html

Carson, R. (2002). *Silent spring.* Boston, MA: Houghton Mifflin Harcourt. (Original publication 1962).

Casus (2019). Chasing smoke. Retrieved from http://casus.com.au/portfolio/chasingsmoke/

Circus Amok (2019). Retrieved from https://www.circusamok.org/circus/

Circus Oz (2019). BLAKflip. Retrieved from https://www.circusoz.com/sidesault/BLAKflip.html

Cirkus Cirkör (2019). [Video files]. Retrieved from https://www.youtube.com/user/CirkusCirkor/videos

Cirque du Soleil (2019). Ovo. Retrieved from https://www.cirquedusoleil.com/ovo

Compagnie Non Nova (2019). Cie Non Nova. Retrieved from http://www.cienonnova.com/#/en

Cynthia, C. (2006). *Watching wildlife.* Minneapolis: University of Minnesota Press.

Davis, J. M. (2002). *The circus age: Culture and society under the American big top.* Chapel Hill: The University of North Carolina Press.

Extraordinary Bodies (2019). Circus for every body. Retrieved from http://www.extraordinarybodies.org.uk/

Flipside Circus (2019). Retrieved from http://www.flipsidecircus.org.au/

Fricker, K., & Malouin, H. R. (Eds.) (2018). Circus and its others. *Performance Matters, 4*(1–2).

Funk, A. (2018). Gender asymmetry and circus education. *Performance Matters, 4*(1–2), 19–35.

Garland-Thomson, R. (Ed.) (1996). *Freakery: Cultural spectacles of the extraordinary body.* New York, NY & London: New York University Press.

Garland-Thomson, R. (2017). Preface to the twentieth century edition. In *Extraordinary bodies: Figuring physical disability in American culture and literature* (pp. vii–xvii). New York, NY: Columbia University Press.

Gilcher-Holtey, I. (2014). *A revolution of perception? Consequences and echoes of 1968.* New York, NY and Oxford: Bergahn Books.

Goffman, E. (1963). *Stigma: Notes on the management of spoiled identity.* New York, NY and London: Simon and Schuster.

Harrison, R. (2013). *Animal machines.* Wallingford: CABI. (Original publication 1964).

Hawkes, J. (2019). The history of Circus Oz. Retrieved from https://www.circusoz.com/circus-oz/history.html

Héritier, F. (2002). *Masculin-Féminin II. Dissoudre la hiérarchie.* Paris: Odile Jacob.

Kuoni, C. (1993). *Joseph Beuys in America/energy plan for the Western man.* New York, NY: Four Walls Eight Windows.

Lavers, K., & Burtt, J. (2017). BLAKflip and beyond: Aboriginal performers and Contemporary Circus in Australia. *New Theatre Quarterly, 33*(4), 307–319.

Maleval, M. (2016). An epic of New Circus. In P. Tait and K. Lavers (Eds.), *The Routledge Circus Studies reader* (pp. 50–65). Abingdon, Oxon. & New York, NY: Routledge.

Moore, J. (2018). Circus Amok - "Enough is Enough" - video excerpts. [Video file]. Retrieved from https://www.circusamok.org/circus/

Mullett, J. (2005). *Circus alternatives: The rise of New Circus in Australia, the United States, Canada and France* (Unpublished doctoral thesis). Melbourne, VIC: La Trobe University.

Oldenburg, R. (1999). *The great good place: Cafes, coffee shops, bookstores, bars, hair salons, and other hangouts at the heart of a community*, New York, NY: Marlowe and Company. (Original publication 1989).

On the Couch (2014, June 16). On the couch with Dale Woodbridge-Brown. *Arts Review.* Retrieved from http://artsreview.com.au/on-the-couch-with-dale-woodbridge-brown/

Peacock, J. (2010). Vale Pierrot Bidon. *RealTime, 97* (June–July), 14.

Polytoxic (2019). Polytoxic loves you. Retrieved from http://www.polytoxiclovesyou.com/about/

Preciado, B. (2013). The pharmaco-pornographic regime: Sex, gender, and subjectivity in the age of punk capitalism. In S. Stryker & A. Z. Aizura (Eds.), *The transgender studies reader 2* (pp. 266–277). New York, NY: Routledge.

Robertson, T. (2001). *The Pram Factory: The Australian Performing Group recollected*. Carlton, VIC: Melbourne University Press.

Sandahl, C. (2016). The Jim Rose Circus Side Show: Representing the postmodern body in pain. In P. Tait and K. Lavers (Eds.), *The Routledge Circus Studies reader* (pp. 267–277). Abingdon, Oxon & New York, NY: Routledge.

Schechner, R. (2004). *Performance theory*. London and New York, NY: Routledge.

Scott Heron (2019). Retrieved from http://www.scottheron.org/

Simpson, M. (2013). Ruth Harrison and other animals. *Oxford Magazine, 340* (2nd week, Michaelmas Term), 6–7.

Singer, P. (1990). *Animal liberation*. London: Jonathan Cape.

Stephens, E. (2005). Twenty-First century freak show: Recent transformations in the exhibition of non-normative bodies. *Disability Studies Quarterly, 25*(3), n.p.

Tait, P. (2005). *Circus bodies: Cultural identity in aerial performance*. Abingdon, Oxon: Routledge.

Williams, S. (2016). Gender in circus – a note from managing director Susie Williams. *Acrobatic Conundrum.* [Blog]. Retrieved from http://www.acrobaticconundrum.com/blog/2016/8/3/gender-in-circus

Wolf, G. (2008). *Make it Australian: The Australian Performing Group, the Pram Factory and New Wave theatre*. Sydney, NSW: Currency Press.

World Sideshow Festival (2019). Retrieved from http://www.worldsideshowfestival.com

Further Reading

Allen, R. C. (1991) *Horrible prettiness: Burlesque and American culture*. Chapel Hill, NC: University of North Carolina Press.

Arrighi, G. (2016). The circus and modernity: A commitment to the 'newer' and 'the newest.' In P. Tait & K. Lavers (Eds.), *The Routledge Circus Studies reader* (pp. 386–402). Abingdon, Oxon & New York, NY: Routledge.

Beissbarth, E., & Jackson, D. (Eds.) (1997). *Women's Circus: Leaping off the edge*. Melbourne, VIC: Spinifex Press.

Belfiore, E., & Bennett, O. (2014). *The social impact of the arts. An intellectual history.* London: Palgrave Macmillan.

Blake, E. (2016, October 27). Sisters behind Black Honey Company push for theatrical diversity. *The Sydney Morning Herald.* Retrieved from https://www.smh.com.au/entertainment/theatre/sisters-behind-black-honey-company-push-for-theatrical-diversity-20161027-gsc0k1.html

Bouissac, P. (1976). *Circus and culture: A semiotic approach.* Bloomington: Indiana University Press.

Bouissac, P. (2010). *Semiotics at the circus.* New York, NY & Berlin: Walter de Gruyter.

Bowers, C. (2017). Comment: Racism in the theatre world is real and it is debilitating. *SBS Life.* Retrieved from https://www.sbs.com.au/topics/life/culture/article/2017/02/15/comment-racism-theatre-world-real-and-it-debilitating

Broadway, S. (1999). Circus Oz - The first seven years: A memoir. *Australasian Drama Studies, 35,* 172–183.

Brooks, D. A. (2006). *Bodies in dissent: Spectacular performance of race and freedom 1850–1910.* Durham, NC: Duke University Press.

Chinn, S. E. (2000). *Technology and the logic of American racism: A cultural history of the body as evidence.* London: Continuum International Publishing.

Davis, J. M. (2011). Bearded ladies, dainty amazons, Hindu fakirs and lady savages: Circus presentations of gender and race in Victorian America. In K. Spangenberg & D. Walk (Eds.), *The amazing American circus poster* (pp. 75–84). Cincinnati, OH & Sarasota, FL: Cincinnati Art Museum and the John and Mable Ringling Museum of Art.

Fiedler, L. (1978). *Freaks: Myths and images of the secret self.* New York, NY: Simon and Schuster.

Garland-Thomson, R. (2008). Foreword. In M. Tromp (Ed.), *Freakery unfurled* (pp. ix–xi). Columbus, OH: The Ohio State University.

Ginsberg, E. K. (Ed.). (1996). *Passing and the fictions of identity.* Durham, NC: Duke University.

Guyez, M. (2015). Cirque et queer. Représentations et mises en scène des genres. In M. Plana & F. Sounac (Eds.), *Esthétique(s) queer dans la littérature et les arts. Sexualités et politiques du trouble.* Dijon, France: Éditions universitaires de Dijon.

Hadley, B. J., & McDonald, D. (Ed.) (2018) *The Routledge Handbook of disability arts, culture, and media.* Routledge International Handbooks. London & New York, NY: Routledge.

Harding, A. (1922). The joys and sorrows of a circus fat lady. *American Magazine, 94*(3), 62–63.

Holland, W. (1999). Re-imagining Aboriginality in the circus space. *Journal of Popular Culture, 33*(1), 91–104.

Kobayashi, A., & Peake, L. (2000). Racism out of place: Thoughts on whiteness and an antiracist geography in the new millennium. *Annals of the Association of American Geographers, 90*(2), 392–403.

Kuppers, P. (2003). *Disability and contemporary performance: Bodies on edge.* London: Routledge.

Kuppers, P. (2007). The performance of disability. *TDR: The Drama Review, 51*(4), 80–88.

Lavers, K. (2015). Horses in Modern, New, and Contemporary Circus. *Animal Studies Journal, 4*(2), 140–172.

Lavers, K., and Burtt, J. (2017). Briefs and Hot Brown Honey: Alternative bodies in Contemporary Circus. *M/C Journal, 20*(1), n.p.

Little, K. (1995). Surveilling Cirque Archaos: Transgression and the spaces of power in popular entertainment. *Journal of Popular Culture, 29*(1), 15–27.

Maleval, M. (2010). *L'émergence du nouveau cirque, 1968–1998.* Paris: L'Harmattan.

Maleval, M. (2014). *Sur la piste des cirques actuels.* Paris: L'Harmattan.

McClintock, A. (1995). *Imperial leather: Race, gender, and sexuality in the colonial contest.* New York, NY: Routledge.

McKenzie, J. (2001). *Perform or else. From discipline to performance.* London: Routledge.

Qureshi, S. (2004). Displaying Sara Baartman, the 'hottentot venus.' *History of Science, 42*(xliii), 223–257.

Reiss, B. (2001) *The showman and the slave: Race, death, and memory in Barnum's America.* Cambridge, MA: Harvard University Press.

Saxon, A. H. (1989). *P.T. Barnum: The legend and the man.* New York, NY: Columbia University Press.

St Leon, M. (1986). The great Con Colleano. *This Australia, 6*(1), 16.

St Leon, M. (2016). Celebrated, implied and finally denied: The erosion of Aboriginal identity in circus 1851–1960. In P. Tait, & K. Lavers (Eds.), *The Routledge Circus Studies reader* (pp. 209–234). Abingdon, Oxon & New York: Routledge.

Tait, P. (1996). Danger delights: Texts of gender and race in aerial performance. *New Theatre Quarterly, 12*, 43–49.

Tait, P. (2000). Fleshed, muscular phenomenologies across sexed and queer circus bodies. In P. Tait (Ed.), *Body show/s: Australian viewings of live performance* (pp. 60–78). Amsterdam: Rodopi.

Tait, P. (2012). *Wild and dangerous performances: Animals, emotions, circus.* London: Palgrave Macmillan.

Tait, P., & Kralj, I. (2011). *Zene & cirkus = Women & circus.* Croatia: Mala Performerska Scena.

3

PERFORMERS IN CONTEMPORARY CIRCUS

Performers in Contemporary Circus – contesting prowess

Circus is an artform which places the peak physical achievements of the human body at its very heart. Physical, bodily prowess is a central element of circus performances.

In Traditional Circus artists displayed their bodily and technical prowess in order to evoke feelings of wonder and awe, as well as, in some of the more daring acts, a visceral or kinaesthetic response from audience members.[1] Hamlin Garland (1860–1940), the Pulitzer prize-winning novelist in his autobiography writes of growing up as the son of an itinerant farmer in rural Iowa and of going to the circus as a boy. He describes the prowess of the performers, saying that 'the stark majesty of the acrobats subdued us into silent worship […] It was an embodiment of all that was skillful and beautiful in manly action.'[2] Janet Davis, in *The Circus Age: Culture and Society under the American Big Top*, writes that 'At a typical Ringling Bros. show, performers heralded from twenty-two countries, including Persia, Japan, and Italy; […] The athletic prowess of these sleek muscular bodies was startling.'[3]

In Traditional Circus the performers, in particular the top aerialists, and circus stars, were often presented as superhumans, or sometimes as aristocrats. For instance, the renowned aerialists Lillian Leitzel (1892–1931) and Luisita Leers (1909–1997) 'were depicted in aristocratic terms: as part of a biological lineage of performers in the press […] whilst wearing the cloaks of aristocracy within the ring.'[4] In addition, the approach to the presentation of high-level skills by the star performers was to perform them as though they were easy, 'Leitzel is frequently described as having made it "look easy"' (Bradna & Spence 1953, p. 150).[5]

Dramaturg Bauke Lievens suggests that this presentation of bodily prowess in Traditional Circus was implicated in reinforcing a particular way of seeing.

Arguing that form and content are inextricably linked, she proposes that within Traditional Circus were encoded the implied narratives of human mastery over nature and natural forces.

> For most of its history the circus was occupied almost entirely with skill and technique, and thus with form. This does not mean that it had no content: in traditional circus, the mastering of physically demanding, dangerous techniques and the taming of wild animals can be seen as expressions of a belief in the supremacy of humankind over nature and over natural forces such as gravity.[6]

This presentation of the bodily prowess of circus artists, in which the performers were presented as superhumans or 'aristocracy,' with the difficult tricks performed as if they were easy, and with the implied narrative of the supremacy of humankind over nature and natural forces, was called into question with the emergence of New Circus in the 1970s.

The radical progressive ideals of New Circus led to circus being opened up to a wide range of people with differing body types and a range of physical abilities. This democratisation of New Circus led to a range of people, some of whom were artists from a variety of different disciplines, entering circus. Many challenged the centrality of the presentation of prowess as the key element in circus performance through the introduction of a range of new aesthetics and new theatrical ideas. A range of hybrid work began to emerge as circus melded with different artforms, and there was a shift in focus with a new emphasis placed on innovation and creation rather than on the display of prowess.

Today, however, with the increasing formalisation of circus training and techniques in the professional circus schools, technical prowess has once again become of paramount importance for graduating students, who are expected to display exceptional technical skill levels in a unique act to be presented at graduation.

Many Contemporary Circus creators and practitioners, however, still retain the progressive political ideals of New Circus in relation to the democratisation of circus. Now, with the highly trained elite graduates entering the field from the professional circus schools, new tensions are emerging within Contemporary Circus. Some of these tensions revolve around the presentation of physical prowess in performance with the Traditional Circus way of presenting prowess now widely problematised within Contemporary Circus.

Many Contemporary Circus creators reject the presentation of circus performers as superbeings, stars, or aristocrats, with a large number of companies aiming to present performers as ordinary people similar to members of the audience.

This can be seen in interviews with performers in The 7 Fingers show *Traces* for the *New York Times* in 2011. Florian Zumkehr, a performer with the show describes how, 'In the early days of circus it was all about, "Look how easy this is" [... but] we kind of show you how hard it is.'[7] In the same article, Bradley Henderson, another acrobat in *Traces*, is quoted as saying,'[we are] really trying to connect with the audience members as if we're just like them. We're not superheroes.'[8]

In the conversation with Jo Lancaster and Simon Yates of Acrobat in the chapter *New Work*, Simon Yates says,

> People are often drawn to things that are heroic in circus performance. Circus performers are often doing things to appear as gods or heroes. In our performances we tend to be doing things to undermine that expectation. Historically we've had a dedication to a very high technical standard but we've also undermined it, or presented it so that it's flawed to make it a bit harder to admire.[9]

As part of this contestation of being presented as aristocrats or 'superheroes,' in *Traces*, as in much New and Contemporary Circus, the glittery sequinned costumes and heavy makeup of Traditional Circus are rejected and instead the costumes most often represent street wear.[10] In an interview with scholar Charles Batson in Montreal in 2012 talking about *Traces*, Shana Carroll, Co-Director of the show with Gypsy Snider,[11] says that it was 'a conscious choice to present the characters as real people' with the performers writing performance texts that are 'built on their own lives.'[12] The aim is to create circus performance on a human scale, embedded within versions of their everyday actions and relationships.

This contestation of the traditional mode of presenting prowess can also be seen in the widespread rejection of the Traditional Circus pause signalling for 'compliments' or applause from the audience after the completion of a trick. In conversations in the *Voices* section in the New Work chapter, Jo Lancaster and Simon Yates of Acrobat talk about their rejection of this traditional 'cue signalling for applause,'[13] while Yaron Lifschitz of Circa later in this chapter states, 'I hate applause in the circus, in my circus' and he says that when it happens the performers work hard to go, 'Why did that happen and how can we stop it?'[14]

It is not just the accoutrements of the Traditional Circus presentation of prowess – the make-up and costumes, and the cues signalling for applause – that are being called into question, at another level still it is the whole notion of the embodied presentation and performance of prowess itself that is being problematised in much Contemporary Circus. This is one of the pivotal paradoxes that informs and drives much Contemporary Circus as physical prowess is required for the performance of circus skills, however the displaying of physical virtuosity, in and of itself, is repeatedly brought into question and contested in embodied ways.

An important indicator of this contestation of prowess can be seen in a widely adopted aesthetic in Contemporary Circus of 'raw' performance. This approach rejects the presentation of circus acts as being 'easy,' and incorporates an emphasis on revealing the performer's effort in performing the circus skills. This is also often accompanied by a rejection of balletic lines and 'polish.' This position is clearly articulated in an interview with performer Cohdi Harrell,[15] Co-Director and Co-Founder of The Ricochet Project, who says, 'I actually like to watch a little bit of a struggle; I want to watch that process [...] I want to see the raw-ness.'[16] This feeling is also expressed in conversations later in this chapter, in particular, in the discussion with Shana Carroll.

In Contemporary Circus, with the traditional presentation of prowess and the portrayal of circus artists as superhuman being called into question, there is instead often an emphasis on conveying the humanity and the vulnerability of the circus performer. One example of this can be found on the website of Gravity and other Myths, the Australian Contemporary Circus collective, in the description of their first show, *A Simple Space*.

> Instead of fine-tuning the performance with makeup, lighting and con-trived theatrical overlay, the cast have deliberately gone the other way. The audience is brought in close to surround the stripped back stage. In that space the acrobats are pushed to the physical limit, breaking down their usual guards and introducing the reality of failure and weakness.[17]

This description of the show could be said to reveal the influence of Jerzy Grotowski's 'Poor Theatre' or 'Théâtre Pauvre' which focuses on stripping back everything that could be considered extraneous, such as lighting and sound, to focus on the use of space, on the actor/audience relationship, and the 'total act' which is described as, 'a moment of self-sacrifice by individual actors where they offer themselves to the audience in a moment of total vulnerability and honesty, to incite the audience to open themselves in response.'[18]

Other approaches enabling the performers to problematise the presentation of bodily prowess and reveal 'moments of total vulnerability and honesty' are apparent in the staging of The 7 Fingers show *Traces*. The performers remain on stage for the duration of the show and, in the sections where they are not actively performing, they can be seen on stage behaving in the way they would if they were backstage, 'joking, tickling, dribbling a basketball, singing in Chinese in full view of the audience. When their colleagues perform, they stand in the back drinking water, wiping off sweat or fiddling with a costume.'[19] Shana Carroll has commented on this saying that she personally found it 'touching when she could see the acrobats training backstage in their training clothes and was aware of their stress and the moment of suspense before they did their trick.'[20]

Other stratagems used in Contemporary Circus to encourage the audience to engage with the performers on a human level rather than seeing them as super-human include performing in silence so that the physical sounds of the artist's exertion can be heard by the audience. In one section of the show *Smoke and Mirrors* by The Ricochet Project, an aerial act by Laura Stokes[21] is performed in silence and is accompanied only by the sound of her breathing.[22] Cohdi Harrell describes how Stokes was rehearsing in the studio one day without music,

> I walked in at that moment and just stopped and watched her, and it was like, 'this is the act, this is the most beautiful thing I've ever seen,' because we're listening to her breath, we're listening to the creaks of the building.[23]

This moment of silence gives space for the viewer to engage with the physical sounds of the performer working with the apparatus in the space, and to become aware of her exertion, her presence, her liveness, human to human. It also offers the performer the opportunity to gain agency giving her the space to time the movements as she wishes rather than in response to the rhythmical pulse of accompanying music.

Other stratagems used in Contemporary Circus to contest the Traditional Circus presentation of prowess include the performer being present on stage for some time before first revealing any bodily virtuosity. This period of time on stage is intended to allow time for the audience to engage with the performer on a human level before any prowess is displayed. As Director Firenza Guidi says in the *Voices* section in this chapter,

> … you have to seduce me well before you do your tricks. And I use the word seduce as from the Latin *se abducere*, 'to bring somebody to you.' For me 'to seduce,' the word 'seduction' is 'bring to you.' It is something or somebody that brings you out of the sort of distracted, bored, absent-minded world of the spectator. The spectator must go, 'Wow, I am so hooked by this.' And the 'Wow, I am hooked' point can be a breathing, a way of moving a hand, a way of contacting you which is totally seductive. And the tricks will be even more spectacular because I am relating to somebody with a life, with a history, with a memory, with desires, with vulnerability, with a past and a future. And not just simply a trained monkey.[24]

One additional element that is sometimes present in Contemporary Circus is an ironic awareness of the paradox inherent in the act of contesting the very prowess that enables the performers to perform the circus skills in the first place. This awareness is expressed in some of the conversations in the *Voices* section of this chapter, in particular in the conversation with Firenza Guidi, in which she says,

> There is a self-irony in performance which is endearing and not arrogant which is about this kind of vulnerability […] Circus performers are trained to say 'I can do it, I can do it, watch me watch me watch me. I can do this, I can do a split, look at this. I am super fit.' But what if you enter a space of not knowing […]? Then within that space you work your abilities to actually narrate your vulnerability.[25]

The complexity visible in these diverse approaches to the presentation of prowess is just one of the range of complexities facing a performer working in Contemporary Circus today.

Training prowess

Many Traditional Circus families working today still have a very particular way of developing prowess in performers. The Wallendas are a Traditional

Circus family whose members pride themselves on their long familial history of performing as wire-walkers, with an unbroken lineage that stretches back to the 1780s, and Nik Wallenda, is keeping this family tradition of wire-walking alive.[26] In June 2012, after two years of complex negotiations with the Canadian and the American governments, he realised his dream of walking across Niagara Falls on a high wire, and this walk was broadcast live for an ABC News special.[27]

In the documentary, Wallenda says, 'People say I'm insane all the time, but they don't understand that this is something I've done since I was two. It's just in my blood.'[28] In the following passage, Wallenda talks more about how he learnt to walk the wire.

> I am a seventh-generation member of the Wallenda family. My family started performing in the 1780s in Bohemia before going over to Germany. We came to the United States in 1928 to perform for Ringling Brothers circus. I started walking a wire at 2. That [was] just 2 feet off the ground; my parents would hold my hand and I would walk back and forth. At 4, I was actually walking on my own. And my first high-wire performance was at 13, and I was about 25 feet above the ground. Once I started performing, I never stopped. It's life to me. My great-grandfather Karl said, 'Life is on the wire and everything else is waiting.'[29]

This method for the transmission of skills through beginning the training at a very young age and imprinting prowess was part of the familial approach to training, and is still used by many Traditional Circus families today.

With the advent of New Circus in the 1970s, this emphasis on the importance of lineage and blood and the hold that the circus families had on circus skills was contested. The politically progressive ideals of New Circus led to widespread workshops and community circus classes, and also the setting up of professional circus schools.

As Circus Studies scholar Pascal Jacob writes, with the development of New Circus, 'the entire sector was brutally and brusquely shaken.'[30] All the traditional identifying elements and codes of Traditional Circus were challenged by the ideas that these new artists brought into circus with them. New Circus, for the most part, jettisoned the big top, the circus ring, the ringmaster, and the acts with wild animals and horses. The secretive transmission of circus skills within the circus families was also contested, and in New Circus, circus skills were taught to anyone who wanted to learn them.

The Traditional Circus emphasis on extreme prowess as a key quality for circus performers was brought into question in many New Circus companies. In Circus Oz, as the ex-Artistic Director Mike Finch discusses later in this chapter, performers were not simply chosen for their level of physical prowess. Other qualities were valued including the ability to input into the creation of innovative work, a range of circus skills which enabled the performer to take part in group acts, the ability to work in a team, and strong political convictions in line with those of the group, were often more highly prized characteristics in prospective performers than extreme bodily prowess. However, as the professional circus schools have become established and more formalised there is once again a strong focus in the training of prowess in students.

The circus schools

Many Circus Studies scholars point to the first professional circus school in the West as being set up in France in 1974 by Annie Fratellini and her husband, the French clown and film-maker Pierre Étaix.[31] In fact another international circus school had emerged in Spain over a decade earlier, the International Benposta School of Circus, created by Father Jesús Silva in 1963, in Ourense, in Gallicia. This school and its touring company, Circo de Los Muchachos, provided living proof that circus could be taught effectively to anyone, and could also act as a radical force for progressive social change.[32]

The background to this pioneering circus school was that in the aftermath of the Spanish Civil War (1936–1939) many orphans were living on the streets. In 1957, a young priest, Father Jesús Silva, seeing the living conditions of these young people, invited 15 orphaned boys to live in his mother's house. His brother later gave him a 30-acre property named Benposta, and on this donated land he created his City of Boys for orphaned boys aged between 4 and 20.[33]

This City of Boys ran as a 'republic' inside General Franco's Spain,

> The young people ran the 'republic' themselves, electing a mayor from among their number, while others took on various civic duties; the city had its own police force, public health officials, financial advisers and guardians of public morals. Racial and social distinctions were not recognised; and attendance at Mass was not obligatory.[34]

Running short of money to keep this community going, Jesús Silva asked his great-uncle, Manuel Feijoo, the well-known Spanish circus impresario who had worked with the Castilla family to create Madrid's Circo Price and the touring Circo Americano, to come in and teach circus skills to the boys.[35] In 1963, Jesús Silva founded the International Benposta School of Circus, and the circus company, Circo de Los Muchachos. The Circus School originally only took boys from within the City of Boys but later expanded to include young people from all over Spain, France, Spanish Guinea, and Brazil. In 1970, *The New York Times* wrote of the City of Boys and the International Benposta Circus School,

> His pupils – now numbering 1,000 – receive academic schooling in preparation for a variety of trades and professions. Some will be bakers, some will be doctors and lawyers and some [...] will emerge as circus stars [...] Circus teachers from all over Europe came as guest professors, and five years ago the Circo de los Muchachos gave its first public performance.[36]

Circo de los Muchachos went on tour in 1965, touring Spain and Portugal for four years. In 1970–1971, over the Christmas period, the company performed at the Grand Palais in Paris with huge success.

> The performers 80 in all – are boys between the ages of 10 and 18 [...] Some are stylish horsemen and some are hilarious clowns. Others form an orchestra that accompanies the numbers and offers a concert as overture. There are fire eaters, nimble jugglers and agile acrobats. A quartet of youths mounts the rope ladders to execute daring trapeze feats at a breathtaking height.[37]

The company later toured to Germany, Italy, Switzerland, Belgium, Russia, North and South America, Canada, Japan, and Australia, and the profits went to keep the City of Boys community going.[38] The international tours of Circo de Los Muchachos demonstrated clearly to a large number of people that circus schools could be successful in teaching circus skills to people who came from outside the Traditional Circus families.

In 1974, Annie Fratellini founded the École Nationale du Cirque Annie Fratellini in France.[39] The École au Carré, which was set up by Silvia Monfort and Alexis Grüss, opened in France a few weeks later.[40] In Brazil the Piolin Academy was founded in 1977, and in 1982, the National Circus School in Rio de Janeiro followed. In 1981, the National Circus School or École nationale de cirque was established in Montreal, Canada, and in the same year, the École Supérieure des Arts du Cirque in Brussels, Belgium. In France, in 1985, the Centre National des Arts du Cirque in Châlons-en-Champagne was founded, and in 1995, the National Institute for Circus Arts was established in Melbourne, Australia.[41] These circus schools all offered access to training to students coming into circus from outside the Traditional Circus families.

Although the New Circus tenet of 'Circus for Everybody' no doubt drove the founding of these schools, one perhaps unforeseen effect of this establishing of the professional circus schools has been the widespread introduction of the Russian approach to circus training. The first professional circus schools set up in the West from the 1970s were founded more than 50 years later than the Moscow State College for Circus and the Variety Arts which had been set up in Moscow in 1927. The remarkable standard of the Moscow Circus artists when they first toured in Europe in the 1950s and the impression they made on spectators, led to the Russian Model of training establishing itself as a strong influence within the circus schools.

This Moscow State College for Circus and the Variety Arts was set up in Russia as a result of a tour undertaken by Charles Hughes, one of Philip Astley's horse-riding students.[42] In 1773, Charles Hughes took a troupe of circus performers to Russia to give a command performance at the court. The performance was a huge success, and the Empress Catherine the Great immediately ordered that two circus rings be built.[43] Most of Hughes' circus troupe stayed on in

Russia to perform for the court, and this attracted a steady stream of performers from the West. The circus in Russia continued in this way until after the Russian Revolution in 1917. After the Revolution, Vladimir Lenin declared that circus, like opera and ballet, was an Art of the People and that it would receive government backing, and in 1927, the first Russian state circus school, the Moscow State College for Circus and the Variety Arts, was set up.

Many of the professional circus schools today still use the Russian Model, an approach to training which is predicated on the pedagogical methods used in the Moscow State College for Circus and the Variety Arts. The Moscow College, now known as the Moscow Circus School, came directly out of the Russian gymnastics programme.[44] The college taught Traditional Circus skills but combined them with gymnastics, and introduced a focus on innovative choreographed acts.[45] Russian circus started to evolve and to develop in its own distinctive way.[46] By 1956, when it toured Europe for the first time, widespread audience excitement led to artists from different disciplines seeing it as a vibrant artform with the potential to reach large audiences.

One example of the influence of the Russian Model can be seen in the origins of the National Circus School in Montreal which was established by the Québécois circus artist, actor, and clown, Guy Caron, a graduate from the Budapest Circus School. Caron along with gymnast Pierre Leclerc, established the National Circus School in 1981, basing the training on the Russian Model he had been exposed to in Hungary.[47]

The pedagogical method known as the Russian Model is usually taught with a one-to-one teacher to student ratio, and uses a direct method of teaching in which the skills are taught in a linear progression. When the performance of a particular skill is considered satisfactory, the coach decides that the student may move onto the next skill. In this method, the student depends primarily on direct feedback from the coach to gauge their progress and performance. This approach teaches the physical skills effectively and quickly; however, its disadvantages are that this type of training can lead to over-dependency on the coach and can limit the development of cognitive skills such as self-regulation and self-efficacy.[48]

The Russian Model focuses on the training of elite levels of physical bodily prowess through the development of a unique circus act for graduation. In this model, developing an act to present the artist's prowess is still seen as the primary focus of the teaching. Pascal Jacob describing the Russian Model writes,

> The teachers aimed to re-create classic artists differentiated by their respective talents. In doing so, they adhered to and ratified a norm. They positioned themselves at the forefront of the market, aiming to produce the very best acts (and therefore the best artists).[49]

In his report for the Federation of Professional European Circus Schools (FEDEC) in 2008, Pascal Jacob writes that around two-thirds of the job market for circus school graduates still actively wants to acquire pre-existing acts for their shows.[50]

This market for existing circus acts that have been designed to demonstrate the physical prowess of the artists, includes many of the larger Traditional Circuses, cabarets, cruise ships, and holiday resorts. Equipping students with an act for this type of market can be seen as a driving force in much circus training.

This kind of training focuses on the development of the prowess to be displayed, rather than exposing the student to issues and aesthetics such as those that arise when the idea of prowess itself is actively problematised as it is in much Contemporary Circus performance. Training in physical prowess is necessary, but as Contemporary Circus Director Firenza Guidi says,

> You need to learn to play the violin otherwise you will not get any notes. Then you can always play a score. But, you could also take this instrument and make it come alive with something that you want to communicate, something you want to say or something which is part of a creative process.[51]

New roles for performers

With new ideas coming into circus from postmodern dance, thinking changed about the role of performers.[52] In postmodern dance performers sought to go beyond their traditional role in ballet and modern dance in which they were required to demonstrate their physical prowess and act as a vehicle for other people's choreographic ideas. They sought instead to gain agency and become contributing creative artists themselves. As Dance Studies scholar Lúcia Matos writes,

> By the final decades of the 20th century the dancer had broken the barriers of 'thingification' – of being a mere performer and reproducer of movements created by a choreographer – to become a creator.[53]

Artists entering New Circus brought with them the idea that circus performers could actively be involved in the creation of new work, through a process which has become known as 'group-devising.'[54] Many circus performers are now actively seeking to move beyond the performing of work solely designed to demonstrate their bodily prowess and instead to become actively involved in the process of creating work.

This thinking has permeated the training in some circus schools, where there is starting to be more of a focus on developing circus performers who can contribute to collaboratively-devised work. However, other circus schools still focus to a great extent on the equipping of the student with a polished act to enable them to enter the job market for pre-existing acts when they graduate. Pascal Jacob writes,

> the circus schools imprint their students with their own ideas and image, so many graduates either come out equipped with an act and with little to no

experience of creating group-devised work, or, vice versa, they come out well versed in group-devising processes and can feel uncomfortable in an environment where they have no input into the creative process.[55]

At a practical level within the diverse field of Contemporary Circus, many performers find themselves moving between working environments and companies which have widely differing expectations of them. The independent circus performer, often working on short contracts, has to become adaptable so as to be able to move easily between these different work environments and expectations. They may need to be able to move from a corporate event where they are asked to rig their own equipment and perform a pre-existing act which demonstrates their bodily prowess, or to be able to respond to and contribute to the differing processes and aesthetics of diverse directors and creators in Contemporary Circus in which they may be asked to problematise their own prowess.

A Contemporary Circus performer may be asked to input and create group-devised movement sequences and autobiographical text, and perhaps also perform in an innovative, newly created, and choreographed acrobatic or aerial act, such as in the work created by Shana Carroll for The 7 Fingers; or work in a company where they are expected to jettison their act and perform continuous flows of ground-based acrobatics in a semi-improvised mode of movement generation in which they problematise the notion of the 'trick' and the 'act' as in Yaron Lifschitz's work *Humans* for Circa; or they may be asked to develop new work by interacting with the environment in a way reminiscent of the approaches to site-specific installation and performance art and, in addition, be required to problematise their own prowess as in Firenza Guidi's work with NoFit State Circus; or work in a show with a commedia dell'arte aesthetic requiring physical theatre skills, such as the works *Nebbia*, *Rain*, and *Nomade* created for Cirque Éloize by Daniele Finzi Pasca; or perhaps work in a company requiring burlesque or cabaret skills as in the political boylesque work of Fez Faanana and his company Briefs.

This required malleability on the part of the Contemporary Circus performer is visible in the work trajectory of artist Valérie Doucet who graduated from the National Circus School in Montreal in 2010.

> Since graduating, Valérie Doucet has performed in German Spiegeltent cabaret circus and worked with the established contemporary circus company Cirque Éloize in Montreal, performing in its signature work *Rain*. She then worked with the stripped-back acrobatic style of the Australian circus company Circa, based in Brisbane, under the direction of the Artistic Director Yaron Lifschitz who is originally from a theatre background. She went on to perform and tour with James Thierrée's Compagnie du Hanneton in the show *Tabac Rouge* in a role that combined comedy, physical theatre and contemporary dance.[56] In addition she has founded her own circus collective named Le Poivre Rose and is creating new work with them.[57] Whilst at the

National Circus School she specialised in hand-balancing, but with each production she has worked on, she has developed new skills and performed new disciplines. By the time she appeared in the production *Rain* in 2011, in addition to hand balancing, she performed contortion, trapeze, aerial hoop, tissu and also sang. In Thierrée's *Tabac Rouge,* with no traditional circus apparatus in sight, she performed contortion in the physical theatre role of the obsequious, whispering confidante to Thierrée's central character, and danced in the work's ensemble contemporary dance sections.[58]

In this environment of such widely differing expectations, with different requirements in terms of how prowess is presented, and also diverse performance aesthetics, many Contemporary Circus performers are now creating their own pathways into circus. They are creating companies and collectives, in the same way as Valérie Doucet has done with her own circus collective Le Poivre Rose, in order to be able to make and perform their own work and give themselves more agency over their performing lives.

Although many of the original New Circus companies started with exactly this aim in mind, for example the Australian company Circus Oz (1977), the French companies Archaos (1986) and Les Arts Sauts (1993), many of these original New Circus companies have been operating for several decades, some for over 40 years, and in some cases their aesthetic, and the creative team, is already established, and firmly set in place. This can limit the possibilities, even with group-devising creation processes in place, for the newer, younger artists to be involved in meaningful contributions to the creation of any new work in terms of there being room for them to explore their own ideas and aesthetics.

In addition, as Mike Finch, Artistic Director of Circus Oz from 1998–2015, discusses later in this chapter, the relationship between the long-established original New Circus companies and their creative teams, and the young graduates now emerging from the professional circus schools and being employed as performers, has over time tended to become more conventional and more hierarchical. This often has the potential to reduce the opportunity for successful creative interchange between the creative teams and the younger performers.

One of the more recent companies, founded with the aim of creating freedom for all the performers in the collective to be able to generate their own work, is The 7 Fingers, based in Montreal. Founded by seven friends in 2002, all of whom were Contemporary Circus performers interested in having opportunities to create their own circus work, The 7 Fingers has had huge success and is now running simultaneous shows that tour widely internationally. The company is now able to offer all six of the remaining founding members the opportunity to make their own new work.[59]

Another collective, the Australian ensemble Gravity and Other Myths (GOM), was also started by seven friends who are all Contemporary Circus performers. This collective of circus artists, based in Adelaide, Australia, was formed in 2009, and presents work that is group-devised by all the company members working together. Like The 7 Fingers, GOM is highly successful, touring the world ten to eleven months of the year, often with several casts touring simultaneously – a model which is becoming more prevalent in small to medium-sized companies.

Part 2 of this chapter, the *Voices* section, includes conversations about performers and performing with 10 Contemporary Circus creators, many of whom have been or are performers themselves, who talk about the ways they choose performers and how they go about developing performers for their own work: Shana Carroll (The 7 Fingers), Yaron Lifschitz (Circa), Firenza Guidi (Elan Frantoio; NoFit State Circus), Mike Finch (Circus Oz), Elizabeth Streb (STREB), Phia Ménard (Cie Non Nova), Daniele Finzi Pasca (Compagnia Finzi Pasca), Philippe Decouflé (Compagnie DCA), Lachlan Binns and Jascha Boyce (Gravity and Other Myths).

Performers in Contemporary Circus – voices

This section begins with a conversation with Shana Carroll, Co-Artistic Director and Co-Founder of the Montreal circus collective, The 7 Fingers. After first training in her native San Francisco she later attended the National Circus School in Montreal. After working with Cirque du Soleil as a performer for seven years, in 2002, Shana Carroll co-founded The 7 Fingers with six friends, Isabelle Chassé, Patrick Léonard, Faon Shane, Gypsy Snider, Sébastien Soldevila, and Samuel Tétreault, all of whom were Contemporary Circus performers wanting to create a platform to enable them to create their own work.

Their first show *Loft,* a mix of circus, dance, theatre, and video, was co-created and co-directed by all seven founders, all of whom also performed in it. Shana Carrol has since created, or co-created, numerous works for The 7 Fingers, and has been Acrobatic Designer and Choreographer for the Cirque du Soleil shows *Iris* and *Paramour,* and Co-Director with Sébastien Soldevila for *Crystal,* Cirque du Soleil's first arena show on ice.[60]

In this short extract she talks about her personal inspiration for becoming a Contemporary Circus performer, and what drew her to Contemporary Circus. She puts forward the idea that showing the performers' vulnerability has the potential to evoke a deep emotional response from the spectator.

★★★★★

Shana Carroll

Is it important to you that The 7 Fingers' performers show their vulnerability on stage?
Shana Carroll: Yes, I think it is one of the other staples of what we do. Really the reason I started doing circus was I saw a trapeze artist who was 18, and I saw her training.

I was working in the office at the Pickle Family Circus, and I had never liked circus because it was a spectacle, it didn't really feel like it was being done by anyone who was actually human, I didn't relate to the performers. But somehow seeing her … I was only 10 feet away from her. She was in training clothes, she was my age and just identifying with her, everything changed. I felt like my muscles were contracting with hers, I was fearful that she would do something that would injure her. It was so moving and beautiful and that has been forever my beacon. I want the audience to go, this is something that could be them, this is someone they know, this could be their son, or their friend, and then they care about the people on stage, and then they will care when they go to any circus show.

There's that, and also this feeling that what I learned when I discovered circus … you know I was an 18-year-old who had never done anything physical really, and just with enough hard work I became a trapeze artist, so I believe much more in this message … that any normal person if they just work hard enough can do these extraordinary things and it's just so empowering. This is as opposed to the feeling you get quite often with Cirque du Soleil or even in the wonderful Russian Moscow Circus – that these are just other worldly beings that are untouchable. There's no way you, or anyone like you, could ever do something like that. And that's wonderful too. There's an excellence involved. That's also empowering in the sense that it's nice to believe there are people in this world who are immortal. But what I like is for people to feel the empowering sense that it could be them.

So, I think that's why quite often vulnerability is mixed in with this extraordinary mix of, 'I'm raw, and I'm sharing my weaknesses, and yes I'll also jump through four hoops.'

FIGURE 3.1 The 7 Fingers, *Traces*. Photo: Alexandre Galliez.

How did it feel when you started changing over from working with the original members of The 7 Fingers who are people that you have worked with for a very long time, to now, when you often have young graduates coming into the process?

Shana Carroll: Well I just want to say one thing that was interesting is that *Traces* [2006] was done with guys we'd known all their lives, and we decided we would do a show with them, and so it was like almost inside the company. *Psy* [2009] was all graduates from the ENC [École nationale de cirque in Montreal], and *Sequence 8* [2012] as well, and when I did *Queen of the Night* [2014] it was a few people who had just graduated from school and a lot of people who had a lot of experience, and I discovered the mix was so good.

So for instance with *Cuisine and Confessions* [2014] we intentionally wanted to have a mix of fresh out of school and experienced performers because with the new kids it was great they brought a lot of energy, and the technical level and everything, but having the well-worn professionals there really brought the young ones up to a certain level, brought a lot of maturity on stage, and Matias [Plaul] who was in *Cuisine* is 40 something now. So I want to mention that, it's tempting, we see the kids in the school, and there is so much talent coming out, and it's sort of tempting just to hire a bunch, but we also really value the professionalism, not just the professionalism, the character that comes with age, first of all, and also the experience.

★★★★★

From Shana Carroll's discussion of how The 7 Fingers collective chooses its performers we move to talk with Yaron Lifschitz, Artistic Director of Circa in Australia, about his particular approach to selecting performers for the company.

Lifschitz originally trained as a Theatre Director at the National Institute of Dramatic Art (NIDA) in Sydney, and took over as the Artistic Director of Rock'n'Roll Circus in Brisbane in 2004, soon changing the name of the company to Circa.[61] Here Lifschitz points to the importance he places on developing the decision-making abilities of performers and how he approaches this by requiring them to not only take responsibility for themselves whilst on stage, but also in every other aspect of their lives.

★★★★★★

Yaron Lifschitz

So how do you go about the initial selection process of performers? What are you looking for?

Yaron Lifschitz: Oh it's like a Geiger counter. You literally walk around and you hear the little clicks going off. The people I look for generally are introverts; they have a dark fire about them; there's something unresolved and deep. They're not too messed up about it, they can function. Sometimes I've made a mistake of having people that don't have enough of that dark fire or have too much of it.

I'm not interested in people who like to show off; they need to have a basic skill level, of course, but they also need to be prepared to cast aside all of their skills. So, one of the performers who joined recently trained in tight wire at the École nationale de cirque in Montreal, and he really wanted to join an ensemble, and I really grilled him and I said, 'Are you sure? You've just spent three years training in tight wire, and you might get a gig, you might get a chance to do it at some special moment but, really, we're not going to start doing tight wire because of you.' But he really wanted to be a part of something, to be part of a group.

How would you describe the way you develop performers in Circa?
Yaron Lifschitz: At the core our circus artform it is about the cultivation of the individual, growing an acrobat from a kind of biomechanical set of systems into an artist, which means getting them to access their humanity, their agility, and their complexity. And you see with artists who've been with us for a long time, you see this extraordinary kind of richness.

After three or four or five years of work you get these extraordinarily rich flavours of performance that are possible because they've spent so much time analysing and thinking, and working and challenging themselves.

How do you go about this process of developing an acrobat into an artist? What is your process at Circa?
Yaron Lifschitz: What I am interested in is the cultivation of artists, the creation of ways of working, and then the products of those ways of working.

So basically, simply put, the artists arrive at 9:00 am, they're never late, I'm very proud of the fact that Circa artists are never late for anything. They do an hour of warm-up, they then do an intensive skill period, generally till about 11:00 am or 11:30 am. Then I come in for an intense period, anywhere between 11:00–11:30 am and 1:00 pm, so an hour and a half to two hours depending on how much work we've got to do. And that's me standing in front of the room, and usually that period is about half an hour, 45 minutes of structured improvisation, not for the show but for language and ideas that go into the show, and performance modality, sensibility, and tuning stuff. And then there's usually a series of group exercises. That sounds too formal – provocations I guess. Then they break between 1:00 pm and 2:00 pm.

In the afternoon they come back and usually do a 20 minute rewarm. Then we spend a couple of hours where I may be there, but I may not, and if I am there I won't be standing at the front of the room; that's more of an act lab, so people will tend to work more on individual things or small groups, particular skills. I'll drop in and out and one of my associates may or may not. With *Humans* [2017] I banned everyone else from the room even the technical crew. But usually there's a few people around.

And then at the end of the day they do about half an hour of warming down and body conditioning, and then we start the next day at 9:00am, and we do that four and a half days a week. We don't do Wednesday afternoons. That came out of work with our physiotherapist and reading about periodisation.[62] On Wednesday afternoon, it's generally a non-physical afternoon. They generally book in treatments on that afternoon, and sometimes we have a meeting or a session – like listening to a piece of music.

Having an afternoon that is non-physical is a good idea because otherwise the schedule can be so relentless, can't it?
Yaron Lifschitz: Before we started doing this you could write Friday afternoons off. Now we can get to the end of Friday, and everyone will go and have a drink and be human, and in that time we get everything done. There's this great sense of inefficiency in circus artforms and they are very traditionalised and are slow to change.

So, again, we got feedback in the tent about 'Oh we saw them doing tricks they didn't do in the tech safety.'[63] And we were like, 'Well yeah, we never do the tricks in tech safety.' The purpose of the tech safety is to check the gear is safe and to check the lights. We want to be able to do our tech safety in an hour maximum, or an hour and a half, we want to do it 'unwarm.' We want to be like, 'What is the most efficient way we can do this?' It's about how few times do we have do it with our acrobats warm in a week, not how much time can they spend doing this. Now that might mean on the first night we are a bit rough around the edges in a few places, but it also means by the last night we're still there and we're able to keep the show going.

There are companies that will take tech until three in the morning. But then again, we don't do Wheel of Death, we don't generally do swinging trapeze, or tight wire or any of the acts that need a lot more tech time.[64] Our bandwidth is narrower in terms of type of apparatus. But generally speaking, I want as fresh bodies as they can be, and that allows them to go on stage and be great and make good decisions and improvise.

FIGURE 3.2 Circa, *Humans*. Photo: Pedro Greig.

We had someone the other day who was associated with our tent when we did this show, and they complained that we didn't have backstage stage managers, so how would we know if we needed to stop the show and they were really saying was, 'This is unsafe.' And we were like, 'We have all these protocols in place. We absolutely do not need someone standing back there.' We don't have stage managers. I don't understand how you can ask people to be grown-ups, and make physical, safety, ethical, and artistic decisions themselves on stage, but not expect them to pick up their clothes from their bedroom floor – I don't think you get maturity that way. You get maturity by saying you're actually responsible for the whole way you are in the world, and it means when you meet our artists at a function, how they deal with the space, how they deal with other people, with crew, employment conditions, with conversation, because it's everything.

It's a discipline and for me it's almost a monastic order. And I like that. I like the fact that it has its own rituals, and it has its own internal focus, and sense of authenticity, and purity. That's part of what I find seductive about it.

Do you ever experience tension or problems with the performers in terms of their adapting to this sort of approach?
Yaron Lifschitz: Yes, I mean I think there's a fair degree of learning difficulties, there's a fair degree of Asperger's, there's a fair degree of stubbornness, chip-on-the-shoulder teenage arrested development, there's a fair degree of masochism, much of which can be harnessed for greater good. I don't think any of those things by themselves are negatives, but I think if you can access their power you can also get people to understand how those decisions made in one place in their lives resonate through and affect them on stage and how they handle their bodies. Cognitive and emotional diversity are valuable attributes for a company.

Another thing is that because no one gets involved with circus because they want to get told what to do by anyone else, there's always this slightly challenging relationship to power.

So how do you negotiate that?
Yaron Lifschitz: So you have to find a way, I find, to meet people, and in a respectful way, but you also need the right people. The thing that they're looking for, and the thing that we have to offer, needs to be roughly the same, even if they don't yet recognise it and we're not sure about it. If we are going to spend two, three, five, six, ten years working together, we're going to need to know that we're digging fertile ground.

Circa presents some extreme acrobatics which include a level of improvisation during performance. What happens in that situation in terms of risk management?
Yaron Lifschitz: I think you just have to have the right people. It's really fascinating. I have a number of very close working relationships in the company. If you don't get stuck on the status or protocols then you just can get on with

FIGURE 3.3   Circa, *Humans*. Photo: Sarah Walker.

the job, and fix it as you go. When it doesn't work and you have somebody who comes into the team and they're not like that, you instantly notice it because you're like, 'Oh, they're nasty, who is this? Suddenly I don't have the information, I don't have the flow.'

My job is to get those ten artists [in Circa] into that flow state and then get out of the way because they know what they're doing. But that requires good communication. When you come to Circa you get asked to read *Crucial Conversations*, it's a structured approach to conversations.[65]

What books are those?

Yaron Lifschitz: They're called *Crucial Conversations*. They're American business books but they're a structured approach to having difficult conversations. Because if you come up to someone and say, 'You know your oral hygiene is making it difficult for me to improvise with you,' that is a very difficult conversation for a 20-year-old who's just come into the company to have with a 30-year-old who's been in the company for 8 years and is a senior artist. Then you can't work with them properly.

If you can have that conversation respectfully and safely in a meaningful way then you can achieve almost anything. That's where the work really happens. It happens where there are the disturbances in the force. Once everyone is in the state where they can communicate, a few things will go wrong, but on the whole these are a group of people working at a very high level to achieve the same result and will achieve it if they are in tune with each other.

But yes, the show on Friday night was exemplary.[66] I mean 41 degrees centigrade in a tent, and the air-conditioning has broken down. Audience members are leaving because it's just too hot. The performers are doing all their tricks, missing a few, getting sticky with many sliding around the stage, and I'm looking at them and I'm absolutely ready to take the sound down and finish the show, or cut a particular scene, but actually everyone just did the thing that they needed to do and it was beautiful.

That was great decision-making on the part of the performers.
Yaron Lifschitz: Yes. Look, when we first went to Montreal they said, 'Look we've seen better skills than you, we've seen better shows than this, but your artists have something, but we don't know what it is,' and I said, 'Well I'm not going to tell you!'

Fundamentally what it is, is that when the artists go on stage they own the show, and so when they stand on the stage they are not in a Yaron production, or in a Circa production. They make those choices and they author it, so it comes from them, and that's what gives it its particular authenticity and flavour, and sometimes also it makes it not that good, we're not always successful in that work.

Sometimes you go to do a show and you go, 'Whoa, you don't want to make those catastrophically bad choices, you nearly derailed the whole show guys. But I'd rather you made the wrong choice than you didn't make any choices.' You can't sort of absent yourself into success. You've got to pursue the thing.

★★★★★

The training of decision-making skills of the individual performers in Circa is part of the process that enables Director Yaron Lifschitz to create acrobatic works that are based on improvisation and task-based creative processes.

In this next extract, picking up on Lifschitz's focus on developing the cognitive and creative skills of performers to enable them to perform in ways that allow them to go beyond being a 'consenting interpreter' and become 'creative artists'[67] in their own right, we move to a conversation with Firenza Guidi, the Italian writer, director, and performance creator, who is Co-Founder and Co-Director of ELAN Wales (European Live Arts Network), and Director of Frantoio, ELAN Wales' sister organisation and Centre for Performative Arts in Fucecchio, Italy. She has created numerous shows for the Welsh company NoFit State Circus, including *Tabú*, *Immortal*, *Bianco*, and *Lexicon*.[68]

Here Guidi discusses her ideas about developing performers, and her interest in ways of empowering artists to express themselves so that their bodies contain dramaturgy in the form of memory and vulnerability. She talks about exploring ways of drawing on these embodied qualities in the performer to enable different forms of connection with the audience to take place.

★★★★★

Firenza Guidi

Many of the circus performers you work with are top acrobats, but how do you go about developing the level of their performance in other areas?
Firenza Guidi: It is one of the things that I am passionate about. In the last 10 to 15 years, I have been creating more and more work for circus performers, and for circus.

My process involves helping circus performers acquire bodies that can be said to contain dramaturgy, so they are no longer simply a display of physical tricks.

Very often, circus performers come to me with, possibly, a very high level of skill, but they don't tell me anything. They don't say anything to me. I can see exactly the same thing in America, and in Australia, and I think 'Why should I look at you?' And very often, I say in a very provocative way, 'Guys,' I enter the creation space, and I enter and I go, 'Guys I am so bored with circus. So, so, bored.' But, it's to provoke them. And so, what is it that makes this thing just a display of tricks: trick A, trick B, and trick C? It's the love that a circus performer has to strut, to show off their skills. I always say, 'You know guys there are many different environments and situations where you can use your skills. It could be a corporate gig, where what you are doing is perfectly alright and where you'd probably earn more money than in my shows.'

But, if I am looking, and if I'm working, and really creating with a circus body that is first and foremost 'a body,' I should really not see the circus. I should actually go, 'Oh, has he or she just done that?' There are some important elements that make the body have meaning, transforming the performer into a being that contains dramaturgy and not just a bunch of tricks.

First, the body has memory and that is what creates depth, dramaturgy, and narrative. These are three words that I use all the time. If the body does not have memory, if the body is just a vehicle for skills, it is empty and just a two-dimensional board. It is the memory in the body that creates depth, creates a living, breathing persona, and which provokes questions in the spectator and doesn't just offer up one answer in the first 20 seconds. I should be intrigued by what is unfolding before me. So, the body has memory.

Second, you have to seduce me well before you do your tricks. And I use the word seduce as from the Latin *se abducere*, 'to bring somebody to you.' For me 'to seduce,' the word 'seduction' is 'bring to you.' It is something or somebody that brings you out of the sort of distracted, bored, absent-minded world of the spectator. The spectator must go, 'Wow, I am so hooked by this.' And the 'Wow, I am hooked' point can be a breathing, a way of moving a hand, a way of contacting you which is totally seductive. And the tricks will be even more spectacular because I am relating to somebody with a life, with a history, with a memory, with desires, with vulnerability, with a past and a future. And not just simply a trained monkey. So, memory, the body has memory, the body has to seduce me before you do the tricks.

FIGURE 3.4 Image from *Bianco*, created and directed by Firenza Guidi for NoFit State Circus. Photo: Mark Robson (Ineptgravity).

And third, there is a self-irony in performance which is endearing, which is not arrogant. Which is about the kind of vulnerability that I talked about. Circus performers are trained to say, 'I can do it, I can do it, watch me, watch me, I can do this, I can do a split, look at this, I am super fit.' But what if you enter a space of not knowing, what I call 'the cloud of un-knowing'? Then within that space you work your abilities to actually narrate your vulnerability. That is what turns me on.

Yes, it's very interesting when you don't know things, because then you're in a mental space that is open to new possibilities.
Firenza Guidi: Yes. You need to learn to play the violin otherwise you will not get any notes. Then you can always play a score. But you could also take this instrument and make it come alive with something that you want to communicate, something you want to say, or something which is part of a creative process. This 'something' becomes the thing that grabs me.

And for this reason, a lot of people come to me saying, 'Ok, I've come out of a circus school, I have all these tricks but I don't know what to do with them.' Or, 'I have been doing this act for five years now and I am totally bored with it and lost within it. How can I say something different?'

I don't say this in an arrogant sort of way, but, there are very, very few form-ative and at the same time creative situations for circus performers. That means that you either get a job with a company, and therefore you create what the company creates, or you are in a workshop, a training situation.

But, the kind of things that I have created, which I call 'performance montage,' offers a formative period, reasonably intensive and reasonably short, where you are mobilizing straight away, through a creative process, something which is not going to require six months to one year of rehearsals. So very often the circus per-former coming to me, paradoxically, has to extend their ability and also their skills because the creative impulse that I give them forcibly takes them into a territory where they have to say, 'Oh, bloody hell, how do I do this with what I know?'

Yes, children are intuitively creative, but, the ability to be creative within an artistic framework is something that develops with training. You learn how to be open, you learn how to engage with the process.

There are some schools, for example Toulouse, where, alongside the circus training, every week the students need to present two minutes of material, good, bad, mediocre, excellent.[69] The point is it takes away this kind of *chrism*, this mystique, or this kind of so-called 'anxiety' about creating. So, every week they present two minutes, and very often some of that work is thrown away. Some of that work goes somewhere else but, equally, they are also trained to enter an unknown space where the question is, 'What do I do with this? What do I do?'

*****

From Firenza Guidi's interest in developing circus performers so they have depth, dramaturgy, and narrative in their bodies, we move to a conversation with Mike Finch and his experience of choosing performers when he was Artistic Director for Circus Oz. In this following conversation Finch talks about his approach to another aspect of the human dimension involved in the running of a successful Contemporary Circus company, that is the balance between the different individ-ual performers in the group.

Mike Finch was Artistic Director and Co-CEO of Circus Oz from 1997–2015 and during that time 'Circus Oz performed to more than 1.7 million people in nearly 150 national and international locations, with tours from Arnhem Land to New York and from the Kimberley to Madrid.'[70]

Here Finch talks about his approach to maintaining the delicate balance of genders, skills, and personalities in a circus company.[71]

*****

Mike Finch

How did you choose performers to work with in Circus Oz?
Mike Finch: For me over the last five years of my time at Circus Oz, there was a gradual sense of the commodification of the circus body – the institute graduate.

The idea that someone comes out of a circus school, they're at a very high level in maybe one or two disciplines. They might not even come from a performance background at all, they could come from gymnastics or something. I would usually avoid those type of performers anyway, going, 'I want people who have done a few years out in the world and I want people who've got a history.'

But you still have the general mass of people coming out of the circus institutions aspiring to getting a full-time job in a circus troupe. Rather than being an artist, who goes, 'I have to make circus whether I'm getting paid or not,' or 'I have to form a troupe with other like-minded artists.' Many of these graduates from circus institutions tend to be people who go, 'what I need is to have a career in circus as a paid employee.'

Then there are the two types of graduates – some who are so excited to have freedom that they go wild, and as a director you need to sometimes say, 'Hang on, this is out of control. This is collaborative, we all need to work together and move across the line together instead of going off in some flight of fancy.' Or other graduates can be like the deer frozen in the headlights. Both those types. I also found myself gradually changing over time. Politically for me, when I started, my whole training and tradition was of troupes of people collaborating together from a diversity of backgrounds who were all intensely egalitarian and equal. My job as the performer is no less or more important than yours as the technician, than yours as the stage manager, and we're all going to get together and make this show, and your idea as the stage manager for the content of the show is just as important as my idea. So we're all in it together. So that's how I arrived at Circus Oz. All of my training in the other companies I worked in was like that.

At the beginning when I started at Circus Oz at the age of 28, most of the performers were in a similar or older age group and experience level as me, and that felt really good to me. By the time I left Circus Oz, I was 46 and the incoming troupe were in their early 20s. I realised that I was older than the lecturers that I'd had at Uni, and I had a grey beard, and I'm now from another generation, and that they were no longer my equal collaborators. They were looking at me thinking, 'You are the establishment and you are the boss and you're my employer,' and the whole dynamic shifted, and I was no longer making the work politically that I wanted to make which was a collaborative process with everyone essentially as equals.

So these days I'd now much prefer to work with a bunch of 40-year-olds, or 50-year-olds, who have got the same ideas. Or younger people who treat me like an equal in an adult-to-adult relationship.

There are some young independent circus artists coming through who might fit the bill.
Mike Finch: All I mean is, it is probably self-selecting because it takes a kind of gutsy, confident, 22-year-old to enter into an artistic relationship with a 47-year-old and feel like they can both bounce ideas in an equal way … and there's this tension. That's one of the inherent dichotomies.

FIGURE 3.5 Circus Oz. Photo: Ponche Hawkes.

Since I left Circus Oz I've had time to think about all the oppositional tensions that exist within circus. The notion that safety is obviously a huge value, innovation is a huge value, and they are absolutely opposite, diametrically opposite from each other. Too much safety is dead boring and too much innovation is really dangerous. New blood is important but old traditions are important. All of these dichotomies … and there are literally dozens of them, are all in tension with each other and that's what's holding them in balance with each other.

You can have a performer who is at the extreme end of a spectrum of irreverence for example. That's a really good one in terms of thinking about clowning and satire. Irreverence is absolutely a central value of a clown. They've got to be able to mock every sacred cow and make fun of them. However, respect and reverence is crucial to maintaining tradition and keeping safety. So that's a major dichotomy. Love for your fellow performers, love for the audience, respect for the structure. So the nihilist anarchist clown and the absolutely collectivist respectful traditionalist, both need to somehow coexist within this organic structure, and they need to have mutual respect for each other and somehow acknowledge the other is watching their back. While the clown gets to do wild clowning, the rigger is keeping an eye on everything and making sure everyone is safe. There are literally dozens of these dichotomies in circus. They form this full circle that surrounds a central point that's keeping everything in balance. That seems to me to be the true craft of maintaining the diverse type of circus.

Most of my time in Circus Oz was spent standing in the middle going, 'Let's try to stay in balance.' So you are going, 'What is this force that holds all this diversity and oppositional tension in balance?' I think it is a combination of love and fear. The notion that it's love for the person opposite you on the disk. The crazy clown has to love the rigger and the rigger has to love the clown. But it's also fear of it all going wrong, someone getting hurt, or losing all your money, or being humiliated in front of the audience.

Another example of opposites. Individuality and group unity. The type of circus I like expresses the individuality of everyone on stage and you get a sense that they're all individual different people. You don't get a chorus of four dancers that are all identical. Everyone has different shapes, and sizes, and styles, but the notion of seeing everyone working together is an incredibly powerful visceral experience. Seeing a team of people all pulling a rope together, or everyone in one human pyramid or all on one bike is like a deep sense of humanity. Like watching those big North Korean displays, it's like, 'Far out, they had to get a 1000 people to do that together.' But, watching Rowan Atkinson on his own being funny is equally as amazing. So those two things are in opposition to each other, so a lot of the casting of Circus Oz was ... we would literally spend hours, days, weeks in the casting process. You do an audition, but it was just like, you would be arguing over stuff like you would argue over wine tasting, or food or something, or gardening, or any of those organic, non-scientific, aesthetic, subjective processes.

So it's not just the strengths of the individuals but it's the individuals in relationship to the other people ... For instance, you can't have too many anarchists in there or the whole thing will disintegrate?
Mike Finch: Exactly, it would all fall apart. So you'd have a situation where you have a performer who's like the best juggler in Australia – total anarchist, crazy, obsessed with juggling, borderline antisocial – you can't cast them in my version of the show, because I require all the performers to be active collaborators, and I know this guy is going to piss everyone off within a couple of months.

And he will not be able to stop practicing his juggling ...
Mike Finch: Yes, stuck in the corner or whatever it is. And then we were always wanting people who could be generous enough to participate in group work that was not their primary skill set. There's a lot of, you would call it, 'excellence' in some cultures and 'snobbery' in another culture. Someone might say, 'I'm not going to be in a pyramid act because I'm not a trained acrobat, I'm going to do

my seven-ball juggling.' You want someone who is prepared to only do six balls, or maybe can only do six balls, but they are prepared to be in a pyramid in order to get that unity, to work with the two or three people who are brilliant acrobats, to make that mix.

It was a constant series of compromises that often worked, but a lot of the time didn't quite work. That's the endless struggle of what we were trying to do. It's more than just the bodies, it's the politics of the person as well. How do they interact? What are they like? My definition of when it was working, it's like the Mandelbrot set fractal. You slice in and at any point you get the same thing. Like you see on stage an equal number of men and women, and then if you were to go to a meeting you would also see a relatively equal number of men and women. The values are expressed through the whole onion. Rather than just, 'Here's the thing we do' and then everything behind it is different.

★★★★★

From Mike Finch and his focus on the dynamics of the group we move to Elizabeth Streb, Director of STREB Extreme Action company, who looks for performers who are team players with generosity of spirit.[72]

Streb founded her own company in 1975. She situates her work as sitting somewhere between dance and circus. The performers in her company are specialists in Streb's own movement technique called PopAction, and she describes them as being able to present 'action as subject not body as object.'

In this next conversation, Elizabeth Streb talks about the type of performers she likes to work with and the attributes of bravery and curiosity that she looks for.

★★★★★

Elizabeth Streb

How do you go about selecting your performers?
Elizabeth Streb: Really, it's always difficult to figure out. I want trained dancers. I've gone from athletes, and gymnasts only, and it's the sophistication of the timing that dancers have. When a movement's finished they're not all crumpled up. They can go faster than any other trained person in a variety of ways. But they're the most fully-trained bodies, and then they can learn the big muscle movements like front flip, the round-the-world, the aerial, all of the big muscle group initiators for actions. Dancers can learn that.

I look for bravery. I look for curiosity. I look for their first time of impacting the floor which, for sure, they don't do that anywhere else. I look for the people who smile when they hit. And then we split people. We have three days of auditions. So I never send anyone away. They self-select to not come back the second day or the third day.

FIGURE 3.6 STREB Extreme Action, Jackie Carlson and Leonardo Giron Torres performing TIED. Photo: Ralph Alswang.

That's an interesting process.
Elizabeth Streb: Yes, and also we're just getting to know each other. I think of it as a workshop and some people, this new group of people have come back three times to audition. I look for people who already know that they are brilliant movers and they're not looking at me to see if I'm looking at them.

People who once they've started to move, something transformative happens to them like once you let a wild animal out of a cage, it's just like you better watch out, and you see this massive life force move out of them because they're addicted to the feeling of extreme action. They're addicted to how, once they start to move, they're out of their normal mental state and that's a pretty rare thing. I look at how people pay attention, not just to when it's their turn to go but that they watch every single person, who is also going and they're not. So there's a generosity of spirit.

People cannot be prima donnas in this company. It's a team. I look for people who are team players. I can, at this point tell who's not, I can just sense it after the third day. Then the STREB dancers break them up at the end of each day into these different groups, different equipment and the dancers are instructing them. So then the dancers come back. We all decide together. How did they take directions? How did they improve after the correction was given? How quickly, and that kind of thing. I look for a wild animal underneath a fairly civilised human being!

If you take dancers into your company, they often come with a particular vocabulary and approach to moving which is trained into their bodies. Is there any way that you actually approach de-habitualising them, or stripping away the veneer, the dance training, so that their approach to movement suits your own movement technique?

Elizabeth Streb: All that unnecessary information, right? Well … it's more the functionality of our technique. They use all the knowledge of the body that they have, they bring that with them as dancers, but some of the things that we do in PopAction just supersede the desire to enact their technical knowledge. For instance, we change our basic support so you're on your feet incidentally at STREB, but then the base of support could be your shin, it could be the backs of your legs, it could be your stomach, it could be your back, your side, it could be one arm, and two feet. So you're constantly switching them depending on how high you're going from. The various amounts of impact will require you to be accurate with that switch of the base, and each base allows support that's here [indicates the horizontal plane with her hand].

So we don't land vertically from high. With the base if your bodies are vertical, you collapse your shin bones and your femurs inwards like an accordion. The bigger the base the more spread out the impact is. The accuracy of taking a hit or landing, it's the same thing, is so time consuming and it takes all of your attention. If you're still attached to doing promenade turns and arabesques and passes … we're the caboose of the dance world, the last car in that train. So if you're interested in that other stuff this is probably the wrong room for you as a practitioner.

You have to get stronger. The women have to train. We adhere to you're only as strong as your weakest link. So if you don't do pull-ups, and you're a woman, or you don't do push-ups, or you don't do a lot of the things required of you to have a unified system to contend with the brutality of this technique … everybody has to be responsible for training their weakest link and making sure it doesn't stop them at the gates … The gate of new moves, the gate of heights, the gate of a certain amount of impact.

Do you expect all the performers to train themselves or do you have some kind of group training?

Elizabeth Streb: I mean the dancers when they're not here, they train apropos to what they have a sense they need. My current Associate Artistic Director gives them a fifteen-minute warm-up that only a hero can get through and then like right now we're doing a trampoline dance that's pretty vigorous. You're jumping on it, you're slamming into the ground on mats but then you're getting up running, jumping back off for eight minutes straight, and then she makes them do two minutes continuation of that dance. So your aerobic and anaerobic powers and strengths are increased based on the extra training she gives them right in rehearsal but they must train their weakest link outside this room.

They cannot come to the first day of rehearsal out of shape. We've had this happen and I didn't think I had to tell young dancers that, 'oh by the way it's your job to be in shape after a two-month break,' because then they start getting injured and then I have to replace them and it's just like a wild circle.

So I think that the training happens in the doing but then there's all these other things. We have two PopAction classes a week that they can come to and they should come to, to really remind themselves what part of the technique they're missing. Some of the dancers just flatline. They never get any better after two years straight. They're scared, usually it's because they're scared.

So it's the mental thing that stops them, not the physical?
Elizabeth Streb: Yes. Absolutely.

So with the PopAction technique is there mental training?
Elizabeth Streb: The whole thing of paying attention. There's coaching going on throughout the rehearsal process. Somebody has never done a flip let's say. You need to have a flip. You really need to have an aerial, you need to have a back handspring, a front handspring, and if you're a trained dancer you can get that, and the STREB dancers teach them to do that. So everybody is sort of their own guru in terms of advancing because you will be stopped by your weakest link at every point, every point.

If it's your fear … I can't help you with your fear. I think fear is about worrying about your own self. Sometimes I think it's a class thing. I was brought up in a very working-class family. My adopted father was a mason and I'd watch his body get – over the years I lived in that home – just broken down, and he didn't feel sorry for himself. This whole thing about how, and it's a very gross exaggeration but still, wealthy people have bigger yards, higher fences. White rich guys don't go into boxing. They have a habit of keeping harm far away from them.

When you walk in this room it's not about you might, you will, get hurt a little, but our job is not to get terribly hurt, and also if you have that kind of concern that I mentioned about, you know, 'People in my world don't get hurt, we have protections.' The protections are really in place in an unrecognised way because of your privilege. This is really not that, and if somebody, if the fear comes in … I respect fear and you have to be afraid, but then you have to banish that and move on; but if I see you're not moving on and I notice it's because of that, then you're not the right person for the company.

How would you characterise your approach to risk when working with the performers in your company?
Elizabeth Streb: 'Extreme' in a word, 'extreme,' and 'foreign' also, because the most observable risks are things that intercept people's paths on a daily basis, tripping, slipping on a banana peel, intercepting with a car or person that's going faster and harder than you are, all of these accidents you could imagine, but we try and invent circumstances so that the risk is not a known risk.

It's an investigative journey into all of the eventualities that could lead to a certain danger but also, more importantly, evoke a vocabulary that hasn't been examined, or exercised, or performed before. I set up a circumstance that is not horizontal, that does not adhere to the body being right side up and only practising on the bottoms of their feet.

It's also, I mean in terms of that type of risk, it's risk that I can't imagine but I do discover. It would have to do with how we construct our machines.

Leading on from this idea of risk, do you think there's a certain state of being or state of mind that risk engenders in your performers? If so, do you train that? How does that come about?

Elizabeth Streb: I'm not really an educator. I think that the manner in which we contend with that is that it all retreats back to what are the formal technical principles of STREB PopAction. And one of them is that this is a present tense technique. This is about believing that only the second, the half second, the millisecond you're in is all that matters. We try not to regret the past, or hope about the future but stay where we are. That in and of itself takes care of everything else. There's only some action practitioners that have the capacity to do that. They have to have this appetite. They have to wonder about things. They have to not worry so much about themselves, not be concerned for their well-being.

I don't mean that I want reckless people in the room. I don't, but I think there's an overarching worry about our bodies and about being careful. That's gone. You dream that your body can handle a whole lot more than you think it can, and then you stay in the moment you're in.

If you stay in the moment you're in, then you can do this thing where you're going higher, faster, sooner, harder just in a glom of an idea, then the timing becomes the content of what STREB does, and the dancers are so focused from one second to the next that they are performing the now.

That's what the performance is about – now. To me that is Zen-like. There's no other real practice towards that. It's just the doing of it. There have been a number of people over these 35 years that have come into the company and after a year, or two years, I can see it's not going to work because they'll do things like hedge. They'll hedge at the jump. Second guess, and that is so dangerous not just for that person but for everybody else. That just means that they can't get over the belief that the right time to go is exactly when everything in your body tells you you're going to crash and it's the wrong time, but it's the right time. It's the only right time. If you wait until it's the right time, you're like way too late. It's millisecond timing that we do.

★★★★★

From the human attributes of bravery and curiosity that Elizabeth Streb seeks in her performers, we move to a conversation with Phia Ménard, performer, and Founder and Director of Compagnie Non Nova.[73] Born into the body of a boy in 1971 when she was named Philippe, in 2008 Ménard made public her[74] decision to transition to being a transgender woman and took the name Phia.

After performing in French juggler Jérôme Thomas' company and touring widely internationally, Phia Ménard began her gender transition in 2008 and her work became 'a redefinition of her theatrical language emphasizing impermanence.'[75]

Here Ménard discusses the danger and risk involved for the performers that choose to work with her. The danger Ménard is referring to is not only the physical danger of working with unconventional materials, such as ice, but also the danger inherent in presenting ideas which challenge orthodoxies.

★★★★★

Phia Ménard

How do you go about choosing the particular performers that suit your vision of your works?

Phia Ménard: So today, there are two situations. When I myself go on stage, it's to perform things that I deem too dangerous for others, as I refuse to endanger others. They are usually solos that will raise central questions related to the fact that I will not escape my story – whatever I do today, I'm a woman, but there will always be something to remind me of the man I once was. It's what I call the trace; the trace that I leave is here. And we will always be interested to look in me for this trace I leave.

So, in order to remove myself from this trace, I choose to do more and more radical performances to allow all types of bodies, both male and female, to look at the subject.

It's the performance that we focus on, forgetting about sexuality, forgetting about gender, forgetting all of that.

Group pieces are political acts addressed to society. In this sense, in a group performance, no emphasis is put on one body more than another – it's the social body that I am evoking. In *Saison sèche (Dry Season)* [2017] for example, I asked seven women to perform a ritual which aimed to break down the walls of patriarchy. Or in a project like *Belle d'hier* [2015] I asked five women to dissolve the myth of Prince Charming and the Princess, and to do humanity's last laundry, and say, 'I will not do the laundry anymore. It will be the last.' These are concepts that are directly addressed to society, and tackle the notions of group, individual, society, and existence in society.

Is there a particular type of performer you're looking for in your company?

Phia Ménard: So … I always have lots of ideas for shows in my head. But the themes are more and more becoming the same. What triggers certain shows to manifest is when, after having accumulated several small pieces of a puzzle, they all suddenly seem to come together.

And the performers (men, women alike) who work with me are always people who come to me. I never organize auditions. So these are people who know my work, who know my artistic process, and who at some point decide to come of their own accord on the basis that my next step has to be with this woman. And the performer and I agree on a contract based on a certain number of important codes and rules. The first one pertains to the repercussions of our actions on stage.

FIGURE 3.7   Compagnie Non Nova, Phia Ménard in *P.P.P.* Photo: © Jean-Luc Beaujault.

All the actions we do have repercussions, and therefore will lead to collateral damage. The performer must be able to de-dramatise this and the potential consequences. And so, I hire the person from the moment they become aware of the consequences for their family, their relatives, and their loved ones, and who show a capacity to control the said potential damage by saying something along the lines of, 'I will know how to explain why this act is important and why I do it.'

This means that the artist is someone who knows how to distance themselves, someone who knows how to perform an act and can state, 'What I do on stage is not necessarily what I am in life, but I can do it, I can play that role, I can play a murderer, I can play something that seems dangerous to me, but it says nothing of who I am other than the fact I am able to keep myself at a distance.'

And the second thing is that I ask the artist to lend their body to the audience. That means that they are aware that the members of the audience must be able to imagine themselves in the performer's own body; and that in order to do so, the performer will also have to accept that the relationship with space, with the work on stage, is a work that stems from a particular method, not a psychological one, but one of continuously maintaining a certain distance; which therefore will allow the viewer to imagine themselves, and not just to be there to forget, but quite the opposite rather to wear the body in space, and almost in some ways, to put themself into the absence of the body.

It's at times a relationship I could almost say of *prostitution*, because part of it requires accepting the viewer's presence by the artist's side, and lending the body to the onlooker in order for them to be able to experience the phenomenon.

★★★★★

Following on from Phia Ménard, in the next conversation Daniele Finzi Pasca, Co-Founder and Director of Compagnia Finzi Pasca, discusses the characteristics he looks for in performers.

Finzi Pasca was sentenced to prison as a conscientious objector, and he finished the writing of his solo show, *Icaro,* in jail in Switzerland. The show forms the foundation of Finzi Pasca and Teatro Sunil's approach to theatre, and has now been performed by Finzi Pasca himself for over 27 years, in six different languages, in 25 countries around the world. As well as creating works for his own company, Compagnia Finzi Pasca, he directed the trilogy *Nomade* (2002), *Rain* (2004), and *Nebbia* (2007) for Cirque Éloize in Montreal; and *Corteo* (2005) and *Luzia* (2016) for Cirque du Soleil.[76]

In this next conversation he talks about the importance of empathy in performers in order that they have an awareness of others in the space, and of performers who are able to simply *be* on stage.

★★★★★

Daniele Finzi Pasca

Can you talk about the make-up of your company?
Daniele Finzi Pasca: So the question is why do people come together? Eighteen nations are represented in our company. Julie [Hamelin Finzi] didn't want the company to grow too big.[77] We have a path, a system, we have a life, a way of thinking, and thus we have people that come more from theatre; and we have people that come from circus and have been part of the company for years, like Stéphane [Gentilini].[78] Some people come from the conservatory like Andrée-Anne [Gingras-Roy].[79] All of us know what we are doing on stage, it's part of how we think about life, how we think about touring, how we deal with certain things. That's why we have come together in this specific format.

FIGURE 3.8 Compagnia Finzi Pasca, *Donka.* Photo: Viviana Cangialosi.

What qualities do you try to instil in the people who collaborate with you in your company?

Daniele Finzi Pasca: For us, there is something like a dance between meditation and confrontation that we learned in Tibet, and in which we observe how to place ourselves in front of one another. If you observe it from the outside, you can see whether the performer is focused on what they themselves are doing, or whether they are more focused on their partner, and what's happening around them. That's how you can recognise it.

The key to our work is centred in the word empathy. It is the quality that makes us so uniquely human in the way that we know. We are empathetic animals and some have this empathetic behaviour hyper-developed, and they are able to be in total harmony. The main idea of our work is to recognise that we have tools that succeed in changing us precisely. So you end up bringing your audience members with you, you ask them to change, or you meet them where they are, and feel who they are tonight, and you slightly change the tone and align yourself. And this comes from a certain mindset.

Does this happen between the performers and the audience?

Daniele Finzi Pasca: Yes, naturally.

But first of all between yourselves?

Daniele Finzi Pasca: When you get up on stage, you sometimes see someone get up there and they are asking themselves, 'What am I supposed to do?' or else you see someone who is there and knows where to be on stage and who keeps on adapting to the space. In languages like those of dance and theatre but even more so in acrobatics, it becomes obvious that if you are working with highly empathetic people, it's easier to move in certain ways because you are always paying attention to those around you.

So I adapt to my environment rather than asking others to adapt. This is the main quality, and as I go around the world, as I observe, sometimes I stumble upon people who have that talent. You can look at Shamans. We worked a lot with Shamans, interviewing them through connections, trips, going to Russia, and meeting some of them, to see how certain things work, how they know who is doing well and who isn't, four villages away. And when you see them, you tell yourself, 'Ok, as a performer, this mind state really interests me.'

So what does it take to have this in our company? It requires us to keep on practicing this artform.

How do you go about developing the performers in your company?

Daniele Finzi Pasca: There is one thing you need to know to understand our approach, a fundamental aspect – it's about the degree of accuracy. Not many people, for instance, in the context of teaching circus arts in the academy or often in theatre, teach about shape. But form itself constitutes the essence of the question, in the sense that in music, in architecture, we know there is a logic, that some proportions make for precision in an object. There are proportion codes; which is why a graphic designer knows exactly where the title must go because

FIGURE 3.9 Compagnia Finzi Pasca, *La Verità*. Photo: Viviana Cangialosi.

of the Golden Rule. You know exactly, which is why when you look at certain buildings, they are precise, shaped correctly.

Studying shapes allows you to see that what you are doing most of the time doesn't essentially depend on the attitude that you have, nor your capacity to perform something, if you aren't strictly precise. You can do what you want, but if you aren't strictly correct then you can alter certain parameters, you can shorten, you can dilate, and then, it becomes more precise, and then it's up to you to perform.

So precision is something to aim for, it is what to look for in a master. A maestro will teach you precision. And precision is passed on. For instance, when you go fishing with a good fisherman, he can't really explain what he is doing. You go and fish with him, you look at how he does it. If he is generous, he will show you everything, he will teach you everything he does.

In the old ways of teaching theatre outside of the training academy, you would stick close to the actors, you would start by playing a small part, but you were always backstage and you would see what they were doing, how they would get ready, how it all worked, how ten seconds before getting on stage, an actor was still smoking his cigarette and would suddenly show up on stage and everything changed. What is happening here?

What does it mean? It means that sometimes, we lose so much time focusing on what doesn't work. But no art, no mastery, no science captures that. If something isn't precise, even a dummy will see it. If you aren't a dance specialist but you see a dancer off tempo, it is obvious. If you aren't a musician but you hear a note that isn't well played, if the violin misses the note, if the trumpet does, it is obvious, there is no need to be a specialist to observe that.

The question that must be asked is when it is precise, when you are in a rehearsal and you can say, 'Ok, what just happened? Why was this moment so right?' We waste so much time focusing on mistakes that are obvious, while masters hand on the art of perfection, they explain it to you, they show it to you. Otherwise, you know you are dealing with a gymnastic coach when he keeps on telling you your mistakes. Masters pass on the art of perfection and you sometimes get a glimpse of it, and you know that this something is right... tac! Sometimes it happens like that and other times, you have to wait for it.

Can you talk about your process of directing performers?
Daniele Finzi Pasca: Often, my way of directing isn't very verbal. I often direct while being on stage, I touch, I move, I try to understand. When I directed opera, at first, it was a bit strange for the singers to have me behind them, and suddenly, they feel that I am helping them to feel that, rather than saying 'go to your right,' 'go to your left,' 'sit down.' We can decide together that this spot could be a better one to start from, to take an attack, to make a suspension. After which, it's easier to bring out emotions.

In one of the shows I was explaining that not many actors wish to share the stage with a horse, especially older actors, they do not want to perform an act with a horse at their side. They don't want to do it because the horse will become the audience's centre of attention. This raises the question, 'Why do we pay attention to the horse? Why? What does this mean?' It's about the ability to *be*.

David Mamet said, and it was his way of being provocative, that he would rather work with people who weren't actors.[80] But in fact, what he meant to say is that he didn't want to work with bad actors. One must transform oneself and cultivate this capacity to *be* on stage, a mastery, a moment of loosening, a fire, a wholesome perception without needing to overdo it.

It's about knowing who the people are in my company. We choose the horse; they all are my horses: one with ruffled hair, one who's injured, they all are horses. That's the required quality to be in the company, the capacity to *be* on stage.

In relation to the circus aspect of your work, it may not always be easy for an aerial performer, or a trapeze artist, or a tight-rope walker to create this empathy with the audience.
Daniele Finzi Pasca: A 90-year-old grandmother on a chair can leave an entire theatre in awe. The risk is there, if she decides to come down from the chair, if she falls, we could imagine seeing a crystal vase break in front of us. So we can feel that this movement is edgy. One of dance's biggest problems is that it becomes aestheticized, the biggest problem in acrobatics is that it remains gymnastics.

We can be an amazing gymnast, but becoming an artist is a question of talent on one hand, but mostly it is a matter of what you have to say, and it mustn't be trivial, it has to be real enough for you that it will resonate for the people in front of you. So it's not so much about how do we make an artist out of a cook, when they can already cook well. Some questions we must all ask ourselves.

As a theatre director you have worked in many different production contexts, for example with Cirque du Soleil, a huge transnational company; with Cirque Éloize which is a mid-to-large sized company; and in addition your own Swiss-based company takes on big events. How do you navigate all those different environments?

Daniele Finzi Pasca: We showed up at Cirque Éloize with a specific logic and way of thinking, and we deeply influenced them. And with some of them, like Julie [Hamelin Finzi] or Daniel [Cyr], or like most of them who were there at that time, we kept on collaborating. Besides, Julie became a leading figure in our own projects.[81]

In the case of Cirque du Soleil, it was different, it was a matter of adopting and understanding a different logic about how to create, but with people who, when it comes to artistic concepts … Guy [Laliberté] was very involved, very hands-on, and he was there with us, and now, the directors and designers are trying to push the limits, so that for each show the known circus formula is shattered.[82] So it was very inspiring. I had the opportunity to work with designer teams by bringing together my own people and meeting new people. And together we succeeded, with *Corteo*, in making a show in a climate of total harmony, that has influenced the history of circus.[83]

In relation to the big events, that was a question of discovery. I keep on doing simple things to stay centred – in contrast to some of my colleagues, stage directors like me, who have found themselves suddenly having to produce massive projects, and haven't gone back to simplicity, and after some time, they've lost their way a little. Simplicity is an artform. So I kept on going back to simple things more and more, and that was mostly Julie's idea – which is why she influenced that world so much, because she wanted to cultivate the ability to prepare simple dishes like our grandmothers used to make, as well as recipes with a degree of complexity because we have to make banquets for kings or ceremonies for princes.

Others chose to stick to the big events in the field, but for us that wasn't interesting. To do those more complex things, you must go back to cooking in your grandmother's kitchen, practicing those small actions.

For my part for instance, I keep on performing *Icaro*. I am the one who strikes the show, I have to do specific actions, I am the one who irons the costumes before the show.[84] I practice these actions, and continue to practice them. And that keeps me in touch with my roots.

Isn't it difficult to maintain a solo show such as *Icaro* with so much else going on?

Daniele Finzi Pasca: I do it for my own benefit – sometimes we accept invitations from festivals. Right now, we only have one date, because I don't know if

FIGURE 3.10 Compagnia Finzi Pasca, *Per te*. Photo: Viviana Cangialosi.

I'll be able to perform it. Since Julie passed away [in 2017], performing *Icaro* has become so strange, this story about confining yourself in a hospital room with another person who is in the final stage of life. At present it is confronting to even start rehearsing it. But I've told myself, 'Well, let's try it the once and see if I can still control those things....'

Other than that, the show has always been great for me. When I was at Cirque du Soleil, when I did the Sochi Gala for the Winter Olympics 2014, I always had, in the midst of it all, one week when I'd go and perform *Icaro* once or twice in a festival, in a small theatre, or in a big theatre. Then when you talk to actors, when you talk to acrobats, when you speak to technicians, they know you are aware of the dangers, the uniqueness, the fear of being on stage, and it is easy to give directions.

★★★★★

From Daniele Finzi Pasca's discussion of how maintaining his own solo performance keeps him connected to the performers he works with, in the next conversation Philippe Decouflé, Director and Founder of Compagnie DCA (the Decouflé Company of the Arts), also talks about how and why he keeps up own solo practice as a performer.[85]

He starts this conversation by describing his recent solo performance in Montpellier.

★★★★★

Philippe Decouflé

When was the last time that you yourself performed on stage?

Philippe Decouflé: The last show I did was a solo in Montpellier last week in the old Opera House, sublime all red and gold, with just a musician and a videographer. In a solo show you have to take care of everything, of the space, of the public. To motivate the audience, to capture them, to take the space for yourself, to manipulate it, to make the audience believe that we are doing very beautiful things, and then afterwards to make the audience happy in such a way that they leave happy. And for me, I did this with an immense enjoyment, and that is the same enjoyment that I felt in the beginning. So for me nothing's changed. The flame is still there.

What is it that you are working on at the moment?

Philippe Decouflé: I'm working with my company in Seine-St-Denis where I develop my projects. At the moment I am in the midst of developing a show with two acrobats and five or six dancers.

What qualities do you look for when you choose performers for a show?

Philippe Decouflé: As a performer myself, when I perform I am pushing myself. I do things that I no longer do in training. We all push the limits when we are on stage. We really push the limits. And we do things that we don't normally do. Energy needs to leave your body, to go out from you, outwards to others. So it can leave your body, you need to project your energy in a way that you don't see regularly in life. So that's a reason to project, to send one's aura out all around. So on stage that is absolutely necessary.

What I ask from people that I work with, I ask for a repertoire of possibilities – of techniques, of different things we could combine to create wonder. I like versatile people who it will be nice to work with, who will be able to involve themselves in the creative process as well.

How do you go about collaborating with other performers?

Philippe Decouflé: Rafaël Cruz is working with me now on developing a show. And I'm happy to have him – he's such a multitalented performer.[86] He's fantastic. The way he uses his talent! I have an easy working relationship with him. [This interview was conducted just months before Rafaël Cruz died in 2018.] So really it all depends on the actual people. It's more a question of getting together with people that you get along well with. Whether they are an actor, a musician, a dancer, or an acrobat, it's the same thing, really. I have the same rapport with them.

Often at Cirque du Soleil when I've worked with the best acrobats, their act is developed as their own particular thing. And, in fact, even though they are at that [high] level, they do often want to create something new together, as a group. That is what is awesome. But it's very delicate! Because at that point you are working on their being. Their act that they've been doing for 20 years. They've been working on this one act and when you touch it you have to be careful! It's delicate. And it's complicated. It's complicated in fact ... the risk element at that level. I'm thinking of the Atherton brothers, of the 'Twins' aerial act.[87] It was a great pleasure working with them on *Iris* and *Paramour*. But I also think if you are working with an acrobat or a circus artist who has a specialty act, you need to speak with them and listen to them. Because with a specialty act, there are constraints, limits, there are certain things to respect. Where is the risk? In the end, you need to talk with the artists to understand how to best work with them.

How do you work with performers when you are directing them?
Philippe Decouflé: In the beginning, when I was directing, I told people what they needed to do, I was fairly precise. Now as time goes on – the older I get the more I draw on the knowledge of others. I do not demonstrate for a circus show, I do not demonstrate everything. And for good reason! I only know how to do a tenth of it. But I draw on words more and more, and on the body less and less, so it changes the rapport with collaborators.

★★★★★

Following from Philippe Decouflé's discussion about the importance he places on having a good rapport with the performers he works with, we move on Lachlan Binns and Jascha Boyce, two of the Founders and Directors of Gravity and Other Myths (GOM), who also talk about the importance they place on friendship when taking a new performer into the company. Founded in 2009, GOM originally consisted of seven ex-members of the Adelaide youth circus company Cirkidz.[88] This very successful company now tours the world ten or eleven months of the year with their shows *A Simple Space* (2013) and *Backbone* (2017) sometimes with multiple casts performing in different locations simultaneously.[89]

Here Lachlan Binns and Jascha Boyce discuss how they have forged new pathways into circus as young performers, through bypassing the professional circus schools and going straight into creating a highly successful company on completion of their training with Cirkidz.

★★★★★

Lachlan Binns and Jascha Boyce

How did GOM come about?
Jascha Boyce: We all started at Cirkidz, that is, the original founders of the company.

   Lachlan Binns: There's five of us [original founders] left in the company now.

   Jascha Boyce: Yes, five of us. Originally, we were seven, and over the course of the years people have come and gone a little bit, so we've gained a musician and lost a few acrobats. But essentially we all grew up together, so we all met when we were eight or nine years old, and went through circus training at the same time, at Cirkidz. When we graduated we decided that we wanted to keep working together, but didn't really have an avenue to do so, so we created a show together, not really expecting much to come of it, and it did really well!

Lachlan Binns: The thing is at the time it wasn't born from a desire to train for circus and become circus artists, and pursue it as a career. I think three or four of the guys were going to study engineering at university. I studied graphic design. The oldest member was already a physiotherapist so everyone had careers mapped out separate to circus.

Jascha Boyce: It was kind of just a thing on the side because we enjoyed hanging out and training together.

Lachlan Binns: We didn't want to stop training, and at Cirkidz when you turn 18 or 19, you have to leave the performance troupe, so me and Jascha had just turned 18 or 19 years old, and we were leaving the group and that was just a kind of an unwillingness to let go of something we'd been doing for our whole lives. Then it took two or three years of doing shows every now and then, slowly building up, keeping training. [Our first show] *Freefall* went on a tour of Australia, and we kind of got a little taste of the touring life, of what the circus performance career could be.

FIGURE 3.11 Gravity and Other Myths, *A Simple Space*. Photo: Chris Herzfeld.

Jascha Boyce: And so then that same year we took [the next show] *A Simple Space* to Edinburgh. It was the first time we'd been overseas with the company. It was planning to be like a last hurrah. We thought we may as well go overseas just once and see what happens, all planning to go our separate ways afterwards, and that was when we met Wolfgang [Hoffman], our agent, and he booked our show and pretty much since then we've been touring ten to eleven months of the year, every year.[90]

Lachlan Binns: We've actually found that a lot of the people that we bring into the company, not everyone, but most have a similar story – that they haven't gone to a high-level circus institution and trained three years, and got their degree, and then applied for a company. They've been friends. Through the networks we've known. We brought in Dan and Rhi [Daniel Cave-Walker and Rhiannon Cave-Walker] who were halfway through a Circus degree in Sweden, and we said, 'Hey guys, want to come and join the company?'[91] So they put that degree on hold, and came and trained and toured with us.

Some people had done the Certificate IV programme at NICA, or one or two years there, and we said, 'Hey, do you want to come and join the company?'[92] A lot of people came from youth circus. That's something we hold up like a really strong source of inspiration, a source of why our work is engaging because we all come from this really tight-knit community of close friends. That's what the Australian youth circus community is.

Do your physical performers come mostly through Cirkidz?
Jascha Boyce: Originally, we all did come through Cirkidz and since then we've hired people from all over the country, acrobats who come from similar [youth] circus schools in different states – Slipstream in Tasmania, Warehouse Circus in Canberra, Flying Fruit Flies in Albury.[93] The way Cirkidz runs within the community, it feels like we're in a big family and all of these schools work in a similar way.

Lachlan Binns: The original seven members of the company were from Cirkidz. We were that original group of friends. Since then we actually haven't brought in any other Cirkidz graduates.

Jascha Boyce: It's because they've started creating a similar thing to Gravity and Other Myths and they're doing incredibly well, so we don't want to affect that in any way. We're trying to help them with their growing company as much as we can.

Lachlan Binns: We're pretty proud of the pathway that's brought us to where we are now and we like that it's an example of an alternative pathway to get into circus.

Notes

1 Although the past tense is used here, forms of Traditional Circus still continue today. For definitions of 'Traditional Circus,' 'Modern Circus,' 'New Circus,' and 'Contemporary Circus' as used in this book see the Introduction p. 6n1.

2 Hamlin Garland (2007). *A son of the middle border*. St. Paul, MN: Borealis Books, p. 110. (Original publication 1917).

3 Janet Davis (2002). *The circus age: Culture and society under the American big top.* Chapel Hill: The University of North Carolina Press, pp. 5–6.

4 Kate Holmes (2015, December 9–11). *Queer circus and gender.* Panel discussion presented at the International Conference CARD 2: Circus on the Edge. Stockholm University of the Arts, Stockholm, p. 61. http://www.diva-portal.org/smash/get/diva2:1044576/FULLTEXT01.pdf#page=61

5 Ibid., p. 61. See also Peta Tait (2005). *Circus bodies: Cultural identity in aerial performance.* London & New York, NY: Routledge.

6 Bauke Lievens (2018). First open letter to the circus: The need to redefine. *Sideshow Circus magazine.* http://sideshow-circusmagazine.com/being-imaging/letter-redefine

7 Florian Zumkehr, quoted in Zachary Pincus-Roth (2011). A circus that lets its freak flag fly. *New York Times.* https://www.nytimes.com/2011/02/13/theater/13seven.html

8 Bradley Henderson, quoted in Zachary Pincus-Roth (2011).

9 Simon Yates, p. 105.

10 Throughout this book the term 'to contest' is used in the sense of 'to call into question' as discussed in the Introduction, pp. 1–6; p. 6n1.

11 Gypsy Snider is the daughter of Peggy Snider and Larry Pisoni, two of the three founders with Cecil MacKinnon, of The Pickle Family Circus in San Francisco. She has directed and/or co-directed The 7 Fingers shows *Réversible, Intersection, Amuse, Traces,* and *Loft,* and created the Tony Award-winning revival of *Pippin* which opened on Broadway in 2013.

12 Shana Carroll, quoted in Charles R. Batson (2016). Les 7 doigts de la main and their cirque: Origins, resistances, intimacies. In L. P. Leroux & C. R. Batson (Eds.), *Cirque global: Québec's expanding circus boundaries* (pp. 99–121). Kingston-Montreal: McGill-Queen's University Press, p. 170.

13 Jo Lancaster and Simon Yates, p. 197.

14 Yaron Lifshitz, p. 184.

15 Cohdi Harrel is a circus artist from New Mexico, USA, and Co-Founder of the Ricochet Project which is currently based in Berlin.

16 Cohdi Harrell, quoted in Ariel Schmidtke (2015, Nov 15). The art of vulnerability: An interview with Cohdi Harrell of Ricochet. *Circus Now.* http://circusnow.org/the-art-of-vulnerability-an-interview-with-cohdi-harrell-of-ricochet/; see The Ricochet Project (2019). https://www.thericochetproject.com/about

17 See Gravity and Other Myths. (2019). Our work. https://www.gravityandothermyths.com.au/our-work/

18 Paul Allain and Jen Harvie (2006). *The Routledge companion to theatre and performance.* New York, NY & Abingdon, Oxon: Routledge, p. 45.

19 Zachary Pincus-Roth (2011). A circus that lets its freak flag fly.

20 Shana Carroll, quoted in Zachary Pincus-Roth (2011).

21 Laura Stokes is Co-Founder, and a performer in The Ricochet Project, see The Ricochet Project (2019). https://www.thericochetproject.com/about

22 See The Ricochet Project (2019). Smoke and mirrors. https://www.thericochetproject.com/smoke-and-mirrors

23 Cohdi Harrell, quoted in Ariel Schmidtke (2015, Nov 15). The art of vulnerability.

24 Firenza Guidi, p. 123.

25 Ibid., p. 124.

26 Nik Wallenda (1979-) is now working with The Big Apple Circus in New York. See R. Scott Reedy (2018, April 1). Flying high with the fabulous Wallendas at Big Apple Circus. *Metro west daily news.* https://www.metrowestdailynews.com/entertainment/20180401/flying-high-with-fabulous-wallendas-at-big-apple-circus

27 ABC News (2012). Nik Wallenda's Niagara Falls megastunt. https://abcnews.go.com/Nightline/video/nik-wallendas-niagara-falls-megastunt-16583602

28 Nik Wallenda, quoted in Alice Gomstyn, Gail Deutsch, and Ed Lopez (2012, June 14). Wallenda family legacy: Nik Wallenda's long line of amazing ancestors. *ABCNews.*

https://abcnews.go.com/Entertainment/wallenda-family-legacy-nik-wallendas-long-line-amazing/story?id=16557997

29 Nik Wallenda, quoted in Erin McCarthy (2011). Nik Wallenda explains how to plan a high wire walk. *Popular mechanics.* (June 23). https://www.popularmechanics.com/home/how-to/a6787/nik-wallenda-explains-how-to-plan-and-rig-a-high-wire-walk/

30 Pascal Jacob (2008). The circus artist today: Analysis of the key competences, p. 11. http://www.fedec.eu/en/articles/325-miroir01---part-1-the-circus-artist-today---analysis-of-the-key-competences-2008

31 Annie Fratellini (1932–1997), the French circus artist, clown, singer, musician, and actress, was a member of the celebrated Fratellini circus family. She was widely renowned as the first female circus clown in France. Together with Pierre Étaix she opened the country's first circus school, the École Nationale du Cirque Annie Fratellini (now the Académie Fratellini) in 1975.

32 See Katie Lavers (2016). The resilient body in social circus: Father Jesus Silva, Boris Cyrulnik and Peter A. Levine. In P. Tait & K. Lavers (Eds.), *The Routledge Circus Studies reader* (pp. 506–525). Abingdon, Oxon & New York: Routledge.

33 Father Jesús Silva named the property City of Boys after the film *Boys Town* (1938) starring Spencer Tracey and Mickey Rooney. The film was based on the life of an American Catholic priest Father Edward J. Flanagan, who set up an orphanage for young boys known as Boys Town in Nebraska, USA, in 1921.

34 Father Jesús Silva, Obituary (2011, September 12). *The Telegraph.* https://www.telegraph.co.uk/news/obituaries/religion-obituaries/8758373/Father-Jesus-Silva.html

35 See Katie Lavers (2016). The resilient body in social circus.

36 Thomas Quinn-Curtiss (1970, December 31). 80 boys and a priest present a Spanish circus. *New York Times* https://www.nytimes.com/1970/12/31/archives/80-boys-and-a-priest-present-a-spanish-circus-enthusiastic-reaction.html

37 Ibid.

38 Father Jesús Silva, Obituary (2011, September 12). *The Telegraph.*

39 Notable graduates of this school included Jérôme Thomas, Philippe Goudard, Maripaule B. (Maripaule Barberet), Antoine Rigaud, and Stéphane Ricordel.

40 Silvia Monfort (1923–1991) was a French actress and theatre director who, together with equestrian circus artist Alex Grüss from the renowned Grüss circus family, directed the École au Carré.

41 See Superior School of Circus Arts (L'Ecole Supérieure des Arts du Cirque). (2019). School. http://esac.be/en/; Centre National des Arts du Cirque. (2019). The national centre. https://www.cnac.fr/article/946; National Circus School (École nationale de cirque). (2019). The school. http://ecolenationaledecirque.ca/en/school; National Institute of Circus Arts. (2019). http://www.nica.com.au/

42 See Introduction, p. 6n1.

43 Catherine II (1729–1796) was Empress of Russia from 1762 until 1796.

44 See Hovey Burgess (1974). The classification of circus techniques. *The Drama Review: TDR, 18* (1), p. 68.

45 See Jon Burtt and Katie Lavers (2017). Re-imagining the development of circus artists for the 21st century. *Theatre, Dance and Performance Training, 8* (2), pp. 143–155.

46 See also Mirian Neirick (2012). *When pigs could fly and bears could dance.* Madison: University of Wisconsin Press.

47 See Pascal Jacob and Michel Vèzina (2007) *Désir(s) de vertige, 25 ans d'audace, l'École nationale de cirque de Montréal.* Montreal: Les 400 coups; and, Louis Patrick Leroux (2016). A tale of origins: Deconstructing North American 'cirque.' Where Québécois and American circus cultures meet. In L. P. Leroux & C. R. Batson (Eds.), *Cirque global: Québec's expanding circus boundaries* (pp. 36–54). Montreal-Kingston: McGill-Queen's University Press, note 7, pp. 312–313.

48 Self-regulation (sometimes termed self-regulated learning) is learning in which students are cognitively active in, and contribute to, their own learning processes.

Although it has long been argued by educational researchers that this is a crucial in-gredient for transformative learning, and although it has been discussed in relation to sports training through the work of sports psychologists such as Laura Jonker and col-leagues (2010), the concept is only recently being considered in relation to performance practices that span the domains of both sport and the arts, such as circus training. See Barry Zimmerman and Dale Schunk (Ed.) (2011). *Handbook of self-regulation of learning and performance.* New York, NY: Routledge; Laura Jonker et al. (2010). Academic performance and self-regulatory skills in elite youth soccer players. *Journal of Sports Sciences, 28* (14), pp. 1605–1614; Sylvain Lafortune, Jon Burtt, and Patrice Aubertin (2016). The introduction of Decision Training into an elite circus arts training pro-gram. In L. P. Leroux & C. R. Batson (Eds.), *Cirque global: Québec's expanding circus boundaries* (pp. 240–265). Kingston-Montreal: McGill-Queen's University Press; Jon Burtt and Katie Lavers, K. (2017). Re-imagining the development of circus artists for the 21st century. *Theatre, Dance and Performance Training, 8* (2), pp. 143–155. The concept of self-efficacy, or the belief in one's ability to succeed in a particular task or skill, is a concept derived from Albert Bandura's (1977) social cognitive theory and inherently linked to the idea of intrinsic motivation, which is self-derived and self-directed: 'In order to succeed, people need a sense of self-efficacy, to struggle together with resilience to meet the inevitable obstacles and inequities of life' (p. x). See Honorio Salmerón-Pérez et al. (2010). Self-regulated learning, self-efficacy be-liefs and performance during the late childhood. *RELIEVE, 16* (2), pp. 1–18; Albert Bandura (1977). Self-efficacy: Toward a unifying theory of behavioral change. *Psy-chological Review, 84*, pp. 191–215.

49 Pascal Jacob (2008). The circus artist today: Analysis of the key competences, p. 16.
50 Ibid.
51 Firenza Guidi, p. 124.
52 The rise of postmodern dance is associated with the Judson Dance Theatre in New York in the 1960s and choreographers such as Trisha Brown, Yvonne Rainer, Steve Paxton, Deborah Hay, David Gordon, and others. See Sally Banes (1993). *Democracy's body: Judson Dance Theater, 1962–1964.* Durham, NC: Duke University Press.
53 Lúcia Matos (2008). Writing the flesh: Body, identity, disability, and difference. In S. B. Shapiro (Ed.), *Dance in a world of change: Reflections on globalization and cultural difference* (pp. 71–92). Champaign, IL: Human Kinetics, p. 79.
54 Group-devising is a way of devising performance collaboratively where there is no written script or performance score prior to the group creation process. See Alison Oddey (1994). *Devising theatre: A practical and theoretical handbook.* New York, NY: Routledge.
55 Pascal Jacob (2008). The circus artist today: Analysis of the key competences, pp. 11–12.
56 James Thierrée (1974–present) is the grandson of the film star Charles Chaplin, and the son of performers Victoria Chaplin and Jean-Baptiste Thierrée. The Swiss direc-tor and performer founded his physical theatre Compagnie du Hanneton in 1999. His theatre performances blend Contemporary Circus, mime, dance, and physical thea-tre. *Tabac Rouge* toured internationally from 2013–2015. See http://www.compagni eduhanneton.com/EN/la-compagnie-du-hanneton
57 Compagnie du Poivre Rose, now based in Belgium, was formed by five artists from Quebec, France, and Belgium including Valérie Doucet and her cousin Claudel Doucet in 2012. See http://ciedupoivrerose.com/frq/compagnie/index.html
58 Jon Burtt and Katie Lavers (2017). Re-imagining the development of circus artists for the 21st century, pp. 144–145.
59 There is currently a five-part case study, 'Les 7 doigts de la main: Un collectif circas-sien qui repousse les frontières,' being undertaken through HEC Business School in Montreal exploring the origins, strategic choices, and management choices taken by The 7 Fingers since their foundation. The articles are written by Professors Wendy Reid and Louis Patrick Leroux, and recent MSc graduates Joanie Leroux-Côté and Maribel Courcy.

60 For video links to Shana Carroll's work with The 7 Fingers, see http://7fingers.com/shows/; for links to her work with Cirque du Soleil, see https://www.cirquedusoleil.com/about-us/our-shows

61 For video links to Yaron Lifschitz's works for Circa see https://circa.org.au/shows/

62 Periodisation is an approach to the training of an athlete that looks at a whole season or annual programme allowing for appropriate periods of muscular overload and recovery across a series of training phases called mesocycles. See Tudor O. Bompa and Carlo Buzzichelli (2018). *Periodisation, theory and methodology of training* (6th ed.). Champaign, IL: Human Kinetics.

63 Yaron Lifschitz is referring to observers watching Circa doing a technical rehearsal of the show *Humans* for its Sydney Festival premiere in 2017. A 'tech safety' is a run-through of a show prior to it being performed to ensure all technical elements such as rigging, lighting, and sound are in place; and some specific performance elements such as blocking and timing are also checked.

64 Originating in the US in the 1930s, The Wheel of Death is a circus act that involves two large steel wheels connected by a truss. Acrobats perform acrobatic skills on the inside and outside of the wheels and use each other's weight to counterbalance each other. See Alex O'Reilly (2011, November 7) Cirque du Soleil – Kooza – Wheel of Death HD. [Video file]. https://www.youtube.com/watch?v=Js2YFgfMza8

65 Kerry Patterson, Joseph Grenny, Ron McMillan, and Al Switzler (2012). *Crucial conversations, tools for talking when stakes are high* (2nd ed.): McGraw-Hill Education.

66 Lifshitz is referring to the premiere of *Humans* in the 2017 Sydney Festival.

67 Pascal Jacob (2008). The circus artist today: Analysis of the key competences, p. 16. http://www.fedec.eu/en/articles/325-miroir01---part-1-the-circus-artist-today---analysis-of-the-key-competences-2008

68 NoFit State Circus (1986–present) is a Contemporary Circus company, school, and training centre based in Cardiff, UK, and is one of the UK's longest-running contemporary circuses, performing a wide range of shows, from street shows to touring tent shows, to site-specific performances in warehouses, and to large-scale community pieces. See https://www.nofitstate.org/en/

For video links to Firenza Guidi's work for NoFit State see https://www.nofitstate.org/en/shows/

69 Centre des Arts du Cirque de Toulouse, also known as the Le Lido, based in Toulouse, France. The Circus Arts Centre was originally created in 1988, and was formed into a professional circus school funded by the Ministry of Culture in 1998. See http://www.circolido.fr/Lecole_professionnelle.html

70 Mike Finch steps down as AD of Circus Oz (2015, 1 April). *Australian Stage.* https://www.australianstage.com.au/201504017227/news/industry-news/mike-finch-steps-down-as-ad-of-circus-oz.html

71 For video links to Mike Finch's work for Circus Oz (all works between 1998 and 2015) see http://archive.circusoz.com/clips/browse

72 For video links to Elizabeth Streb's work with STREB Extreme Action Company see https://www.youtube.com/user/strebvideo

73 For video links to Phia Ménard's work with Compagnie Non Nova see http://www.cienonnova.com/#/en

74 The pronoun 'her' is Phia Ménard's pronoun of choice.

75 Paul B. Preciado (2017). Phia Ménard. *Documenta 14: Daybook.* https://www.documenta14.de/en/artists/13542/phia-menard

76 For video links to Daniele Finzi Pasca's work for Compagnia Finzi Pasca, and collaborations with Cirque Éloize and Cirque du Soleil see https://finzipasca.com/shows/

77 Julie Hamelin Finzi (1972–2017) was an author, Creative Director, Producer, and Co-Founder of Compagnia Finzi Pasca. As a Co-Founder of the Montreal-based Cirque Éloize she was a Creative Associate on the trilogy of Daniele Finzi Pasca works for the company, *Nomade* (Cirque Éloize), *Rain* (Cirque Éloize), and *Nebbia* (Cirque Éloize and Teatro Sunil).

78 Stéphane Gentilini is a juggler and actor who performed with Cirque Éloize. He is the Juggling and Acting Coach on touring shows for Compagnia Finzi Pasca.

79 Andrée-Anne Gingras-Roy is a musician in Compagnia Finzi Pasca.

80 David Mamet (1947–present) is an American Tony-nominated playwright, film director, author, and screenwriter. See Anne Dean (1990). *David Mamet: Language as dramatic action*. Madison, NJ and Vancouver, BC: Fairleigh Dickinson University Press.

81 Daniel Cyr is an acrobat and a Co-Founder of Montreal-based contemporary circus company Cirque Éloize. He also invented the Cyr wheel, a mono-wheel apparatus, in 1996.

82 Guy Laliberté is the Canadian entrepreneur who is Co-Founder, with Gilles Ste-Croix, of the internationally renowned circus company Cirque du Soleil. The company has gone on to become the most successful theatrical entertainment company in the world, with an annual turnover of over $800 million US dollars with up to 10 permanent and 10 touring shows being performed around the world at any one time. See Louis Patrick Leroux (2016). Introduction, reinventing tradition, building a field: Québec circus and its scholarship. In L. P. Leroux & C. R. Batson (Eds.), *Cirque global: Québec's expanding circus boundaries* (pp. 3–21). Kingston-Montreal: McGill-Queen's University Press.; Jean Beaunoyer (2004). *Dans les coulisses du Cirque du Soleil*. Montréal: Éditions Québec-Amérique.

83 *Corteo* (2005) was the first Cirque du Soleil circus show directed by Daniele Finzi Pasca. It was performed as a permanent show from 2005–2015, and was restaged as a touring show in 2018.

84 'Strikes' here refers to clearing the set, or 'bumping out' after the show.

85 For video links to Philippe Decouflé's film and performance works see https://vimeo.com/philippedecoufle, for *Iris* and *Paramour* see https://www.cirquedusoleil.com/shows

86 Rafaël Cruz (1986–2018) was an American clown, acrobat, and actor who played the lead role of Buster, based on American film comedian and director Buster Keaton, in the Cirque du Soleil show *Iris*. He was also a regular performer with The 7 Fingers and part of the original cast of The 7 Fingers show *Traces*.

87 The Atherton Brothers, also known as the Atherton Twins, Andrew and Kevin Atherton, are aerial straps artists who have performed with Cirque du Soleil on various shows since 2002 when they appeared in *Varekai*, performing over 3000 shows during the 10 years they were with the show. See also https://www.athertontwins.com

88 Cirkidz (1985–present) is a circus school for young people based in Adelaide, Australia. The school was founded by community arts pioneers Tony Hannan and Michael Lester. See http://www.cirkidz.org.au

89 For video links to Lachlan Binns and Jascha Boyce's work with Gravity and Other Myths' works see https://www.gravityandothermyths.com.au/our-work/

90 Wolfgang Hoffmann is Gravity and Other Myths' representative agent for international touring. He set up the Berlin-based Aurora Nova, a theatre booking agency and consultancy firm in 2001. The company also represents other circus companies including Circa.

91 Daniel Cave-Walker and Rhiannon Cave-Walker are circus artists who, after working with Gravity and Other Myths, formed Fauna Circus (2016-present), an ensemble of six acrobats, five of whom were graduates of DOCH, Sweden's University of Circus and Dance. For DOCH see http://www.uniarts.se/english/about-uniarts/doch-school-of-dance-and-circus/department-of-circus

92 Certificate IV programme is a one-year training course offered by NICA (National Institute of Circus Arts) in Melbourne, Australia as a preparation for the Bachelor of Circus Arts course.

93 Slipstream Circus (2000–present) is a youth circus organisation and training centre based in Ulverstone, Tasmania, see http://www.slipstreamcircus.org.au/about

Warehouse Circus (1990-present) is a youth circus organisation and training centre based in Canberra, Australia, see https://warehousecircus.org.au/

Flying Fruit Fly Circus (1979–present) is Australia's National Youth Circus school and performing company based in Albury, Australia, and was set up by the Murray River Performing Group (MRPG), see https://fruitflycircus.com.au

References

ABC News (2012). Nik Wallenda's Niagara Falls megastunt. Retrieved from https://abcnews.go.com/Nightline/video/nik-wallendas-niagara-falls-megastunt-16583602

Allain, P., & Harvie, J. (2006). *The Routledge companion to theatre and performance*. New York, NY and Abingdon, Oxon: Routledge.

Atherton Twins. (2019). Retrieved from https://www.athertontwins.com

Bandura, A. (1977). Self-efficacy: Toward a unifying theory of behavioral change. *Psychological Review, 84*, 191–215.

Banes, S. (1993). *Democracy's body: Judson Dance Theater, 1962–1964*. Durham, NC: Duke University Press.

Batson, C. R. (2016). Les 7 doigts de la main and their cirque: Origins, resistances, intimacies. In L. P. Leroux & C. R. Batson (Eds.), *Cirque global: Québec's expanding circus boundaries* (pp. 99–121). Kingston-Montreal: McGill-Queen's University Press.

Beaunoyer, J. (2004). *Dans les coulisses du Cirque du Soleil*. Montréal: Éditions Québec-Amérique.

Bompa, T. O., & Buzzichelli, C. (2018). *Periodisation, theory and methodology of training* (6th ed.). Champaign, IL: Human Kinetics.

Burtt, J., & Lavers, K. (2017). Re-imagining the development of circus artists for the 21st century. *Theatre, Dance and Performance Training, 8*(2), 143–155.

Burgess, H. (1974). The classification of circus techniques. *The Drama Review: TDR, 18*(1), 65–70.

Centre des Arts du Cirque de Toulouse (2019). Le Lido, École d'Art. Retrieved from http://www.circolido.fr/Lecole_professionnelle.html

Centre National des Arts du Cirque (2019). The national centre. Retrieved from https://www.cnac.fr/article/946

Circa (2019). Shows. Retrieved from https://circa.org.au/shows/

Circus Oz Living Archive (2019). Browse. Retrieved from http://archive.circusoz.com/clips/browse

Cirkidz (2019). Retrieved from http://www.cirkidz.org.au

Cirque du Soleil (2019). Our shows. Retrieved from https://www.cirquedusoleil.com/about-us/our-shows

Compagnie du Hanneton (2019). James Thierrée, Compagnie du Hanneton. Retrieved from http://www.compagnieduhanneton.com/EN/la-compagnie-du-hanneton

Compagnia Finzi Pasca (2019). Shows. https://finzipasca.com/shows/

Compagnie du Poivre Rose (2019). Cie du Poivre Rose. Retrieved from http://ciedupoivrerose.com/frq/compagnie/index.html

Compagnie Non Nova (2019). Cie Non Nova. Retrieved from http://www.cienonnova.com/#/en

Davis, J. (2002). *The circus age: Culture and society under the American big top*. Chapel Hill, NC: The University of North Carolina Press.

Dean, A. (1990). *David Mamet: Language as dramatic action*. Madison, NJ & Vancouver, BC: Fairleigh Dickinson University Press.

DOCH, School of Dance and Circus (2019). Department of circus. Retrieved from http://www.uniarts.se/english/about-uniarts/doch-school-of-dance-and-circus/department-of-circus

Flying Fruit Fly Circus. (2019). Retrieved from https://fruitflycircus.com.au

Garland, H. (2007). *A son of the middle border.* St. Paul, MN: Borealis Books. (Original publication 1917).

Gomstyn, A., Deutsch, G., & Lopez, E. (2012, June 14). Wallenda family legacy: Nik Wallenda's long line of amazing ancestors. *ABC News.* Retrieved from https://abcnews.go.com/Entertainment/wallenda-family-legacy-nik-wallendas-long-line-amazing/story?id=16557997

Gravity and Other Myths (2019). Our work. Retrieved from https://www.gravityandothermyths.com.au/our-work/

Holmes, K. (2015, December 9–11). *Queer circus and gender.* Panel discussion presented at the International Conference CARD 2: Circus on the Edge. Stockholm University of the Arts, Stockholm, p. 61. Retrieved from http://www.diva-portal.org/smash/get/diva2:1044576/FULLTEXT01.pdf#page=61

Jacob, P. (2008). The circus artist today: Analysis of the key competences. Retrieved from http://www.fedec.eu/en/articles/325-miroir01---part-1-the-circus-artist-today---analysis-of-the-key-competences-2008

Jacob, P., & Vèzina, M. (2007) *Désir(s) de vertige, 25 ans d'audace, l'École nationale de cirque de Montréal.* Montreal: Les 400 coups.

Lafortune, S., Burtt, J., & Aubertin, P. (2016). The introduction of Decision Training into an elite circus arts training program. In L. P. Leroux & C. R. Batson (Eds.), *Cirque global: Québec's expanding circus boundaries* (pp. 240–265). Kingston-Montreal: McGill-Queen's University Press.

Lavers, K. (2016). The resilient body in social circus: Father Jesus Silva, Boris Cyrulnik and Peter A. Levine. In P. Tait & K. Lavers (Eds.), *The Routledge Circus Studies reader* (pp. 506–525). Abingdon, Oxon & New York, NY: Routledge.

Leroux, L. P. (2016). A tale of origins: Deconstructing North American 'cirque.' Where Québécois and American circus cultures meet. In L. P. Leroux & C. R. Batson (Eds.), *Cirque global: Québec's expanding circus boundaries* (pp. 36–54). Montreal-Kingston: McGill-Queen's University Press.

Leroux, L. P. (2016). Introduction, reinventing tradition, building a field: Québec circus and its scholarship. In L. P. Leroux & C. R. Batson (Eds.), *Cirque global: Québec's expanding circus boundaries* (pp. 3–21). Kingston-Montreal: McGill-Queen's University Press.

Lievens, B. (2018). First open letter to the circus: The need to redefine. *Sideshow Circus magazine.* Retrieved from http://sideshow-circusmagazine.com/being-imaging/letter-redefine

Matos, L. (2008). Writing the flesh: Body, identity, disability, and difference. In S. B. Shapiro (Ed.), *Dance in a world of change: Reflections on globalization and cultural difference* (pp. 71–92). Champaign, IL: Human Kinetics.

McCarthy, E. (2011). Nik Wallenda explains how to plan a high wire walk. *Popular mechanics.* (June 23). Retrieved from https://www.popularmechanics.com/home/how-to/a6787/nik-wallenda-explains-how-to-plan-and-rig-a-high-wire-walk/

National Circus School (École nationale de cirque) (2019). The school. Retrieved from http://ecolenationaledecirque.ca/en/school

National Institute of Circus Arts (2019). Retrieved from http://www.nica.com.au/

Neirick, M. (2012). *When pigs could fly and bears could dance.* Madison: University of Wisconsin Press.

NoFit State Circus (2019). Shows. Retrieved from https://www.nofitstate.org/en/shows/

Oddey, A. (1994). *Devising theatre: A practical and theoretical handbook*. New York, NY: Routledge.

O'Reilly, A. (2011, November 7) Cirque du Soleil – Kooza – Wheel of Death HD. [Video file]. https://www.youtube.com/watch?v=Js2YFgfMza8

Patterson, K., Grenny, J., McMillan, R., & Switzler, A. (2012). *Crucial conversations, tools for talking when stakes are high* (2nd ed.). New York, NY: McGraw-Hill Education.

Pincus-Roth, Z. (2011). A circus that lets its freak flag fly. *New York Times*. Retrieved from https://www.nytimes.com/2011/02/13/theater/13seven.html

Preciado, P. B. (2017). Phia Ménard. *Documenta 14: Daybook*. Retrieved from https://www.documenta14.de/en/artists/13542/phia-menard

Quinn-Curtiss, T. (1970, December 31). 80 boys and a priest present a Spanish circus. *New York Times*. Retrieved from https://www.nytimes.com/1970/12/31/archives/80-boys-and-a-priest-present-a-spanish-circus-enthusiastic-reaction.html

Reedy, R. S. (2018, April 1). Flying high with the fabulous Wallendas at Big Apple Circus. *Metro west daily news*. Retrieved from https://www.metrowestdailynews.com/entertainment/20180401/flying-high-with-fabulous-wallendas-at-big-apple-circus

Salmerón-Pérez, H., Gutierrez-Braojos, C., Fernández-Cano, A., & Salmeron-Vilchez, P. (2010). Self-regulated learning, self-efficacy beliefs and performance during the late childhood. *RELIEVE, 16*(2), 1–18.

Schmidtke, A. (2015, November 15). The art of vulnerability: An interview with Cohdi Harrell of Ricochet. *Circus now*. Retrieved from http://circusnow.org/the-art-of-vulnerability-an-interview-with-cohdi-harrell-of-ricochet/

Slipstream Circus (2019). About. Retrieved from http://www.slipstreamcircus.org.au/about

Strebvideo (2019). [Video files]. Retrieved from https://www.youtube.com/user/strebvideo

Superior School of Circus Arts (L'Ecole Supérieure des Arts du Cirque) (2019). School. Retrieved from http://esac.be/en/

Tait, P. (2005). *Circus bodies: Cultural identity in aerial performance*. London & New York, NY: Routledge.

The 7 Fingers (2019). Shows. Retrieved from http://7fingers.com/shows/

The Ricochet Project (2019). Retrieved from https://www.thericochetproject.com/about

The Ricochet Project (2019). Smoke and mirrors. Retrieved from https://www.thericochetproject.com/smoke-and-mirrors

Warehouse Circus (2019). Welcome to Warehouse Circus. Retrieved from https://warehousecircus.org.au/

Further Reading

Andrieu, B. (2018). *Apprendre de son corps une méthode émersive au CNAC*. Rouen, France: Presses universitaires de Rouen et du Havre.

Auslander, P. (1999). *Liveness*. London: Routledge.

Bourdon, A-M. (Ed.) (2005). *Une école pour un cirque de création: Les parti pris pédagogiques du CNAC, La formation pluridisciplinaire de l'interprète du spectacle vivant*. Paris: Éditions du CNRS.

Burgess, H. (1977). *Circus techniques*. New York, NY: Thomas Y. Cromwell.

Butler, J. (1990). *Gender trouble*. New York, NY: Routledge.

Butler, J. (1993) *Bodies that matter: On the discursive limits of 'sex.'* New York, NY: Routledge.

Coessens, K., Crispin, D., & Douglas, A. (2009). *The artistic turn: A manifesto*. Leuven, Belgium: Orpheus Instituut, Leuven University Press.

Cordier, M., & Salaméro, E. (2012). *Etre artiste de cirque*. Lyon, France: Lieux dits.

Dumont, A. (2013). S'entraîner à une virtuosité du sentir. Le cas des activités physiques et artistiques. *Staps, 98*(2012/4), 113–125.

Fratellini, A. (1989). *Destin de clown*. Lyon, France: La Manufacture.

Goudard, P. (2005). *Arts du cirque, arts du risque, Instabilité et déséquilibre dans et hors la piste*. Lille, France: Atelier National de Reproduction des Thèses.

Heddon, D., & Milling, J. (2006). *Devising performance: A critical history*. Basingstoke: Palgrave Macmillan.

Hurley, E. (2016). The multiple bodies of Cirque du Solei. In L. P. Leroux & C. R. Batson (Eds.), *Cirque global: Québec's expanding circus boundaries* (pp. 122–139). Kingston-Montreal: McGill-Queen's University Press.

Journeyman Pictures (2007). Inside the world's first circus school, Russia. [Video file]. Retrieved from https://www.youtube.com/watch?v=BaFw-TBCzeI

León, F. P. d. (2010). *Daniele Finzi Pasca: théâtre de la caresse*. Desarrollo, Montevideo: Tradinco.

Sizorn, M. (2013). *Trapézistes*. Rennes, France: Presse universitaire de Rennes.

Streb, E. (2010). *How to become an extreme action hero*. New York, NY: The Feminist Press at CUNY.

4

NEW WORK IN CONTEMPORARY CIRCUS

New work in Contemporary Circus – contesting the circus act

Traditionally the circus act is the basic structural unit of circus shows. A circus act is generally structured by assembling a series of tricks which are then linked together by flows of movement that act as segues between skills.[1] Within Traditional Circus the act is usually a six to seven-minute choreographed work individually created for the performer to show the tricks they have mastered and to display their bodily prowess. Many Traditional Circus acts have as their principal focus the aim to elicit wonder, and sometimes also, depending on the type of act, a kinaesthetic response from spectators.[2]

The act holds an iconic status within circus because to possess a unique, high-level act offers an entry point into the performing world of professional circus. In Traditional Circus, artists may perform the same act for many years and even in New Circus and Contemporary Circus this is not unusual. Philippe Decouflé, talking about his experience working with top artists at Cirque du Soleil, says, 'Often at Cirque du Soleil when I've worked with the best acrobats their act is developed as their own particular thing […] that they've been doing for 20 years.'[3]

Shana Carroll performed as a trapeze artist for many years before she co-founded The 7 Fingers in Montreal, and she performed the same solo trapeze act in Cirque du Soleil's show *Saltimbanco* for seven years. Although some circus artists enjoy the repetition and the familiarity with their act, others speak of the experience of continually performing the same act as being like a form of imprisonment. Director Firenza Guidi, talking about the workshops she gives to professional circus artists, says that she often has high-level circus artists coming to her, saying, 'I have been doing this act for five years now and I am totally bored with it and lost within it. How can I say something different?'[4]

The circus act could perhaps be seen as choreography in one of its most heightened forms, in which the work created, although usually only six to seven minutes in length, often takes as much as three years or more to develop the component skills. In many cases this work may, with slight variations, go on to be performed by the circus artist for their entire professional career.

The choreographed circus act with its assembly of tricks can be described in the way that dance scholars Ric Allsopp and André Lepecki speak about choreography in general, as

> an apparatus of capture (Deleuze and Guattari) or a body-snatcher (Franz Anton Cramer) that seizes bodies in order to make them into other(ed) bodies – highly trained (physically, but also emotionally, artistically, and intellectually) variations of what Foucault once called 'docile bodies.'[5]

In order to be able to identify the arts version of Michel Foucault's 'docile bodies' that Allsopp and Lepecki point to, the authors use the term 'captured bodies' to reference this highly trained 'docile body' within the performing arts. This idea of the 'captured body' is particularly applicable in circus in relation to the feeling of imprisonment by their act that has been described by many circus artists.

There are numerous choreographic and parachoreographic imperatives involved in the lengthy process of developing an act. Allsopp and Lepecki, commenting on dancers, but their comment could equally well be about circus artists, write,

> Indeed, it is known but seldom theorized how dancers have to subjugate themselves to the commands of all sorts of choreographic and parachoreographic imperatives – from dieting to gender roles; from strict physical discipline to the precise enactment of positions, attitudes, steps, gestures [...] all for the sake of exact repetition.[6]

The choreographic and parachoreographic imperatives involved in developing a circus act can take many years of arduous training. The acrobat, Philip Rosenberg, Co-Founder of Cirque Le Roux based in France, describes the long process of training as 'bitter.'[7] At the age of seven, Rosenberg transferred from early gymnastics training, to study at the San Francisco Circus Center training in Chinese acrobatics under Master Lu Yi, and he then entered the National Circus School in Montreal where he refined his hand-balancing act for a further three years. Rosenberg, in an interview for *The Stage* in which he was asked about his training, says, 'Training is bitter. The training aspect is very hard and sometimes really difficult, and sometimes you just don't want to get up and do handstands. It's a bitter life of training, but the reward afterwards is the performance.'[8] It could be said that the notion of the circus artist who undertakes 'bitter' training to become someone with a unique act who will then go on to perform that same act for most of their professional life is one of the most entrenched ideas in circus.

In most Traditional Circus there is a widespread practice of inserting pre-existing acts into shows as circus artists become available, and this is still the practice in corporate work, and shows on cruise ships, in resorts, and in clubs. Although widely contested, inserting pre-existing acts into shows is a practice that still occurs in some Contemporary Circus, but most directors prefer to create new material and new acts whenever possible.[9] As Tilde Björfors, Artistic Director of Cirkus Cirkör says,

> When I have the opportunity to work the way I prefer, I set up research labs with some artists for at least a year but more often two years before the new show opens. That way we have time to research and test new material. Our creative process is a lot more complex than just putting people's finished acts together.[10]

The act still remains in much Contemporary Circus as a highly problematised structural element of many shows. As the Circus Scholar Pascal Jacob writes,

> To be simply an 'act' in a show is a return to the simplified idea of the individual and his capacities to exist and create. This principle is at the core of the difference between a consenting interpreter and a creative artist.[11]

It could be argued that many of the professional circus schools, through focusing largely on the development of the circus act in order to provide an entrée for graduating students into the professional world of circus, are still currently training students to be 'captured bodies' or 'consenting interpreters' of their act instead of artists capable of working to their full creative potential. In some professional circus schools, comparatively little attention is paid even now to developing the student's capacity to create work and make creative decisions.[12]

Within New Circus the role of the artist as being a 'captured body' or a 'consenting interpreter' of their act was challenged and this role is still actively contested in Contemporary Circus today.[13] One of the major ways in which this role was challenged in New Circus was through the upsurge in the creation of new work. As artists from a wide range of disciplines came into New Circus, innovative work began to be created with a range of different aesthetics, politics, approaches to costuming and staging, and new technologies. Circus hybridized with different disciplines including street theatre, postmodern and contemporary dance, opera, postdramatic theatre, and performance art, and in the process new exciting possibilities opened up for what circus could be. However, for the most part the traditional act structure remained in place as the basic structural unit for circus even though innovative text, or movement was sometimes generated as segues between the acts, and on occasion the acts were offset or sometimes overlapped to blur their structural boundaries.

Many Contemporary Circus companies are now actively contesting the act in a number of ways. Innovative work is being created which focuses on the potential of the act to go beyond the display of bodily prowess and instead to hold meaning, and to communicate directly on a human level with audience members. This is often achieved through the involvement of the artist in the creation process. Movement is sometimes created which draws on the performer's own lived experience and generates a resultant level of physical and cognitive investment in the work by the circus artist. In turn the performer's personal investment in the content of the creative material has the potential to create a direct emotional connection with audience members.

Other companies are now moving in a more radical direction and actively contesting the act itself, along with its component tricks, as being the only structural unit possible for circus performance. Gandini Juggling and Circa, for example, have both broken away from the stop-start rhythm of the act, and in some of their works have adopted an approach focused on an ethos of flow and continuity of movement. In Gandini Juggling's collaboration with the English National Opera on the Philip Glass Opera *Akhnaten*, the notion of the act and the performance of tricks is abandoned and the juggling forms a seamless flow of abstract patterns correlated precisely to the patterns in the minimalist score.[14]

In *Humans* (2017), a work by Circa's Artistic Director Yaron Lifschitz, the acrobatics are reconfigured into a continuous flow of movement throughout the 70 minutes of the show.[15] In *Humans* the acrobatics throughout the show is semi-improvised in a way that Lifschitz compares to improvising jazz. This acrobatic improvisation on stage can be seen as actively contesting the fixed choreography of the traditional circus act, or the 'imprisonment' of the choreographed act. As Allsopp and Lepecki write:

> 'choreography' initiates, immediately and alongside its project, all sorts of resistances and counter-moves, anti and counter- and meta- and conceptual- and carnal-choreographies. We could call these acts 'Improvisational' – not at all to invoke a particular dance style or school, but in the sense William Forsythe once defined it, as an exact technology made to destroy choreography.[16]

The ability to introduce improvisation into such a high-risk physical area as acrobatics is accomplished by the approach that Yaron Lifschitz takes to developing the artists in the company, by empowering each of them to make decisions, not only in the development of new performance material, but also in every aspect of their working lives.[17] Lifschitz's approach is to develop the performer's decision-making skills, and their self-regulation, self-efficacy, and self-reliance.[18] These skills can ultimately be identified as some of the key cognitive qualities vital to escape being captured bodies, to escape from the imprisonment of the act and its choreography, and to become instead an artist involved in creative decision-making moment to moment, and in the development and creation of new work.

The act in Traditional Circus

From the beginnings of Modern Circus with Philip Astley in London in 1768, circus shows have been defined and structured by circus acts.[19] A Traditional Circus show included 'on average 10 to 12 acts [...] each of a pre-defined length of six to seven minutes.'[20] These acts were often created to showcase all the particular tricks that the artists had mastered. The act was a display of bodily prowess and was designed to evoke feelings of wonderment in spectators, and, also with some of the more daring acts such as the aerial acts, a kinaesthetic response.

In Traditional Circus, these acts often started with a group acrobatics act by the acrobats and clowns, termed a 'charivari.' This would be followed by a succession of different acts, such as equestrian acts, wild animal acts, juggling, aerial acts, magic acts, or wire-walking. These distinct acts were often linked by clowning or musical interludes to keep the crowd entertained during the changeover of apparatus required between each act. When the upcoming act was set up, in place, and secure, the Ringmaster, acting as a Master of Ceremonies, would introduce the next act to the audience. In this way the Ringmaster acted as a guide leading the audience through the different parts of the show.

Many of the most famous Traditional Circus acts were hugely popular, becoming favourites with the crowds and often staying almost identical from one year to the next with audiences coming back to see them again and again. These acts were also taken out to new audiences through the extensive touring undertaken by many Traditional Circus companies. One such act, 'Billy Buttons or the Taylor's Ride to Brentford,' a comic equestrian act created by Philip Astley, proved such a huge favourite that it went on to be performed for decades, and was toured by different circuses to countries around the world.[21]

The skills for many of these favourite circus acts were tightly held by particular circus families such as the Wallendas, famous for their wire-walking;[22] the Konyots, well known for their equestrian acts;[23] and the Fratellinis, renowned for their clowning.[24]

The acts themselves were generally structured in similar ways adhering to 'strict rules in terms of rhythm and intensity,'[25] usually consisting of a series of skills, or tricks, of increasing difficulty leading up to the final most difficult trick. Often one of the most difficult tricks would be marked by one, or often two choreographed 'failures' before the trick was successfully achieved. This was to underscore the difficulty of the trick to the audience. The successful completion of each trick would be marked by the performer assuming a pose designed to elicit applause from the audience, often by standing with one arm held high in the air after performing the trick successfully. These conventions set the norm for the structure of the act.

New Circus and the act

Many of the conventions in Traditional Circus were challenged by New Circus when it emerged in the 1970s.[26] New Circus contested almost everything in

Traditional Circus. Perhaps the most radical position taken by New Circus was to contest the inclusion of the animal acts. New Circus, which developed in the midst of a new, widespread controversy about animal rights, jettisoned the wild animal acts altogether, and for the most part, also abandoned the equestrian acts, focusing on human animals only as the performers.

New Circus challenged the tight hold on the transmission of circus skills held by Traditional Circus families. This contestation led to the development of widespread circus workshops open to everyone, the development of community circus classes, and the setting up of professional circus schools.

This opening up of circus skills to everyone, combined with a new and widespread interest and excitement about the potential of circus as an artform, led to new artists beginning to enter New Circus from widely different disciplines. These included artists from agit-prop theatre, postdramatic theatre, postmodern dance, street theatre, site-specific art, installation art, video installation, and music.[27] New innovative, hybrid forms of circus emerged as circus began to meld with these diverse artforms. These artists entering circus also brought with them a strong interest in creating new work. As Pascal Jacob writes, 'the traditional codes and conventions of the circus were broken down by artists who were more concerned with creating than reproducing.'[28] They brought with them not only a desire to create new work and new aesthetics, but also diverse approaches to creating new material.

Circus Oz, one of the earliest New Circuses, was formed in Melbourne at the end of 1977. The company began to create innovative work by bringing together elements from two very different artforms, namely agit-prop theatre with its accompanying political activism, and a form of New Circus that was human performers only. The company's style and aesthetic developed through this hybrid combination, resulting in the creation of a new politically activist circus.[29]

The aesthetic of this new form of circus created by Circus Oz was shaped directly by its political convictions. Tim Robertson, one of the original founders of the Pram Factory in Melbourne, points to what he calls the 'cultural super-hero' of 'the Group,' which functioned as 'an energy field of a set of individuals that created a charismatic surplus value' as being part of the cultural milieu from which Circus Oz developed.[30] The investment in the group led to the jettisoning of the idea of the circus 'star' and the development of many innovative and original group circus acts. The commitment to feminism resulted in an equal number of female and male performers on stage, and the deconstruction of normative gender roles in performance with male artists performing acts normally performed by women such as spinning web, and often performing as the flyers in the air, the role most often reserved for light small women. The female performers often acted as bases, taking the weight-bearing roles normally reserved for men.[31]

Circus Oz, although contesting many of the norms of Traditional Circus, did retain the conventional Traditional Circus structure of the show as consisting of a succession of acts, although there was significant innovation within the content of the acts themselves, for example Tim Coldwell's roof walk, in which he walked upside-down along the top of the circus tent to play an upside-down drum solo.[32] Although the circus act itself was retained, the conventional rhythm and pacing of the acts within the show was challenged. Mike Finch, ex-Artistic Director of Circus Oz, says that,

> In terms of show structure we very much avoided announcing each act or back-announcing acts. The intention was to roll the acts together, over-lapping them, or at least carrying the energy from most acts into the start of the next.[33]

One of the most influential New Circus companies, with its commercial success and huge audience reach, is the Quebec company, Cirque du Soleil, which began in 1984.[34] Over the years Cirque du Soleil has brought many different perfor-mance genres and styles into their shows. It was in the early shows, however, that the influence of Franco Dragone, the Belgian theatre director, set in place the innovative combination of theatre and circus that is central to the Cirque du Soleil brand. Dragone directed almost all of Cirque du Soleil's early shows, including *Saltimbanco* (1992), *Mystère* (1993), *Alegria* (1994), *Quidam* (1996), *O* (1998), and *La Nouba* (1998), until 2000 when he formed his own company based in Belgium.[35]

Cirque du Soleil, like Circus Oz, retained the Traditional Circus act structure of their shows, with the acts often being linked by clowning or musical interludes to cover the change of apparatus. In Cirque du Soleil, a central figure, the Ring-master or sometimes a character within the show, leads the audience through the show and acts as a guide. This figure often takes the form of a traveller, or seeker, who, finding themselves in a new world, moves through it taking the audience with them. Cirque du Soleil shows often have the meta-structure of a journey or odyssey through this new, often imaginary world, and this acts as a narra-tive arc for the audience, enabling them to encounter the different inhabitants in the world, namely the different characters in the circus acts. One of Cirque du Soleil's major innovations within New Circus is this mixture of circus with narrative-driven and character-driven theatre.[36]

From these two vastly different, trail-blazing New Circus companies, Circus Oz and Cirque du Soleil, and from the myriad of other innovative New Circus companies, including Archaos, Cirque Baroque, Cirque Plume, and The Pickle Family Circus, each of whom brought a distinctive aesthetic into New Circus, Contemporary Circus has now grown to encompass a huge range of work and aes-thetics so that 'the notion of a uniform and indivisible circus is no longer possible.'[37]

Approaches to the act in Contemporary Circus

Many Contemporary Circus companies have kept the structure of circus acts within a show, in the way that Circus Oz and Cirque du Soleil have. In much Contemporary Circus work there is now a widespread focus on moving beyond acts which function simply to display an artist's prowess and instead to create acts with the potential to hold meaning, and elicit a wide range of differing emotional responses from audience members. This is sometimes achieved by creating a physical and visual narrative related to the performer's own lived experience or by uncovering new metaphorical potential within the traditional act structure in terms of the relationship of the performer to the apparatus. These metaphorical resonances have the potential to create an innovative kind of physical and visual narrative within the circus act, often with striking visceral and emotional power.[38]

Some Contemporary Circus companies who choose to work with a traditional act structure, as well as developing these new forms of acts which focus on holding meaning, also innovate in terms of the material, or the connective tissue, that segues between each circus act. Companies such as The 7 Fingers in Montreal, and Company 2 in Brisbane, create text that serves as linking material between the circus acts. This textual material is often generated by the circus artists themselves, using improvisational and task-setting approaches taken from postdramatic theatre, and often draws on the performers' personal experiences to create autobiographical texts. These are then performed in a kind of meta-structure, in which the performers play themselves on stage, recounting fragments of their own lived experience.[39] The circus acts may then sometimes be created, or reimagined, in response to these texts, as in Shana Carroll's description, in the *Voices* section of *Apparatus* chapter, of how she developed a Chinese pole act in response to autobiographical text developed by the performer Matias Plaul.[40]

Other new work in Contemporary Circus is made using creative processes from contemporary and postmodern dance to generate movement material which can segue between each circus act and sometimes function to blur the boundaries between the end of one act and the start of another. This movement material is often group-devised. Based on a process of improvisation predicated on task-setting, and often generated around a specific theme, the fragments of movement material that are developed are then drawn together, sometimes by the group themselves, or sometimes by a choreographer or director, to create cohesive movement sections. This approach is used by numerous companies including The 7 Fingers and Company 2. In these shows the circus acts themselves may still remain but they are connected by ground-based movement flows developed in response to the theme of the show, which serve to reinforce a narrative or thematic thread throughout the performance.

Another approach to creating new work in Contemporary Circus, is one in which the work is created out of responses to the particularities of a space. This is an approach and a sensibility that emerged out of sculpture in the mid-1970s with the development of site-specific installations.

Miwon Kwon, in her book *One Place after Another: Site Specific Art and Locational Identity*, observes that within the visual arts in the 1970s there was a widespread reaction against the plain white gallery space of modernist art. In installation art,

> the space of art was no longer considered a blank slate, a tabula rasa, but a real place. The art object, or event in this context, was to be singularly or multiply experienced in the here and now through the bodily presence

of each viewing subject, in a sensorial immediacy of spatial extension and temporal duration [...] rather than instantaneously perceived in a visual epiphany by a dis-embodied eye.[41]

These ideas about the importance of the particularities of the space also began to emerge in theatre at around the same time. One of the influential pioneers in this area is Mike Pearson, who was one of the original founders of the influential Welsh site-specific theatre company Brith Gof, and now Emeritus Professor of Performance Studies at Aberystwyth University, who has written extensively about site-specific theatre.[42] This approach to the creation of work can now be seen in the work of the Contemporary Circus director Firenza Guidi and her creations for the Welsh Contemporary Circus Company, NoFit State Circus. In her descriptions of her working processes Firenza Guidi discusses how she wants to move away from the specular nature of much Contemporary Circus which is often performed in traditional proscenium arch theatres and 'read' by the audience from left to right. Instead, Guidi focuses on situating her circus works within a phenomenological world in which the whole body of the spectator is involved in the experiencing of the circus performance.

For the development of new site-specific performance, extensive research into the site is involved, and, in addition, it requires an intuitive response on the part of the artist to the specific characteristics of the space itself, as the space is considered to retain traces of archaeological memories and histories in its walls and building materials that can be sensed by the responsive artist. These ideas and research approaches are visible in Firenza Guidi's devising processes and the language she uses to describe them.[43]

Guidi has created and directed site-specific Contemporary Circus works such as the performance of *Tabú* by NoFit State Circus which took place in 2010 in La Tohu, the purpose-built circus space in Montreal. This performance was processional and involved the bodies of the audience members in the actual phenomenological experience of the event. It was immersive in intent with the performance surrounding the audience. Working with the specifics of the tall, cylindrical space of La Tohu, Guidi placed some performers above the audience in the roof running along the lighting grid, while positioning others beneath the floor, and in alcove spaces in the walls, creating a new awareness of the particularities of this performance space for audience members. The work was structured around circus acts which had been created to hold meaning and were based on the performers' lived experiences, which were designed to engage with audience members on an emotional level.[44]

French circus artist and Director of Cirque Ici, Johann Le Guillerm creates new work employing a studio-based approach which, in many respects, is similar to the working approach of a sculptor. He works alone in his studio developing maquettes for his innovative sculptural objects which eventually evolve to become his performance apparatus. His work can be seen as a hybrid mix that draws on approaches from sculpture in the creation of his three-dimensional objects; on installation art, in the interrogation of space and the involvement of the audience in an immediate and sometimes immersive experience; and on a form of performance in which the movement material draws on circus disciplines such as juggling and acrobatics.

Contemporary Circus is a hybrid artform combining multiple disciplines and some creators take this hybridity itself as a major point of focus, working on the connections and interrelationships between the various diverse elements in their work, while still retaining the circus act. Founder and Director of Compagnie DCA in France, Philippe Decouflé, for example, works in his laboratory to research and develop both live and recorded approaches to using video as a fully integrated part of his dance and circus performances.

Other Contemporary Circus artists, such as Jo Lancaster and Simon Yates from the Australian company Acrobat, resolutely reject the use of any analysable method in the creation of new performance work, believing that any recognisable process that is determined beforehand holds the potential to mark and shape the final result in its own image. These artists prefer instead to generate the performance material through an intuitive creative process in the studio which allows them to access their subconscious, with the aim of discovering unique and unpredictable imagery and material.

Another radical approach underlies those circus performances in which the companies have worked to create new work which dissolves the structure of the 'act' altogether, and also the recognisable circus 'tricks.'

Sean Gandini and Kati Ylä-Hokkala, the Co-Founders and Co-Directors of the London-based Gandini Juggling, in some works, have sought to dissolve the juggling act along with the whole notion of the juggling trick to contest what they describe as the imprisonment of skills.[45] The company has developed a particular approach to the relationship between music and juggling by creating a precise score for the performers through the use of a software called Siteswap, specifically developed for juggling. This enables the split-second correlation of the juggling material with the musical score, and allows for the development of juggling patterns to emerge through the precise relationship of the juggling to the dynamic structure of the music.

This approach is visible in the Gandini Juggling collaboration with the English National Opera on the Philip Glass Opera *Akhnaten* (2016), in which the patterns of the juggling balls and their precise relationship to the music score, create a three-dimensional realisation of the patterns, rhythms, and complexities of the music in space, and generate a form of abstract narrative that flows throughout the opera.[46]

Some of Yaron Lifschitz's work with Circa, the Brisbane-based Contemporary Circus company, has broken away from the tightly orchestrated choreography of the self-contained circus act. In *Humans* he has worked with the acrobats in the studio to create a free-flowing movement language with the aim of disrupting the circus vocabulary of 'the act' and 'the trick.' The Circa performers are empowered to make improvisational decisions about their movement in real time, not only in the creation period leading up to the performances, but also during the performance itself, while they are on stage. Lifschitz describes the on-stage improvisational process as being similar to improvisation in jazz, in that it is improvised but retains set reference points. *Humans* is a work that is improvised by the cast in every performance, so that each time it is performed the show is different, although retaining set points of reference.

Through the calling into question of the act, new possibilities and new dynamic forms of Contemporary Circus are being generated which focus on flows and dynamic patterns of movement as opposed to the stop-start rhythm of the conventional circus act.

In Part 2, the *Voices* section of this chapter, 12 creators, known for their innovative and distinctive work, discuss their creative processes. We speak with Shana Carroll (The 7 Fingers), Chelsea McGuffin (Company 2), Lachlan Binns and Jascha Boyce (Gravity and Other Myths), Sean Gandini (Gandini Juggling), Yaron Lifschitz (Circa), Firenza Guidi (Elan Frantoio; NoFit State Circus), Johann Le Guillerm (Cirque Ici), Philippe Decouflé (Compagnie DCA), Jo Lancaster and Simon Yates (Acrobat), and Jennifer Miller (Circus Amok).

New work in Contemporary Circus – voices

We start by talking with Shana Carroll, Co-Founder and Co-Artistic Director of Montreal-based company, The 7 Fingers, about how she begins the creative process with the performers.[47]

Carroll is renowned for her success in creating innovative Contemporary Circus shows, and has also created acts for performers that have to date won six Gold Medals at Cirque du Demain in Paris. She has directed or co-directed numerous works for The 7 Fingers including *Loft* (2002), *Traces* (2006), *La Vie* (2007), *Psy* (2009), *Séquence 8* (2012), *Le murmure du coquelicot* (2013), *Cuisine & Confessions* (2014), and *Passagers* (2018).

Shana Carroll starts this conversation by describing how she uses group-devising and improvisation as the starting point for the development of new work.

★★★★★

Shana Carroll

What is your starting point for your creative developments, where and how do you start making a new work?
Shana Carroll: One thing we do now as a standard, is start the first month of creation in workshop mode, and allow ourselves to really get to know the people we are working with, by excavating, and improv, and figuring out how to hone in looking at this theme, this character, going deeper with them, so when we create the show it is like butter, it is like everyone has been churned.

FIGURE 4.1 The 7 Fingers, *Passagers*. Photo: Alexandre Galliez.

I guess if we created a show again with those same people having gone through that process well I think it would be faster, but especially because we are coming in with these new bodies, it's really that, even with people you think you know, once you put them in a context where you are pushing them further, it's like, 'Woah I didn't realise that you have this dark side, or this silly side.' So we always do that, and I always start with that. Sometimes it is just pure, no theme, you're 10 minutes alone on stage, just different directions, and you just bond as a group, then more and more incorporating the theme of the show, and the numbers, so we are heading towards the show we're going to create.

Then we have so much raw material with the improvs that when we start creating the acts we know what we can pull from, and the way I always refer to it is, it's almost like you find the essential oil. So even if it's just one gesture, like one teeny gesture they did in an improv, you go back to it, that's the compass, this is where we are going. You feel when it goes off. You felt that one quality you can build everything on.

Do you record everything on video in the improv situation?
Shana Carroll: Well we do now. I'm actually really bad because I never want to watch the video. I'm not from that generation and so we video, and I just forget about it, and the performers are there and they want to watch the video, and they're actually going to get frustrated, because I'm like 'Oh no don't watch yourself.' Because with improv the energy is palpable in the room, and on video you lose all of that, and some of it is kind of awkward and funky looking, and I'm worried they're going to judge themselves, and start censoring what they do.

However, I should use the video more because when we sit down and start looking at it, it's like, 'Hey there's that move. Let's do this. Let's do that.' It does bring a lot of material, and I encourage people to video and to watch the videos, but it's just I haven't got really into the habit of watching them regularly.

Are there any particular artists making physical material, or even film-makers that have been influential in how you approach making new Contemporary Circus work?

Shana Carroll: There was this piece by Ulysses Dove, the choreographer for the Alvin Ailey [dance] company, called *Episodes I* in the early '90s.[48] It was about a friend of his that died of AIDS, and when his friend died, he wished he'd had just two more minutes to spend with him. But what if we live our lives so fully, leaving nothing unsaid, or undone, that we never feel like we need those two minutes?

So the whole piece is just like so intensely connected, these passionate exchanges, and that really had a great influence on me, and I feel like it's something that a lot of my work in different ways sometimes touches, that urgency of connection. And even the vocabulary there I feel like that influenced things a lot as I was fairly young at the time.

How do you address this sense of a need for urgency and intensity that you were talking about within the way you work?

Shana Carroll: Actually, I think that circus is so urgent and intense. Quite often due to the nature of acrobatics there is a lot of adrenalin that's happening, there's fear, there's courage … it's very difficult!

One of the things we were saying with *Traces* [2006] is we wanted it to be really intense, and they don't even have to fake it because they are so out of breath after the first half, and it's so sincere because what they are doing is just pushing themselves to the absolute limit. The whole idea in circus, in its essence, is that it is pushing the limits of human possibility, so it is urgent, and intense, and elemental.

And yet what I find creating with that quality with circus artists in that way is easy, what's hard is once we put a show up and it gets easier for them, and they relax, it's hard to maintain it, it really is. It gets better like with humour because they get more relaxed and they find jokes, but always the intense quality of the shows always goes down. It's always like the thing of going back to remind them, 'We did these improvs and it was soul-baring.' It becomes really routine and easier, so sometimes the show really depends on the intense quality, and I go back and see shows and it is almost like the whole meaning has gone and it is a shell of what it was in that sense.

Do you feel like going in and changing little things to keep the immediacy or urgency?

Shana Carroll: There's a limit to how much we change as there is a certain safety element as quite often that's involved as well, but changing little things is a good idea. The one variable is that first of all we have injuries and a cast changes sometimes, so quite often they are happy to do new versions of the show, or a part they don't usually do, or a trick they don't usually do. On the one hand it can be stressful and weaken the show a bit but on the other hand at least it keeps them fresh in that way.

FIGURE 4.2 The 7 Fingers, *Passagers.* Photo: Alexandre Galliez.

One thing I think is an advantage with the fact that we work so much with improv is that when they do lose that intensity with time, we can always say, 'Remember when you created it?' We can always go back to the source, and say, 'Remember that feeling that day, remember?' And it works. I mean sometimes it may only last a show or two, they just need the discipline to do it themselves and not have me remind them.

✶✶✶✶✶✶

From Shana Carroll's approach to the use of improvisation to develop new work, we move to a conversation with Chelsea McGuffin, Co-Founder and Co-Director of Company 2 in Australia, who describes how she begins each new work with a period of embodied research to create new vocabulary for the generation of movement material.

McGuffin originally trained as a dancer at the Adelaide College of Contemporary Arts (CPA) before training in circus with Circus Monoxide. She learnt the acrobatic 'Toss the Girl' act from Cletus Ball, and went on to perform with the Brisbane-based Contemporary Circus company Circa for 10 years before founding Company 2.[49]

McGuffin has created nine shows for Company 2 including *Cantina* (2010), *She Would Walk the Sky* (2014), *Sediment* (2014), and *Kaleidoscope* (2017).[50] Her embodied research for new work creation can vary from studying dance styles such as the waltz form which underpins the show *Cantina*; to researching the lived experience of fellow collaborators, for example in her work *Kaleidoscope* in which she investigates Asperger's Syndrome, or in *Fallot* (2017), which was based on the medical heart condition of one of the performers.

In the next conversation Chelsea McGuffin talks about her diverse approaches to creating new work.

****

Chelsea McGuffin

How do you approach making new work?
Chelsea McGuffin: It depends on the show. Each show we create, my part-ner, David [Carberry], gets inspired by a type of music because he comes from a music background and is driven by sound, and I get inspired by movement, so *Cantina*, for example, was inspired by waltzing.[51] At the time my partner and I were doing an acrobatic routine called the *Dance Apache*. It originates from a waltz, but a street-style waltz, so all the pieces came from that, from the idea of the waltz, and we had researched all the different styles, from across many years and many countries, of forms of waltzing and acrobatic waltz, and then we would learn that as a straight form and then go, how can that now in-fluence what the scene is, and what we'd like it to be, and what the acrobatics are inside that.

So each piece has had a little starting point like that and gets driven by that, other than *Kaleidoscope* which has been the only one that hasn't had a fixed kind of dance form, though Ethan [Hugh] as a young boy did a lot of spinning, and so we did do a lot of spiralling movement, and we went, 'Let's turn and get ourselves really dizzy and see what comes out of that, let's spiral down to the ground, let's think about moving things like that,' and everything through the show moves in a curved kind of way.

FIGURE 4.3   Company 2, *Le Coup*. Photo: Mik Le Vage.

What are you working on at the moment?

Chelsea McGuffin: We just created a new piece called *Fallot*. This piece has four artists in it and it's based on the story of one of the performers who has a heart condition. In her life so far she's had two open heart surgeries and she possibly will need one or more in her life to come. So it's all based on her story, and how that experience has changed and shaped her life, and whether you hold on to that, or move on.

It's been really amazing, a really beautiful project. She's coming to circus quite late in her life. She came from an acting background and so the piece is really theatrical.

***She Would Walk the Sky* was a commissioned collaboration with a playwright. Is using text something you're moving more towards now?**

Chelsea McGuffin: Definitely. *She Would Walk the Sky* was a commissioned work and we were put together with [the playwright] Finegan Kruckemeyer, and that was our first taste of doing that kind of work.[52] Then we've explored from there. We did *Sediment*, which is based on a story, there are bits of text in it, and then *Kaleidoscope* which is also inspired by somebody's story. I've become interested in telling or being inspired by real stories. I find with *Sediment* to

FIGURE 4.4 Company 2, *Scotch and Soda*. Photo: Sean Young Photography.

some degree, but with *Fallot* and *Kaleidoscope*, I've gone, 'This is exactly what I'm loving doing, where I can see art and circus and movement and all the things I like, actually affecting people's lives right away, from the people who are in it, to the people who are coming to see it.'

With *Fallot* are you exploring the poetic metaphors connected with the heart, or are you constraining the work into a physical examination of what it is actually like to have a heart condition?
Chelsea McGuffin: Both ideas. One of the things we talked a lot with Marianna [Joslin] about was, 'Is this a show that goes beyond you, or is it a show that's for you to tell your story?' She was really clear; 'I want this to be a show that goes beyond myself.' So we look at the heart in terms of her experience, but also other people's experience. We look at the heart being a muscle, scientifically what we now know about the heart, and how it can drive your body and connect with your brain. We use a whole lot of elements to try and get people in the audience to personally connect with their own heart.

Are you devising the text or do you have someone writing for the show?
Chelsea McGuffin: We are group-devising mostly. I feel like if we get a writer in then it doesn't necessarily stay so personally connected to Marianna's story, and that's what feels really real about that text at the moment. So I've made the choice for now to keep exploring without having a writer coming in, to see how far we can take it.

★★★★★

The collaboration and group-devising that Chelsea McGuffin describes as key elements of the development of new work for Company 2 is also a central part of the creative process for the Australian circus ensemble Gravity and Other Myths (GOM).[53]

Here, Lachlan Binns and Jascha Boyce, who originally set the company up as a collective with five other performers, talk about how the group goes about collaborating during the development of a new work, and, in particular, how they go about the process of group-devising task-based creative work.

★★★★★

Lachlan Binns and Jascha Boyce

Gravity and Other Myths is a collective, and so how does that collectivity work in the creative process? How do you start creating material in the studio?
Jascha Boyce: The collective has evolved a lot over the years. We started with seven people, who made our first show *Freefall*, and we very much created the show together collectively. We had a few outside eyes but definitely no one that was acting as a director. The process was the same for our second show

A Simple Space. We started off just with five of us making that show, and added a few more people and collaborated with them, and helped them grow their part of the show as well. Then most recently *Backbone*, our newest work, we began devising again in the same way, and then actually decided to engage our director, Darcy Grant, in a very collaborative way so he wasn't the 'strict' director at all.[54]

Lachlan Binns: No, it's not the traditional director role.

Jascha Boyce: We worked very collaboratively with him on the floor. All of our work is very task-based so whether it's set by us or by the director, all the work is created by the acrobats on the floor.

So what sort of tasks are used to generate material?
Lachlan Binns: It's actually a whole range of things. It depends on what stage of the work we're at. In the initial phase, it's actually a lot of written tasks, a lot of spoken tasks where we'll talk through all the ideas. We'll have big conversations. We'll separate and spend five minutes writing down our ideal show on a piece of paper and then come back together and compare those.

So if you could talk us through that process say with the show *Backbone*, what were the ideas that you were working with in the studio when you were separating out and writing?
Jascha Boyce: The show from the beginning has been based around 'strength.' So we often start with a really strong word or theme of some sort.

Lachlan Binns: It's interesting though. Before that phase, before we settled on 'strength,' there was a phase where we knew we wanted to make a new work, but we didn't really know what we wanted to make it about. So what we did is we got together and we brainstormed a whole bunch of ideas about things we were potentially interested in, or things we thought could be seeds for physical language, and at that phase we split up, and we all wrote a few ideas about potential shows that we would be interested in making. I think we went so far as to

FIGURE 4.5 Gravity and Other Myths, *Backbone* in rehearsal. Photo: Darcy Grant.

plot our whole show and come back and pitch it to the crew. After that phase we narrowed it down and I think we settled on the idea of 'strength' and, after we'd whittled it down to one idea, we then exploded that back out and explored that in a more thorough way.

Was 'strength' the common element in everyone's ideas or was it one particular person that came back with this idea of 'strength'?
Jascha Boyce: I think it was more a common element in everyone's ideas and pitches, and none of the shows that we created in that little creative session actually became what *Backbone* is at all. It was more just of just a starting point to get the thinking going, about what we wanted to do as individuals, and then what the group wanted to do together.

Lachlan Binns: If you trace back the journey of how the show's developed, there would be a number of different starting points that you could trace, that would weave all over the place and then come back to what *Backbone* is now.

So through a process of playing with the ideas, the physical material began to emerge?
Jascha Boyce: Yes, exactly. It began before we engaged with Darcy, the director, as well.

Lachlan Binns: We had two or three developments.

Jascha Boyce: Yeah, I think three developments in total, some just with the acrobats, and some with outside creatives as well who set tasks that we wouldn't necessarily have done ourselves to give us the chance to figure out what direction we wanted the show to go in, which helped us to decide to engage Darcy.

Three developments is quite an achievement in Australia at the moment with the current dire funding situation.
Jascha Boyce: We've been incredibly lucky. The three developments prior to our big development for *Backbone* were actually when we had time off from our normal touring schedule, and we squeezed in some developments. Some overseas, some in Australia, mostly unfunded. I think one of them was funded.

Lachlan Binns: Yes, two of them were just off our own back. We had a little bit of time in between seasons overseas, so we just decided to spend some time at a residency in Germany that we had organised through our agent, and we spent time on it together there, and then back in Australia at Cirkidz.[55] We have a really good relationship with them so we can often use that space without needing to fund it too much.

Jascha Boyce: And I guess those developments gave us a chance to really figure out what we wanted the show to be, to create a really strong application to get the funding that we needed. We did an eight-week, full-time funded development period leading up to the show.

Seeing *Backbone* you could imagine that it emerges out of physical improvisations in the studio, but when you talk about it in terms of the starting points, the beginnings of the show are really ideas-based, aren't they?

Jascha Boyce: I think some of our physicality and the unique skills, as well as some of the acts, would come about from us training together. Because of our style of touring, we tend to train together every day and have a chance to grow our material as a company. So that physical stuff is continually happening. Whereas the conceptual stuff, we need to make sure that that happens a little bit more, so it is often a set time that we do that.

Lachlan Binns: It's broken down into a couple of kind of layers I guess. There is that physical, structural, more skills-based technical element which happens in the exact way you described, but with the set element, the rocks, and the sticks for *Backbone,* that actually came after we'd done a little bit of the physical stuff. So it kind of does happen in stages and it loops back on itself occasionally as well. We do loop around a lot!

We come back to our starting point so we'll find that seed. We'll develop it a little bit and then we'll come back to the beginning and investigate why we wanted it to be a seed in the first place, and maybe take it in a different direction, or maybe at the end we'll add an extra thematic, or set element on top that will change it slightly. It is a little bit cyclical, it's not quite so linear that it moves from the theme, to the physical material, to the show.

There's an element in that show that feels Zen-like with the use of the rocks, the bamboo, and the sound component – how did that come about?

Jascha Boyce: Part of that was to do with the formation of the soundtrack. The two musicians that wrote the soundtrack based the whole music for the show on an Indian raga, so that really meditative kind of sound really informed the movement, as well, Darcy really liked the idea, and we all gripped onto the idea, of the strength of having to go about your everyday life and push through, no matter what, which everyone does every single day. So it was very relatable, and that comes across a lot in that repetition and the Zen meditative feeling in the work.

How did you find the experience of working with a director?

Lachlan Binns: Yes, it worked really well. It's not something we used to do in the past. I think we really stayed away from it intentionally. We always wanted to make work that was thoroughly ensemble-created, and *Backbone* still is. It still really has that feeling. The only difference is when you bring in a director, there's a slight difference in responsibility. They are responsible for the whole show – from the outside looking at the whole show – whereas as individual artists, we are responsible for our own contribution and our own pathway.

So there's a different level of responsibility for the work, but the process of creating was actually exactly the same. It would be a lot of everyone throwing in

FIGURE 4.6   Gravity and Other Myths, *Backbone*. Photo: Benoit Leroux.

their ideas and talking about the decisions that needed to be made. The obvious difference is that we come from the inside of the work, and the director would be sitting on the outside of the work. So what it does is it offers that outside perspective which is what we didn't have initially.

So in the past we would have to do things like film the work and watch it back ourselves, which obviously isn't quite the same, or we would bring in outside eyes to watch it and get feedback, but we always found that not having a longer relationship with that outside eye meant that the feedback wasn't always exactly what we wanted, or it wasn't as useful. Whereas working with Darcy [Grant] for a long period of time meant the contribution, and that relationship, was a little more meaningful, and a little stronger from beginning to end.

And being an Acrobat meant that he had an understanding of those biomechanics that you are constantly playing with.
Jascha Boyce: Part of the reason we chose to work with him is that we've had a very long relationship with him, so we all knew him well. The founders of GOM all met him before we started our company, when we were teenagers. He was one of the first people to teach us a bunch of the skills that we now use all the time. We have quite a strong personal relationship with him which I think really helped that transition into working with a director.

★★★★★

Following on from Lachlan Binns and Jascha Boyce of Gravity and Other Myths and their discussion about how the ensemble creates new work, we move to Sean Gandini, Co-Founder and Co-Director of Gandini Juggling in the UK, who in turn discusses how he develops the company's shows.[56]

Gandini, with the company's Co-Founder Kati Ylä-Hokkala, started the process of the precise correlation of their juggling patterns with musical scores in the early 2000s, with the use of Siteswap, a juggling notation that enabled absolute precision and also increased the vocabulary of juggling.[57]

Sean Gandini begins by talking about how the company contests the traditional idea of a circus show as a series of 'acts' with each act structured as a series of tricks. He discusses his interest in patterns, shapes, and dynamics, and how the company's collaborations with artists from other artforms act as informing influences in the creation of new work.

★★★★★

Sean Gandini

In *4x4: Ephemeral Architectures*, the juggling is extraordinary. It seems almost like an animated 3D realisation of the patterns in the minimalist score.
Sean Gandini: Well that's interesting. We do another piece which is a Philip Glass opera [*Akhnaten*].[58] Actually, we're doing it at the Metropolitan Opera House this year (2019). This piece takes Philip Glass' music and the patterns in it, and repeats them a lot, and one of the things that appeals to me is that the director uses it as a hovering narrative, a very abstract form of narrative.

But to me what's interesting is I've always liked the idea that you could use juggling as patterns, and not juggling as, 'And now I will do one more than you've ever seen before.' I think that's our imprisonment in circus. The skill is sometimes an imprisonment that is so hard to break.

That ballet piece (*4x4: Ephemeral Architectures*) is part of a trilogy and we've just performed the trilogy in Europe. It's a dialogue with ballet, then there's the dialogue with Bharatanatyam, the Indian dance form (*Sigma*). Then the one we just finished (*Spring*) which is larger scale, which is contemporary dance and colours, but they are all about patterns. I mean at the end of the day you can't get away from them. But also choreography, and whether it is rhythms or shapes, or how do you get from one shape to another, or is it the rhythmic patterning between the shapes, or the dynamic? I mean there are so many questions. But it's also about how one communicates to the audience those questions without the audience going, 'Oh that's clever!'

Ballet is in a similar place because ballet has its tricks, its pirouettes, and its big jumps, so in ballet, the choreography is often choreographic information … choreographic information … a trick!

FIGURE 4.7 Gandini Juggling, *4 x 4: Ephemeral Architectures*. Photography by Ash.

The crossover between the dancers and the jugglers was fascinating in *4x4: Ephemeral* Architectures – how the patterns in the movement language were taken up by the jugglers and vice versa.
Sean Gandini: Yes. In the latest piece, *Spring*, I feel like we go a lot further into that complex dialogue between the two things. One of the other things we had in our head for *4x4: Ephemeral Architectures* was a classicism, in that ballet has a classicism as in these are the correct positions, these are the incorrect positions, and juggling doesn't have classicism, or its classicism would be street performance or vaudeville. We wanted to imagine a more regal history – if Louis Quatorze had been obsessed with juggling as well as dancing, and juggling was in the big opera houses of the world, how would that be done and would there be a formality?[59]

I do a lot of ballet myself recreationally and the teacher will sometimes go, 'Well you don't do that position because that position's ugly.' You would never say in juggling that the pattern is ugly … the whole beginning [of *4 x 4: Ephemeral Architectures*] is imagining a juggling classicism. You hold the clubs like this and you throw the first one like this always. You must always throw the first one like that. That's an alternative history. But in terms of the trilogy, that show [*4 x 4: Ephemeral Architectures*] feels like ballet and juggling, they went on a date. It is about the spaces they both inhabit, and it feels like sometimes ballet is in a room and then juggling goes into the same room.

With *Spring* we tried to think that ballet and juggling spoke the same language from the start, so that it's merged. With *Spring* it is more like if you're watching you can't tell who's the juggler and who's the dancer. That was our challenge.

Who were you working with in *Spring*?

Sean Gandini: A choreographer called Alexander Whitley, one of the more interesting choreographers working in the UK at the moment.[60] He really dug deep. I feel like with the other two choreographers, they were very respectful of me, and let me suggest to them what they did, whereas Alex just loves manipulating forms and objects, and straight away immersed himself in 'What was the juggling? What are the patterns? What's a shower? How does that go? Can they do that juggling catch here?'

What is Alexander Whitley's movement background?

Sean Gandini: He was from the Royal Ballet originally, but then he danced with Rambert, and Wayne McGregor, and all the big contemporary companies. Then he's been making his own work for about six years.

Your piece *Smashed*, that is influenced by Pina Bausch isn't it?

Sean Gandini: *Smashed* is a homage to Pina Bausch.[61] We do it with 100 apples and that's a show we do all the time. It's a weird show because in a way I don't think it reflects the essence of who we are and yet it's the show that's been the most seen out of all the company's work. So a lot of people have come into our world by that piece.

In what way do you think *Smashed* doesn't reflect your company's essence?

Sean Gandini: Because when we started the company it was very much about nurturing juggling through dance, and in a way Pina Bausch is dance, but it has a theatrical side, but for the first decade that we made work we had a phobia about theatricalness. We were very much in the kind of Merce Cunningham, Tricia Brown aesthetic.[62] When we started our first shows we were at The Place Theatre in London. We used to work with a woman called Gill Clarke.[63] She was very much Tricia Brown and not necessarily the Cunningham technique, but the Cunningham aesthetic, 'Dance is dance, and the stories that are there, are whatever stories the viewer wants to put on to the thing.' And we did that for about 12 years, and then for fun we made a dramatic piece just to see.

Last year with Dominique Mercy from the Pina Bausch company, he came to help us rework *Smashed* for 22 people so we did a version of *Smashed* with 22 performers which I loved doing.[64] It's with a live opera singer.

Could you talk about your creative process with Kati Ylä-Hokkala?

Sean Gandini: So the company's very much the two of us, and it's always been the two of us. She's an ex-rhythmic gymnast, and when we met she hadn't juggled per se, but she picked up juggling very quickly, and because of her movement background, straight away we started to do a lot of dance and we thought, 'Gosh! There's something here.' She's more shy than me so I tend to get more credit than her, more because she doesn't necessarily do the interviews but she's contributed as much, if not more than me, to everything.

FIGURE 4.8   Gandini Juggling, *Smashed*. Photo: Ludovic des Cognets.

It's unusual to see high level women jugglers like her.

Sean Gandini: Juggling has more men than women, and that's a whole other complex question why that is, but then ballet's the exact opposite. I often go and do ballet classes in the afternoon and I'm the only man in with 30 women, so I don't know if it's cultural, genetic, a mixture of both. Who knows? But in terms of creativity that's an interesting one – there's very few, considering how much good work is being made.

Would you say that it was through your connection with her that your juggling started to move into dance?

Sean Gandini: Yes, absolutely. I was interested in dance a little bit before I met her because I used to do street shows in Covent Garden, and the independent dance classes used to happen in that gym. A very nice man called Scott Clarke used to come by and watch me juggle and he said, 'Come and do dance class,' and I had no idea what a dance class was but he just dragged me along, and they were all very supportive with us.

But it would be something completely different if Kati hadn't been there. The company is very much a bouncing backwards and forward. Even our personalities – she's quiet and considered, so I'll say, all excited, 'Let's do this, this and this,' and she will say, 'No, actually, that isn't working. What about this?' I think the reason we've survived 27 years, is because of the duality of the relationship, which creatively is sustaining.

At what point did you actually start juggling so that it correlated so precisely with the music?

Sean Gandini: Actually, there was always an element of that, but the work we did with Gill Clarke because of its Cunningham aesthetic, often would have sounds that related but weren't precise. I would say about 15 years ago we started working with scores and being millimetre precise. Something I think that's quite important in contemporary juggling is the use of notations, and there's a notation called Siteswap which came about in the mid '80s.

One of the people who discovered it, Mike Day, worked in our first company.[65] So there are strings of numbers, so 531, 441, 7531, 97531, and they give you pathways of juggling balls in space and you can get really in depth into how they work and what they do. The main thing it did to juggling was that juggling had a limited amount of vocabulary. So it's as if you were writing with 15 words, and then somebody all of a sudden gives you a dictionary and goes, 'There you go.'

And then there were other things added on top of that vocabulary like dynamics, so the language of juggling has just exploded, more than I would say probably any other circus discipline. Sometimes it's too much. It's a bit like when we had our first computers, and you write stuff in every font. So it's so many patterns. It's like you go, 'I've got to use them all.'

Then we've done a reasonable amount of work with contemporary classical music, working with a score. So we have a score, they have a score, and we put them together.

Which contemporary composers are you working with?
Sean Gandini: *Spring* has a score by Gabriel Prokofiev, who is the grandson of Sergei Prokofiev. We have worked a lot with the composer Tom Johnson, who's a contemporary of Steve Reich and Philip Glass.[66] He's the lesser known but in my money, just as interesting in that he never let go of the minimalist repetitive aesthetic. So he wrote a piece for us that's called *Three Notes for Three Jugglers* and it has three balls that go 'do, do, do,' (sings three notes). Juggling so it makes sound, and then we do one permutation so that the notes are in a slightly different order. The build-up to it being complex is about 17 minutes.

Tom wrote various pieces for us and we've done a couple of Steve Reich pieces. We do Steve Reich's *Clapping Music* with bouncing balls, and then we did John Cage's *4'33* piece.[67] What's quite nice in John Cage's *Silence* piece is that it's in three parts, so we don't juggle balls in the first part, we don't juggle rings in the second part, and we don't juggle clubs in the final part. The Cage Foundation was really nice. They gave us permission. I sent them an email and they went, 'Yes, that would be great, do it.' I hoped they wouldn't go, 'No, you can't!'

Or say, 'It's copyright!'
Sean Gandini: Copyright, yes! It's a beautiful score! Then there's Philip Glass which we do, there's this piece which will probably be around for a decade which is *Akhnaten*. It's the second ever large-scale version and the director had a dream where he saw juggling in it, and so he ended up with us, and then he didn't know this but the first illustrations of juggling are Egyptian hieroglyphics. I love the fact that it's women as well. Yes, it's three women. There's three balls above each one.

How do people know they are juggling?

Sean Gandini: You would think it's juggling, but it could be like say if you were drawing tennis, you could put more than one ball above somebody if you were representing motion. Egyptologists have argued over this a lot. I think they're jugglers. We'll say they're jugglers!

So in a way, acrobatics and juggling are the forms of circus that go back the farthest.

Sean Gandini: Yes. I guess they're quite primal. I mean there's unfortunately very little known about what patterns were juggled up until maybe the early twentieth century. There's very little information on what was juggled and how. Whereas acrobatics, I think one would have a sense because drawings can be clear, and dance and music are so clearly notated. So we have a very young artform. I argue that it's in its golden age, and maybe that's why there's such a creative impetus, because one is finally realising its possibilities.

In *4x4: Ephemeral Architectures* it seems that somehow, suddenly, juggling has become elevated to a high artform in the way that ballet is.

Sean Gandini: That was at the back of my mind, that whole higher, lower divide. Ironically when I started, I was in Covent Garden downstairs on the Piazza, while the Ballet and the Opera were in the building next door upstairs, and then when we made *4x4: Ephemeral Architectures* we were in the studios upstairs. A funny journey but actually that's really just arbitrary cultural histories. For example ballet in a way, it's such a perverse random thing that the women are on little stilts. The fact that that's considered high art, or that the falsetto singing of opera has become … I think they're arbitrary cultural divides, because other cultures have different forms of dance which are elevated in the same way.

★★★★★

From Sean Gandini and his focus on abstract patterns both as the generator of content, and as a means to subvert and bypass the structure of the traditional juggling act, we move to the next conversation with Yaron Lifschitz, Artistic Director and CEO of Circa in Brisbane, Australia, who in some of his work with the company also contests the traditional act structure in circus.[68]

Yaron Lifschitz took over as Artistic Director of Rock'n'Roll Circus, as it was then known, in 2004, soon changing the name of the company to Circa. Since then he has directed all the Circa shows, and has developed a company which has now become highly successful, touring to over 30 countries.

Here he discusses his approach to making new work, and his role as director in which he sets out to function as a creative catalyst for the performers.

★★★★★

Yaron Lifschitz

When you think about creating circus shows, what is it that you aspire to?
Yaron Lifschitz: When I first came to circus, I was in a rehearsal room in an old museum, there was a shaft of light, dust motes in the air, and someone was doing some backflips, and it created this emotional response within me that I couldn't explain.

One of the lines that inspires me is a line by the American poet, Donald Hall, where he says, 'Poetry is a human inside talking to a human inside,' and I think that's probably the condition I would like our work to aspire to. It's not going to reach there very often. It's just a casing for this kind of real human experience. We have to feel something, we feel a strong emotion where you know it's beyond words. I like to think about circus shows as emotional holotypes. A holotype is that thing that is the first of a species that every other member of the species gets defined as. In the Australian museum there is this room with all different types of jars with fish holotypes in them. I like to think about it that there's a sort of human emotion or holotype that is beyond normal emotion.

The only way I could describe it is as the thing I felt when I saw that show. You don't have any words for it, but each show should aspire to be an emotion that does not yet have a name.

Is that the thinking that drove the creation of *Humans*?
Yaron Lifschitz: For *Humans* I'd been thinking a lot about what is the circus equivalent of folk dance. Before ballet came folk dance, where a lot of the dance connected the body to the ground. Ballet emerged as a courtly dance not an entertainment. Ballet removed the sense of the ground, the genitals, and torso, and codified a set of gestures and basically said, 'well, we aren't folk, we are aristocracy.'

Acrobatics does a very similar thing. It creates biomechanically incredibly efficient pathways and, although in some ways we have been able to deconstruct that alignment and break it apart, for me it's still balletic in its form. One way you can break it apart is to add another kind of urban dance on top of it, so that's what a lot of Canadian companies like Cirque Éloize and The 7 Fingers do. This requires you to do dance, and then stop and then do your classical acrobatics, and that's fine, that's their approach.

For me, I was interested in what would folk look like in the acrobatic form. How can we add groove and rhythm, and torso, and genitals, and the connection to the ground back into this? What happens if instead of walking along to someone and stopping, what happens if the body is in motion and flux? Does that change reconnect us to a sense of our humanity?

I think the answer we have found in some shows of ours is occasionally 'Yes!' and more often 'We're not there yet.' It's a very counter-intuitive style for the artists to work with, to find that point where something doesn't stop. You know, we're very good at going 'bam!' and stopping, but how do you go 'bam!' and keep moving, keep a sense of flux.

FIGURE 4.9 Circa, *Humans*. Photo: Pedro Greig.

If we can live with this show *Humans,* then in a year's time there will be a kind of authentic *Humans* style. That will actually then make the next show we do more difficult because you realise, 'Hang on, everything is moving now. I don't want it to stop and it feels so good when we do this'… but that's the risk of testing boundaries and exploring so it's really part of the show, that attempt to find out the contemporary folk line into Contemporary Circus.

What exactly do you mean by folk?
Yaron Lifschitz: If you go to a Greek or a Jewish wedding, and you see a group dancing, when you see it, it's a connection between the rhythm, the body, and the music. It is present and unselfconscious, less a performance than an event. And if you watch the difference between an orchestral violinist and a gypsy violinist, in just the way they hold their body and their relationship to the music, one has the music flowing through their body much more than the other.

One is more about purity and remoteness and taking the body out of performance, and most codes operate that way across the arts. For me it's really interesting to look at this because our bodies have lots of ways of coming together, and usually we can explore only a few of the most efficient pathways, and in *Humans* we're looking for different flavours and textures.

One of the constants in *Humans* seemed to be side-stepping anything that's expected. For example, all the normal kinds of signals that usually indicate that a partnering lift is coming up are omitted, as is the conventional pause for applause or 'compliments' from the audience. Also, the fact that the section that you would normally think of as being the finale actually starts the show.
Yaron Lifschitz: Yes, though it wasn't quite as perverse as that sounds. Those things were actually coming from quite separate places. I've done a lot of

'noodling' starts to shows, you know, five, ten, twenty minutes of slow-building stuff, and I was really keen to break that. Also I hate applause in the circus, in my circus. In other people's it's great, but in my circus I hate it. We consider that any time the audience applauds where we don't want them to, it's a failure. So we work very hard to go 'Why did that happen and how can we stop that.' Applause is a kind of simian gesture, like monkeys we bang the hands together.

Well, it can indicate you're having fun!
Yaron Lifschitz: Oh absolutely, but you know, having fun which is at the end of a phrase is fine, but I'm having fun when I go see a piece of great orchestral music. I don't want to clap in the middle of it because I want to hear what's happening.

So, a different kind of fun?
Yaron Lifschitz: Yes, a different kind of fun. So it's like changing the audience's responses, the normal responses of an audience where they're trained to applaud at this point in the act, and at this next point in the act, and the end of the act.

Are you looking at ways to bypass the moment of applause?
Yaron Lifschitz: Yes, but it's not as calculated as how can we prevent that or how do we do the opposite of that. It's more a kind of consequence of this thing that happens when you do start to get in touch with these different rhythms.

But what is interesting is that the normal rhythm of moments of applause in circus is really like a predetermined sense about what the act is, predetermined like in ballet with a sarabande, or an allemande, or some other form. It's a form. Once you get into folk or social movement, those forms stop mattering because there is a certain amount of energy you have. That interaction, that expression of those things takes over from, 'Well it should be like this' because it actually just isn't. So you end up with this kind of slightly shaggy set of things and then, of course, you have to check, 'How can I get that into a show in a way that makes sense.'

So it's not like a particular approach to the language of circus where you're taking normal structures and cutting them up and reassembling them?
Yaron Lifschitz: We're applying pressure and heat, and sometimes that produces diamonds and sometimes it just produces a great big mess in the pressure cooker all over the ceiling. The way I see it is, we're kind of distressing them. I don't really have a creative process. We've got a kind of theoretical framework that we work loosely within, but mostly what I think I do is, essentially I'm the grain of sand in their oyster. It kind of irritates them into producing a pearl and basically all I do is disrupt them and just say 'What happens if you do it that way? What happens if don't do it that way?'

One of the exercises that produced quite a lot of material for the show, it's not staged as a section though it easily could have been, is called 'One Trick Wonders,' where what we looked at was what happens if the entire act is only allowed to have one skill. Usually it started off as duos and then grew from there, but how can you turn that trick that might last five seconds or ten seconds, how can you turn it into two minutes, three minutes but not by adding to the skill, but by adding new and interesting pathways, by adding intent but not acting?

The two things at Circa you get told from day one and every day you work is, 'Don't act and don't dance.' Again, we're not always successful at that, and sometimes in our shows there are moments of both from time to time.

Sometimes you are described as a choreographer. How do you react to that?
Yaron Lifschitz: I often get described as being a choreographer, but I'm not, and the work gets described as being dance, but it's not. Generally in my personal life I'd choose to see dance more than I would see circus if I was going to a festival, and I would rather see Pina Bausch than any number of circuses, including my own frankly!

But the difference is there's always a point in dance where the aesthetics of the gestures are in and of themselves. I spend a lot of my time saying, 'Yeah, that was good but it looks good.' I don't care what it looks like. We never ever choreograph a sequence the way where 'You put your hand here, you put your ...' I wouldn't know where to start.

Our work is essentially jazz. It's essentially based on a set of languages, and codes, and rules, and algorithms that create structures. You can keep those structures very alive or you can freeze them almost entirely, but if you freeze them completely you can kill them, and if you leave them completely to run away, they can end being flat. But essentially I don't ever want to tell my performers where they should stand, I want to give them a way to find an amazing way to stand.

I've taught a lot of dance classes, like at Tisch and at Jacob's Pillow.[69] One of the first exercises I get the dancers to do is I get them to cross the stage and they do that for a bit. And then I say 'I want you to cross the stage without your feet touching the ground,' and they do it stunningly, some roll, some do a handstand, some get carried by other people. They find all these extraordinary pathways.

The interesting thing is I ask them to do it again but to do it better, and what they always do is they do it nicer, more refined. Actually, in my world, that's worse. If you're rolling, I want you to roll faster or, you know, in a more complex or a different pattern. I don't want you to roll prettier. Pretty is easy if you're an 18-year-old ballet dancer, they can't easily help but be pretty, but the first time they do it, this kind of extraordinary energy gets unlocked because they can do something with their full body, their full spirit that's actually challenging to them, rather than, 'I'm going to spend the next six months working out how to get an extra one degree of extension on that thing,' while the rest of my body – my mind and my genitals – are completely disconnected from that foot. Whereas, actually, if I'm rolling across the stage, it's me rolling across the stage and I believe that the audience can powerfully connect to that kinetic response in their cells. You feel it in your skin when they roll.

So when that ballerina hits the ground and rolls with everything they've got, the audience members do the same in some way. The fact that we're locked into a chair creates torque and tension in our intestines, and in our upper body, and that's fantastic, that's the goal. And that's the bit that interests me. You don't get that when you go back into the prettiness of codifying it or recreating it, that really connecting with the impulse.

So part of my notes session for the performers in *Humans* tonight is to get people to start again. You take a dozen things in the show and breathe new life into them. This is that crux point after three shows. It's been pretty successful and the audiences like it, where we can be safe, artistically safe. This is the point to start stress-testing, more like kind of breaking it, and some of those choices will be catastrophically wrong. That's okay, that's honest.

And how does that relate to the whole notion of managing risk, if you're in a performance situation where there are groups and partnering and duos, if people start leaving out material that the other performers are expecting, how does that work?

Yaron Lifschitz: Well, the structure of most of our scenes is a couple of big things that need everybody in a particular place, and the rest is essentially improvised.

Not set?

Yaron Lifschitz: No. I mean it becomes set. The way I imagine it is a sort of curve between rehearsed and improvised. If you've got the highly rehearsed level of the Paris Opera Ballet here, and if you have a free jazz ensemble here, Circa excels in a zone somewhere between the two. If we get too rehearsed the shows get quite dull, and lifeless, and brittle. If we don't have enough rehearsal they get too unfocused. The reason for wanting to ask people to remove or change a number of different things in the show is to ensure that we're getting back that freshness. So the challenge for anyone in the company that comes from a dance background, their challenge is that they're used to pushing work up to a refined level, up here all the time.

Except with contact improvisation perhaps?

Yaron Lifschitz: Yes, that's right. But if they have a formal dance training then, honestly, the first year in Circa is the hardest year of their life because I'm like, 'Bring me something, show me the idea that I'd sketched in.' I'll say like, 'Can you finish this, I have to go to a meeting,' and I come back, and the idea's been done beautifully. 'No, no, no. What I wanted you to do is to take that, break it and take it somewhere else, see what happens and then … not refine it.'

And the other thing that often happens with dance is that movements get set to counts.

Yaron Lifschitz: We don't count. We use music in a way that I didn't realise was eccentric until Libby [McDonnell], Circa's Associate Director and also my partner, was watching me doing some bad dancing in the kitchen.[70] She went, 'I've never been able to explain it but the thing you ask for musically from performers is the way you dance. It's not like anyone else does it because it's completely bizarre.'

What exactly was it? Were you counting across the bars?
Yaron Lifschitz: I imagine that a piece of music has two train lines and one essentially is roughly the melodic flow of the thing. The other is the flow of information which might be percussive beats but it might also be a word you really like or a particular phrase. And basically you leap ... like an electron or an atom ... you do quantum leaps between the two. You'll be in this thing, but then you'll hold that moment, or word, or beat, and then you'll come back into this thing but the logic is not the logic dictated by the music, it's dictated by your own response to it. How do we deal with music? I'd say we deal with it inquisitively, and sometimes we lead, sometimes we follow, sometimes we hold moments.

I often think about when I was a kid, we used to go to water parks and water slides, and five or six of us would be at one end, then we'd stop and the water would build up on our backs. Sometimes it's like the weight of the music behind you and you're holding back all that water, and sometimes you should go with it, being pushed out with it, and that kind of dramatic interplay is much more involved with the music than just kind of moving to counts.

When you finish your day at Circa, like every other circus, you're physically very tired but I think, unlike some circuses, you're certainly also mentally tired. Our guys work very hard here [indicates his brain] as well as here [indicates his body].

★★★★★

From Yaron Lifschitz's interest in keeping 'a sense of flux' in the performance in order to disrupt the normal stop start rhythm of acrobatics, we move to a conversation with Firenza Guidi.

Guidi is a writer/director, and performance creator, who is the Co-Founder and Co-Director of ELAN Wales (European Live Arts Network) and Director of Elan Frantoio, ELAN Wales' sister organisation and Centre for Performative Arts in Fucecchio, Italy. Guidi often uses her investigations into the nature of the performance space as a starting point for the generation of new work. Her work with NoFit State Circus, the Wales-based Contemporary Circus company, includes *ImMortal* (2002), *Tabú* (2008), *Bianco* (2012), and *Lexicon* (2018).[71]

★★★★★

Firenza Guidi

We would like to talk to you about the way you use space in your works, especially in relation to *Tabú*.
Firenza Guidi: *Tabú* was created in 2010. The idea of that creation was that it would be created for the NoFit State tent, but that it could also, with a meaningful amount of work, be reinvented in circular spaces. And so I recreated *Tabú* in the Roundhouse in London, and at La Tohu in Montreal. When I arrived in Montreal, very lovely people, very collaborative, very beautiful to work with, but the staff said I was completely crazy. Nothing like that had ever been done

before. You do not take the seating out. You do not lay bare the entire space. The space was cleaned out. In fact, the technical manager was saying, 'Firenza, you've asked me to move things that have not been moved for 13 years.' I was also interested in what was below the space and what was above.

There was a grid in the floor, which was, again, filled with a lot of rubbish that people had accumulated over a number of years. I got all of that, got the area underground emptied, and filled it with lights to create a world underground. And in the same way, the tech tower had two women, these two beautiful Argentinian women, dancing a tango at some point; and the rigging grid was activated at a particular time by people running on it and creating a big, disruptive noise.

Now, the space first of all, every nook and cranny of the space was inspiring. Yes, it was circular, so I could give the show the same resonances as in the tent. But because of the fact that it was a building with doors, I created a pathway for people to come in. So, they came in from the back door, and not from the front door. The docking bay where normally people unload their rigging

FIGURE 4.10 Image from *Lexicon*, created and directed by Firenza Guidi for NoFit State Circus – Brighton and Avignon Festival. Photo: Mark Robson (Ineptgravity).

equipment, or anything to do with scenography, became a boxing ring. People were suspended at different points along the pathway even before the show started. This was to create a world that was not just, 'You come to the foyer, you buy your ticket,' a world which obeyed the theatrical convention where we read things from left to right, and watch things from the safe space of the auditorium. In this show, in both the pre-show and the show itself, you as a spectator became a co-player in the same way that the space itself did.

Where does your interest in the particularity of the space come from?
Firenza Guidi: As a child, as a little girl, I was taken ritually, almost every week, to La Scala in Milan to watch everything from opera, to ballet, to concerts, because a friend of the family was a member of the claque.[72] So, as a child, I experienced quite a lot of different kinds of performances of a very large scale. And most of the time, when the opera was too difficult for me to understand, or the ballet, I would start looking around. I loved the big chandelier of La Scala. I loved the little boxes where people sat. I loved watching from above, from below, and I really started making my own shows even as a child.

My love has always been live performance, whether it was opera, or ballet, or theatre. But I also started very early on creating, on a small scale, the environments where people would be performing.

For me, it is impossible to imagine a performer without imagining the world. The world is a little bit like the costume. It's all one thing. Even if the costume is simple and just a T-shirt, it's got to be right. It's got to be a second skin. And the environment cannot arrive, as it does sometimes in theatre, in production week.

FIGURE 4.11 Image from *Bianco*, created and directed by Firenza Guidi for NoFit State Circus. Photo: Richard Davenport.

There has to be an organic process of actually living, responding, listening to it, working with it, and also whispering in the space. I always say that walls have wrinkles, and stories, and memories. Every space, even a car park.

Are you interested in the way that performance can explore the archaeology of the memories in the space?

Firenza Guidi: Absolutely. That is, in fact, my passion. It's what excites me. In about two days' time, I will be creating a performance in Italy here, in a tower which has just been built. It's been built to prevent another building from falling down. The tower is attached. So, it's new. It's not always been there. But nevertheless, I spent two hours just sitting in this tower, which has a beautiful resonance. I can use the voice in a beautiful way at the bottom of the tower, and you can hear the voice at the top, and vice versa. So you can just whisper. Those are the things that immediately say to me, 'Okay, the main element here has got to be the voice.' The main element is both body and voice. The main element is not theatrical lights. The lights will be very small, and directional, and tracked. It's almost like a Tower of Babel going up. So, I totally believe that there is a process of 'listening to' the space without getting too new age about it. I don't want to be one of these new age people saying like 'Oh, yes! I go in, then I'm psychic.' But nevertheless, there is a process of listening.

I remember when I had to create this show in the catacombs of Indianapolis. It was a whole underground, almost like an Alice-in-Wonderland network of corridors and alleyways. Absolutely no electricity, no concrete floor. You could get lost in there. And for 10 days, I didn't know where the audience would come in from, and what their journey would be, until this beautiful epiphanic moment where I looked at the map of Indianapolis by accident. I looked at it, and I said, 'That's the answer!' I can't explain it, but suddenly even the underground began to make sense. I had a wonderful Icelandic electrician that managed to rig the entire catacombs with light of a very particular nature using a 1940's American panel fuse block.

I did the same thing in NICA [National Institute of Circus Arts], in Melbourne. But there as well … in *dreams from the second floor*, it was almost bringing into this space my great-great-grandmother, immigrants, and professions, and objects that made the space resonate with the feeling of a melting pot, which that place in Melbourne was for me, which I absolutely loved.

★★★★★

Firenza Guidi's ideas on how the creation of new work often emerges from investigation into a particular space we move to a conversation with the French juggler and installation artist Johann Le Guillerm, who also investigates space. Le Guillerm's investigations of space however occur through his creation of unique sculptural objects which he interacts with during the performance and uses as a form of apparatus.[73]

Johann Le Guillerm is a performer and the Co-Founder and Co-Director of Cirque Ici. A juggler and wire artist by training. Le Guillerm studied at the Centre National des Arts du Cirque (CNAC) in Châlons-en-Champagne, France. He then went on to work with Archaos, La Volière Dromesko, and also to co-found Le Cirque O. In 1994, he founded Cirque Ici and created his first solo show *Où ça?* which toured internationally for five years.

Le Guillerm describes how he needs to have complete control over his working process from concept through to performance outcome in order to realise his unique visions.

★★★★★

Johann Le Guillerm

How would you describe your body of work?
Johann Le Guillerm: The entirety of my work is called *Attraction*. It hinges around the observation 'the nothing much' [French, 'le pas grand chose']. The *Secret* show is a work that's constantly mutating. Up to now, my career has been built on some 40 sequences that make up the subject matter, and my shows are always created from this same subject matter.

Half the show contains entirely new sequences. There is always about a quarter of the show that is made up of sequences from the previous show. And about a quarter comes from the show before that. That is to say that this subject matter, each time, grows with each new mutation, and there are always things that come back from before, things that return. It's really subject matter that I use a bit like how in a kitchen you will have things you use and reuse. And you change some things. And some things are always there.

There's one sequence, you know, that I have always performed. It's never been cut – it's always been there.

What's that?
Johann Le Guillerm: It's a section with a paper plane, where I construct a plane from paper on stage and I make it fly.

And it's there in all your shows?
Johann Le Guillerm: Up to the present, right since the beginning.

Could you talk about the evolution of your work to your current solo practice?
Johann Le Guillerm: So, I needed a place and space to figure things out. And I always went to studio spaces. It's rare to see a studio-based artist work with others to produce a work. It happens, it's possible, but it's not very common. I like to have complete control over my space, my work, the whole thing.

It bothers me to work with several collaborators on what I would call a multi-authored work. With several people you compromise. You make compromises instead of doing other things. Everyone has to make a few compromises,

FIGURE 4.12 *Secret (temps 2)*, Creation 2012, Johann Le Guillerm. Photo: © Philippe Cibille.

and so you can never achieve the whole of what the work should be. You compromise. Whereas when I am by myself, I can build things, develop my ideas in their entirety, without having to make compromises. In all of my work, it's important to be able to go to the end point of what I want to achieve. Because it's simpler that way. I need to be left alone with what I'm working on.

And when you are getting yourself ready to perform, do you have a specific mental and physical preparation for performance?
Johann Le Guillerm: When I work, first thing in the morning when I wake up I know I am going to work. It shapes my day. I sleep a lot. I never rehearse. I work a lot during the show. So the show serves as its own rehearsal. But I never rehearse during the day. Right now, since I am performing late, I get up fairly late. I eat. After that, I have a short sleep. Then, I work with the objects for a while then afterwards, at 4:00 pm, I have another sleep. Then I warm up. Then I go back to sleep and I allow my mind to wander inside myself. And then, there we are, the show begins. And then the next day it's the same.

Your presence on stage is remarkable. Would you say that you enter a particular state of being for performance? How would you describe your state of mind when you are performing?
Johann Le Guillerm: Well, I'm there.

'There' as in *present*?
Johann Le Guillerm: Well, it depends – it can really depend. Even juggling, the attitude that I take on, it depends really on my state, the state of the team, the state of the audience, the feel of the audience. It can be very changeable. Sometimes it can be very difficult, at other times it can be very funny, a lot more comical, and it changes. It depends on the general atmosphere.

What is the role of games and play in your work?
Johann Le Guillerm: Well, I often ask myself whether I am serious or not. Where are the boundaries? It's like the world – is it serious or not serious?

★★★★★

From the singular vision of Johann Le Guillerm we move to Philippe Decouflé, the performer, and Founder and Director of Compagnie DCA in France. Like Le Guillerm, Decouflé also uses a 'lab-based' creative process, but to experiment with ways of combining film, video, and dance choreography with Contemporary Circus.

Decouflé originally trained as a circus artist at École Nationale du Cirque Annie Fratellini, and as a mime artist at the Marceau Mime School. He trained in dance with Matt Mattox and performed as a dancer with Alwin Nikolais, Karole Armitage, François Verret, and Régine Chopinot. In 1983, at the age of only 21, his work *Vague Café* won the International Prix Bagnolet award for choreography, and he founded his own company Compagnie DCA the same year.[74] Philippe Decouflé has been Artistic Director of two Cirque du Soleil shows, *Iris* and *Paramour*, and he created the opening and closing ceremonies for the 1992 Winter Olympics.

Here Decouflé speaks about the necessity of finding a balance between the different hybrid elements that he uses in his Contemporary Circus or dance performances so that one element does not dominate the others.

★★★★★★★

Philippe Decouflé

Could you speak about your video work, especially in circus?
Philippe Decouflé: I had the luck to grow up with a good camera, and it interested me right away. First, because I loved watching musicals on television when I was a little kid, and so I could see that filming dance was interesting. Filming the movement, and filming the background. And, also a film like *Freaks* for which I have an admiration without bounds.[75] Really, that film could only have been done at that time, with the help of that incredible circus.

Film allows us to freeze things for eternity. You know when you have an extraordinary artist, film allows you to capture them. Chaplin at the peak of his form, we captured him. It's really amazing – the film of his performance remains, so it is still possible to see him. These films remain as an example of a great master for all clowns and all actors, so that is fantastic. So there is something about the image that fascinates me. Because it stays fixed for eternity.

Another thing is movement, and acrobatics are not easy to notate. It takes a long time to write roles down! It's laborious and complicated to read. So, as a result, I've always used a video camera fairly early on in the process of creation to fix, to remember, to note down choreography, and to catch ideas for movement, spatial ideas, and all sorts of other ideas.

Then after that I had the desire to mix – this was my research into magic – fake with real characters. There is a field of possibilities that opens itself up with cinema that is really super interesting.

From early on there was a film by Segundo de Chomón from the early 1900s – as always with magic, it's the mixing of several different tricks that makes illusion work – and it intrigued me. Video is complementary; it allows for, as in 'Kiriki,' a little break in the show.[76] A pause to change the set decor.

Also the use of the live video, now, effectively, with the quality of technology, we can film something and then project it live. The big danger with this is that the projected image has an extraordinary power to attract the eye, and make you watch it. Most often, the use of video in live performance is poorly done and so it attracts the eye too much, it pulls focus and we no longer watch the real action.

And so I work a lot – I have my own laboratory, in fact, in Saint-Denis and we work on that. To balance the relationship between real and recorded action. To find a way to balance the two, to find how to do it, because the advantage of the live technology is that you can do a live close-up, and right away everyone will see that the performer has beautiful eyes. It's marvellous. You experience it almost like a 'zoom.' So if it's well done, it's extraordinary. If it's poorly done, then you are looking in the wrong direction and it's pulling focus. So it's interesting, but it's dangerous.

What is very interesting is that we can also create our own décor, live. For example, we can create the visual effects, like we did with the Mongolian contortionists with *Cirque du Soleil,* and the effects allowed us to keep the traces of their movements, to add planes that leave traces, and to create traces that surrounded them physically, that outline the performers and surround them. And that created a magnificent visual effect. As far as I remember it was done with infrared.

FIGURE 4.13 Compagnie DCA Philippe Decouflé. Image: © Laurent Philippe.

But also I don't really want to be too hi-tech. At *Cirque du Soleil*, in the end, there was an army of projectors, and at some point it becomes a little too complicated. And that's the inconvenience of doing big things. It doesn't change anything, in reality. It's a bit longer to set up when we have eighteen video projectors instead of two.

★★★★★

From Philippe Decouflé's approach to finding a balance between the diverse elements in his works, the next conversation is with Jo Lancaster and Simon Yates, Co-Founders and Co-Directors of the Australian company Acrobat, who talk about their motivation for contesting all orthodox approaches to making new work.

Acrobat was founded by Simon Yates and Jo Lancaster in 1995, and since then has toured to major festivals and venues all around the world.[77] The company's most recent show *It's Not for Everyone* (2015) can be seen as a contestation of conventional power structures.[78] The work problematises received genres and categorisable artforms, and their process in creating work could be said to reflect this, showing a deep reluctance to adopt any particular, predetermined approach. Jo Lancaster and Yates start by talking about their working process in which they often work with musician and composer Tim Barrass.[79]

★★★★★

Jo Lancaster and Simon Yates

How do you go about making new work?
Simon Yates: We have avoided having any kind of process that we can articulate very easily, and so when we've made material for performances the process has been quite varied.

Why is it that you resist articulating what your process is?
Simon Yates: I reckon there's a couple of things. When people use the same tools to make something, there may be some degree of variation, but ultimately there tends to be the mark of the tool used in the making of it.

Also, when you want to make some performance it's unnerving. It's intimidating. You feel very insecure and so having a process that gets you through that by helping you forget your insecurity can be reassuring. Belief in the process you're using helps to deal with the discomfort of self-doubt. Aside from that comfort though, I'm not convinced that a clearly articulated process gives you a more desirable outcome. It's not that I don't think you should use any kind of particular approach, as much as I think you need to be very careful. It's like worshipping false idols.

We fumble around a lot in the dark, not knowing what the fuck we're doing or what the next step will be. It is a decision to do that though, it's like an expression of non-compliance. In actuality, all three of us are very self-disciplined, and there's a lot of toiling over the practical side of making a performance. Our process is undefined but we are particular and thorough. Our approach remains unnerving, but we like the results.

So how does the collaborative process work between you?

Jo Lancaster: Simon and I have ideas and we conduct experiments. Tim Barrass, who creates the sound element of our performances is also very much a part of the whole chemistry. We come up with material to present and he usually has a wry comment to make about it, which can be stimulating and helpful. He beavers away creating sound or noise that reflects what he sees, the tracks he develops bring their own layers of meaning and humour and we also respond to them. I see it as a circular dynamic, which adds depth and potency to the ideas.

There are experiments that might not work, and we'll see if there's another way that they can succeed. We'll give them a few goes, and then if they still don't succeed, they go out. If they succeed they get built on some more.

FIGURE 4.14 Acrobat, *It's Not for Everyone.* Photo: Karen Donnelly.

How do you judge if they're succeeding?

Jo Lancaster: I guess if we like them. Sometimes it's laughter. We don't really know until we're in front of an audience, and that's kind of part of the excitement and the fun too.

I think usually by the time we've got in front of an audience we are fairly confident with what we want to present. Whether we know it's going to work or not I don't know, but we know what we want to present.

Simon Yates: Yes, we know what we want to present, but it's interesting the relationship with the audience. We make our performances very much in order to perform them for an audience, but we aren't looking for their approval. I would say that our performances, even though I reckon they are funny, are not necessarily the kind of funny that makes you laugh out loud. When we've done performances that are technically very difficult and potentially impressive, we've often done them in a way that might make it a bit difficult for the audience to clap. We definitely structure performances so that there are no …

Jo Lancaster: … cues, like 'this is where you show appreciation.'

Simon Yates: I like to feel aware of the audience, but within our performances it can be very difficult to tell what their experience is. Also, the intention of what it is that we are wanting to represent is more important than what we think the audience may want. It's more important for us to stay true to making the ideas communicate, than it is to indulge audience expectations. But it is for them that we make that effort.

What for you constitutes a successful performance?

Simon Yates: When you look at what people put their efforts into, clearly there are different ideas of what will constitute success. I know that if I'm watching a performance, I'm going, 'Why is it that I find that compelling?' or 'Why is it that I'm bored?' trying to understand the experience.

I've heard directors say, 'You need to perform with confidence or certainty, that's what'll make the performance work.' But I've seen things that have been evocative because the person was vulnerable and unsure of themselves. People are often drawn to things that are heroic in circus performance. Circus performers are often doing things to appear as gods or heroes.

Like Superbeings?

Simon Yates: Yes. So in our performances we tend to be doing things where we undermine that expectation. Historically we've had a dedication to a very high technical standard, but we've also undermined it, or presented it so that it's flawed, to make it a bit harder to admire.

The simple transaction with circus skills is that you're doing stuff that people don't expect you to be able to do. Also there's a dichotomy in performing with that because when you focus on technique you're working on efficiency, but on the other hand, with creating art the idea is for what you're doing to be unique. So there's an efficiency required in the reproduction of a skill, but that's kind of at odds with it being unique, and so there's this layer in creating work that is a tug of war between those two things. Maybe the more we go against the grain and still manage to present something that's satisfying, particularly to those who, like ourselves, are often uncatered for, the more of a success it is for us.

Empire building is the prevailing model and that leads to monocultures, even in circus. To contribute to diversity is rebellion. To be able to survive and maintain a voice of dissent for as long as we have has been a real privilege. If we have provided a glimpse of the existence and value of possibilities outside of the dominant model, it will have been a real success.

All your works are made outdoors, is that right?
Simon Yates: Yes, outdoors. The vast majority of our performances. *It's Not for Everyone* is the only one that we've created indoors.

Jo Lancaster: We've built a hangar, a purpose-built space in our backyard.

Simon Yates: We've been attached to the idea of not being answerable to anyone else. You need to be careful about what it is that influences what you do. We've tried to have as much independence as possible. So for *It's Not For Everyone* we'd go into the hangar and go about constructing the things we're interested in, or feel compelled to do.

Jo Lancaster: There's also a trajectory that we aimed at, like the overarching shape of the performance.

Simon Yates: We got to the point quite early in *It's Not for Everyone* where there's two poles in the show. At the beginning, there's the 'saccharine clowns,' brought through to some kind of …

Jo Lancaster: … singularity of some sort.

Simon Yates: Yes, with mud, and so then we both had a sense of those two things.

Jo Lancaster: It's just amazing how things just serendipitously kind of emerged. You're just turning things over in the back of your mind and it takes shape, and it just ties together, it organically pulls together. It's like things crystallise. It can be an amazing experience making the show.

Simon Yates: When we work like this, the thing that I like about it, it's kind of inefficient and it's painful. There's no comfort, but it's from the gut. We will laugh a lot at times, but at other times you're going 'what the fuck am I doing?'

Jo Lancaster: But then I like that stage. There's a bit of a chemistry that happens when we're in a room together. It's fun to play and there's a lot of joy to be had and all that becomes a show eventually.

Simon Yates: Even though watching some other processes I can see that they are a lot more defined than ours, the thing that I like is that generally when we come up with something you go, 'Yeah I don't reckon anyone else is barking up this tree.' It's very idiosyncratic and I like that. I like that.

★★★★★

From Jo Lancaster and Simon Yates and their rejection of conventional approaches to making work, we move to Jennifer Miller, the juggler, fire-eater, writer, and director, and the Founder, Director, and Ring Mistress of Circus Amok in New York City.[80]

Miller's approach to creating new work involves combining different artforms and drawing on numerous diverse creative processes. Her work has been described as 'borrowing drag fabulousness from Charles Ludlam's Theater of the Ridiculous, large-scale transformation using whole-body masks from Bread and Puppet Theater, and the outdoor bally and verbal rhythm and repertoire from the sideshow, as well as movement vocabulary from postmodern dance.'[81]

Here Miller, who is Associate Professor in Performance Studies at the Pratt Institute in New York, starts by talking about her experiences of teaching circus within academia and about teaching different approaches to creative practice.

★★★★★

Jennifer Miller

What is your experience teaching creative process and Circus in Academia?

Jennifer Miller: Well I don't teach in a broader circus context. I'm teaching performance classes in an art school. We're starting an MFA [Master of Fine Arts] programme in Performance and Performance Studies so in the future I will be teaching people who are in the world of performance. Right now at Pratt I'm teaching undergrads who are very individually oriented studio artists, I find it's a revelation for them to be physical with each other, to be playful, to have a skill to practice, to work collaboratively, and to think politically.

I do teach a circus class, 'Making Big Outdoor Spectacle: Theory and Practice, The juggle,' they read Brecht and Muñoz, they write about queer utopias and make puppet shows about local elections. There is skill work, juggling, basic partner acrobatics, slack-rope walking, stilt walking, but I think the most expansive parts of the practice for them is the big physicality, when we are running around warming up. The contact improvisation, vocal work, clown schtick, physical comedy, all of this is a great release for them. They access a playfulness that informs their creative practice. The skill stuff is very grounding for them, the fact that they're learning something that is quantifiable. They can see their progress.

I teach 'Introduction to Performance Practice' which is about presence and improvisation. Sometimes I teach 'Gender in Performance' and I love those classes, but the circus class sells out in a minute. It has that reputation. I'm teaching a class now with a few of my other colleagues on 'play.' I do it with a graphic designer, and a poet, and an architect.

So how does that work?

Jennifer Miller: Well, we had a faculty development research group which met for a semester and shared work. Out of that we decided our next project would be to collaboratively teach a class about play. I tend to the physical. I get the bodies up and moving. I teach improvisation. I bring in movement scores and theatre scores. We focus on engaging the mind in shaping and shifting the rules of the game as it is being played. My colleagues talk about computer programmes as play spaces, algorithms and how they work to generate creativity, collaborative design, play in animal behaviour. It's wide-ranging and delicious.

Do you take that approach to developing your Circus Amok shows?

Jennifer Miller: I came up in dance improvisation and postmodern contemporary dance, so those improvisatory practices made me in many ways. We spent a lot of time experimenting with what a score would be, what the rule set would be in order to make a dance. I love this process-based stuff, but in Amok we use a more a traditional way of making work. We research. We write some text, we improvise some text, we improvise some schtick, we set it, we play with the characters, and we make a clown act.

With the Circus Amok show that you're currently developing, how is that shaping up?

Jennifer Miller: This circus has eventually found its hook. Opening with a somewhat hysterical recitation of the destruction Trump is creating daily, and ending with a dance number celebrating activist groups locally and nationally, with some good juggling, slapstick acro, a ferocious lion, and a bit of opera in between!

FIGURE 4.15 Circus Amok. Photo: © Circus Amok.

Notes

1 Pascal Jacob (2008). The Circus Artist Today: Analysis of the Key Competences, p. 16. http://www.fedec.eu/en/articles/325-miroir01---part-1-the-circus-artist-today---analysis-of-the-key-competences-2008

2 See the Introduction, p. 6n1 for definitions of the terms 'Traditional Circus,' 'Modern Circus,' 'New Circus,' and 'Contemporary Circus' as used in this book.

3 Philippe Decouflé, p. 142.

4 Firenza Guidi, p. 124.

5 Ric Allsopp and André Lepecki (2008). Editorial: On choreography. *Performance Research, 13* (1), p. 3.

6 Ibid., p. 3.

7 David Hutchison (2015). Philip Rosenberg: 'Circus training is bitter but rewarding.' *The Stage.* https://www.thestage.co.uk/features/interviews/2015/philip-rosenburg-circus-training-bitter-rewarding/

   Cirque le Roux was formed in 2014 and consists of four circus artists, Yannick Thomas, Gregory Arsenal, Philip Rosenberg, and Lolita Costet. Their show *Elephant in the Room* (2015) has been performed in over 10 countries. See http://www.cirqueleroux.com/en/

8 Liz Arratoon and Adrian Arratoon (2017). Philip Rosenberg, hand-balancer and acrobat, Cirque Le Roux. *The Widow Stanton* [Blog]. http://thewidowstanton.com/post/155291187143/philrose

9 Throughout this book the term 'to contest' is used in the sense of 'to call into question' as discussed in the Introduction, pp. 1–6; p. 6n1.

10 Tilde Björfors (interview with Katie Lavers and Jon Burtt, December 11, 2017).

11 Pascal Jacob (2008). The circus artist today: Analysis of the key competences, p. 16. http://www.fedec.eu/en/articles/325-miroir01---part-1-the-circus-artist-today---analysis-of-the-key-competences-2008

12 There are examples of schools that take a different approach, as Firenza Guidi mentions in her interview, 'There are some schools, for example Toulouse [Centre des Arts du Cirque de Toulouse, France] where alongside the circus training, every week the students need to present two minutes of material, good, bad, mediocre, excellent. The point is it takes away this kind of *chrism*, this mystique or this kind of so-called "anxiety" about creating,' p. 125. See Centre des Arts du Cirque de Toulouse. (2019). Le Lido, École d'Art. Retrieved from http://www.circolido.fr/Lecole_professionnelle.html

13 For a discussion of the authors' concept of the 'captured body' see pp. 156–7.

14 See Sean Gandini, 158; p. 176.

15 See Yaron Lifschitz, p. 182.

16 Ric Allsopp and André Lepecki (2008), p. 3.

17 See Yaron Lifschtiz, p. 122.

18 Self-regulation (sometimes termed self-regulated learning) is learning in which students are cognitively active in and contribute to their own learning processes. See pp. 147–8n–8.

19 See definitions of different types of circus in The Introduction, p. 6n1.

20 Pascal Jacob (2008). The circus artist today: Analysis of the key competences, p. 15.

21 See Marius Kwint (2016) The circus in late Georgian England. In P. Tait & K. Lavers (Eds.), *The Routledge Circus Studies reader* (pp. 331–348). Abingdon, Oxon: New York, NY: Routledge.

22 See The Wallendas (2018). The world famous Wallendas. http://wallendaenterprises.com/

23 See Tina Konyot (2018). Induction into the Circus Ring of Fame – Konyot Family. http://tinakonyotdressage.com/HTML/Family.htm#Family

24 The Fratellini Family was a European Circus family widely known for the famous clown trio, The Fratellini Brothers: Paul (1877–1940), François (1879–1951), and Albert (1886–1961). Another famous member of the family was Annie Fratellini (1932–1997), the first female clown in France and granddaughter of Paul.

25 Pascal Jacob (2008), p. 15.

26 Ibid., p. 11.

27 For agit-prop theatre, see Lynn Mally (2003). Exporting Soviet culture: The case of agitprop theater. *Slavic Review, 62* (2), pp. 324–342; for postdramatic theatre see Hans-Thies Lehmann (2006). *Postdramatic theatre* (K. Jürs-Munby, Trans.), London & New York, NY: Routledge; for postmodern dance see Sally Banes (2011) *Terpsichore in sneakers: Postmodern dance.* Middletown, CT: Wesleyan University Press. (Original publication 1987); for site-specific and installation art see Miwon Kwon (2002). *One place after another: Site-Specific art and locational identity.* Cambridge, MA: MIT Press; for video art, see Michael Rush (2007). *Video art,* London: Thames and Hudson Ltd.

28 See Pascal Jacob (2018), p. 12.

29 Tony Wright (2018, March 12). Circus Oz at 40: From self-made tent to global success in many tricky moves. *Sydney Morning Herald.* https://www.smh.com.au/ entertainment/circus-oz-at-40-from-selfmade-tent-to-global-success-in-many-tricky-moves-20180309-h0x8vw.html

30 Tim Robertson (2001). *The Pram Factory: The Australian Performing Group recollected.* Carlton, VIC: Melbourne University Press, p. 1

31 See Mike Finch, 64; pp. 66–8.

32 See Circus Oz Living Archive (2018). Roof walk, from a 2004 show in Melbourne. [Video file]. http://archive.circusoz.com/clips/view/56923

33 Mike Finch (personal communication with Katie Lavers and Jon Burtt, July 13, 2018).

34 See https://www.cirquedusoleil.com

35 Franco Dragone's company, Dragone, is based in his home town of La Louvière in Belgium and produces major shows throughout Europe, Asia, and North America. See http://dragone.com/en

36 See Katie Lavers and Louis Patrick Leroux (2018). The multiple narratives of Cirque du Soleil. In B. Sellers-Young & J. R. McCutcheon (Eds.), *Narrative in performance* (pp. 111–132). London: Red Globe Press/Palgrave Macmillan.

37 See Pascal Jacob (2018), p. 12.

38 See Shana Carroll, 22–4.

39 See Charles R. Batson (2016). Les 7 doigts de la main and their cirque: Origins, resistances, intimacies. In L. P. Leroux & C. R. Batson (Eds.), *Cirque global: Québec's expanding circus boundaries* (pp. 99–121). Kingston-Montreal: McGill-Queen's University Press.

40 See Shana Carroll, p. 24.

41 Miwon Kwon (2002). *One place after another,* p. 11.

42 See Mike Pearson (2010). *Site-specific performance.* Basingstoke: Palgrave Macmillan; Geraldine Cousin (1994). An interview with Mike Pearson of Brith Gof. *Contemporary Theatre Review, 2* (2), 37–47.

43 See Firenza Guidi, p. 190.

44 For video footage of *Tabú* at La Tohu in Montreal see La TOHU (2010, July 13). Nofit State – Première Tabu Premiere. [Video file]. https://www.youtube.com/ watch?v=O29Wqxql4r4

45 See Sean Gandini, p. 176.

46 Ibid., p. 176.

47 For video links to Shana Carroll's work with The 7 Fingers see http://7fingers.com/ shows/; for links to her work with Cirque du Soleil see https://www.cirquedusoleil. com/shows

48 Ulysses Dove (1947–1996) was a dancer and choreographer in the New York-based modern dance company Alvin Ailey American Dance Theater. He danced with the Merce Cunningham company, with Mary Anthony, Pearl Lang, and Anna Sokolow, before joining Alvin Ailey in 1973. He choreographed *Episodes* for the company in 1987.

49 See Hamish McCormick/Carnival Cinema (2012). Carnival chronicles: Lady Torpedo and The Big Swing Brothers – 'Toss the Girl' – National Circus Festival 2009. https://vimeo.com/45183460

  Cletus Ball is an Australia vaudevillian and circus elder from whom Chelsea McGuffin learnt the 'Toss the Girl' act. He was part of this touring acrobatic act from the 1950s onwards.

50 For video links to Chelsea McGuffin's work with Company 2 see http://www.company2.com.au

51 David Carberry is an acrobat, musician, director, and Co-Director and Co-Founder of Company 2. He is a graduate of Flying Fruit Fly Circus, and has performed with Tom Tom Crew, and Circa.

52 *She Would Walk the Sky* was commissioned by the Brisbane Powerhouse for the World Theatre Festival 2014.

53 For video links to Lachlan Binns and Jascha Boyce's work with Gravity and Other Myths' works see https://www.gravityandothermyths.com.au/our-work/

54 Darcy Grant, Director of Gravity and Other Myths' show *Backbone*, is an acrobat, and a circus and theatre director who has performed with the Australian company Rock'n'Roll Circus (1987–2004) or, as it is known today, Circa (2004–present). He also co-directed Circa's 2018 show *Aura*. He is an Associate Artist with Northern Rivers Performing Arts (NORPA) in Lismore, Australia.

55 Cirkidz (1985–present) Circus school for young people based in Adelaide, Australia. The school was founded by community arts pioneers, Tony Hannan and Michael Lester, to provide access to arts activities for disadvantaged young people in Adelaide's industrial inner-western suburbs. See http://www.cirkidz.org.au

56 For video links for Sean Gandini's works for Gandini Juggling see http://www.gandinijuggling.com/en/our-shows/

57 See Colin Wright and Andrew Lipson (1996). SiteSwaps. http://www.juggling.org/help/siteswap/ssintro/

  See Bengt Magnusson and Bruce Tiemann (1989). The physics of juggling, *The Physics Teacher,* pp. 584–588, and (1991). A notation for juggling tricks. A lot of juggling tricks, *Juggler's World, 43* (2), n.p. http://www.juggling.org/jw/91/2/notation.html

58 Philip Glass (1937–present) is an American minimalist composer. He has collaborated with choreographers such as Twyla Tharp for her work *In the Upper Room* (1986), and has composed music scores for film including *Koyaanisqatsi* (1982), *Powaqqatsi* (1988), and *Kundun* (1997). His works for opera include *Einstein on the Beach* (1976), *Satyagraha* (1980), *Akhnaten* (1984), Robert Wilson's *The Civil Wars* (1984), and *The Voyage* (1992). See Richard Kostelanetz and Robert Flemming (1999). *Writings on Glass: Essays, interviews, criticism.* Berkeley: University of California Press.

59 Louis Quatorze – Louis XIV (1638–1715), also known as the Sun King, was King of France from 1643 to 1715. A generous supporter of the arts, he founded the Académie Royale de Danse in 1661, and the Académie d'Opéra, in 1669.

60 Alexander Whitley (1980–present) is the Founder and Artistic Director of the London-based Alexander Whitley Dance Company which was formed in 2014. He has created works for some of the UK's leading Dance Companies including the Royal Ballet, Rambert, Balletboyz, Candoco, and Birmingham Royal Ballet. See http://www.alexanderwhitley.com

61 Pina Bausch (1940–2004) was a German choreographer, and Founder and Artistic Director of the dance company Tanztheater Wuppertal Pina Bausch, which still performs her work. Bausch's dance theatre works include *Café Müller* (1978), *The Rite of Spring* (1975), *Vollmond* (2006), and *Kontakthof,* first created in1978, but subsequently restaged with different casts: *Kontakthof – Mit Teenagern ab 14* (2008) with a cast of teenagers, and *Kontakthof – Mit Damen und Herren ab 65* (2000) with a cast of untrained dancers all aged over 65. See the Wim Wenders' (2011) film *Pina.* https://vimeo.com/31227698

62 Merce Cunningham (1919–2009) was an American modern dancer and choreographer, and Founder and Artistic Director of the Cunningham Dance Company, which still performs his work today. Cunningham was an innovator exploring the relationship between music and dance through his long-term collaboration with the composer John Cage, and also the use of technology with dance through his development of the software programme DanceForms, which enabled the creation of complex new choreography. See https://www.mercecunningham.org, and David Vaughan (1999). *Merce Cunningham: Fifty years.* New York, NY: Aperture.

Trisha Brown (1936–2017) was an American postmodern dancer and choreographer. She was one of the founders of the Judson Dance Theater, and part of the postmodern dance movement. See https://www.trishabrowncompany.org, and Hendel Teicher and Maurice Berger (Eds.) (2002). *Trisha Brown: Dance and art in dialogue, 1961–2001.* Cambridge, MA: The MIT Press.

63 Gill Clarke (1954–2011), British contemporary dancer, choreographer, and teacher, was a founder member of the influential English contemporary dance company Siobhan Davies Dance. See Sanjoy Roy and Rosemary Lee (2011). Gill Clarke. *The Guardian.* https://www.theguardian.com/stage/2011/dec/20/gill-clarke

64 Dominique Mercy (1950–present) is a French contemporary choreographer and dancer, and a member of Tanztheater Wuppertal Pina Bausch which he joined in the late 1970s, and where he is now the company's Rehearsal Director. See http://www.pina-bausch.de/en/

65 Mike Day is a Juggler and Co-Founder of Siteswap notation. He performed in the first two Gandini Juggling shows in the 1990s. See Mike Day's 1994 *Solo 2 from Caught – Still /Hanging,* choreographed by Gill Clarke at the Place Theatre, London from Gandini's second show, https://vimeo.com/2157079

66 Tom Johnson (1939–present) is an American minimalist composer. He collaborated with Gandini Juggling creating the music for the 2013 work, *Three Notes for Three Jugglers,* creating the score from working with mathematical algorithms. See Sean Gandini and Tom Johnson (2012). Preview: Juggling Balls, presented by the Steim Centre for Research and Development of New Musical Instruments in the Electronic Performing Arts in Amsterdam, https://vimeo.com/29421406

Steve Reich (1936–present) is an American Composer of minimalist music. He incorporated innovative tape loops to create 'phasing' music as part of the compositional process, and 'process' music such as in *Pendulum Music* (1968). He has collaborated with choreographers such as Anne Teresa De Keersmaeker, and key works include *Drumming* (1971), *Music for 18 Musicians* (1976), and *Electric Counterpoint* (1987). *Clapping Music* was created in 1989. See Steve Reich and Paul Hillier (2004) *Writings on music, 1965–2000,* Oxford: Oxford University Press, and http://www.stevereich.com/

67 John Cage (1912–1992) was an American composer, music theoretician, and writer, and a pioneer of avant-garde music. He was an innovator in the use of indeterminacy, electro-acoustic music, and chance-based environmental music. His most radical work *4'33"* (1952) used the ambient sound in the recital hall as the music. He is also known for his lifelong collaboration with the American dance pioneer Merce Cunningham. See John Cage (1991). Autobiographical statement. *Southwest Review, (76)* 1, pp. 59–76, and Alex Ross (2010, October 4). Searching for silence, John Cage's art of noise. *The New Yorker.* https://www.newyorker.com/magazine/2010/10/04/searching-for-silence

68 For video links to Yaron Lifschitz's works for Circa see https://circa.org.au/shows/

69 Tisch (1965–present), The New York University Tisch School of the Arts, is a performing and media arts School based in New York City. The school is one of America's leading centres for the training of artists, film-makers, and arts scholars. See http://tisch.nyu.edu

Jacob's Pillow (1931–present) is a dance centre in Becket, Massachusetts, home to the internationally recognised Jacob's Pillow Dance Festival and a professional dance school. See https://www.jacobspillow.org/about/pillow-history/jacobs-pillow-story/

70 Libby McDonnell is a designer, choreographer, director, and performer who has worked with Circa since 2010, and is now an Associate Director. She was Co-Director on Circa's *Peepshow* (2018) and *When One Door Closes* (2016).

71 For video links to Firenza Guidi's work for NoFit State see https://www.nofitstate. org/en/shows/

72 A claque is a group of audience members hired to act as professional 'applauders' in theatres and opera houses in France and Italy.

73 For video links to extracts of Johann Le Guillerm's work with Cirque Ici see, for instance, Théâtre Sénart (2017, June 26). SECRET (TEMPS 2) // Johann Le Guillerm. [Video file]. https://www.youtube.com/watch?v=Eqd6f_KrEUM

74 For video links to Philippe Decouflé's film and performance works see https://vimeo. com/philippedecoufle

75 *Freaks* (1932) is a 1932 American film produced and directed by Tod Browning, based on some of Browning's experiences when he left his middle-class family to join a travelling circus when he was aged 16. See https://vimeo.com/257932547

76 'Kiriki' is an act created by Philippe Decouflé which is an homage to early trick photography and films. It features antipodism (foot juggling) and unexpected gravity-defying (trick) acrobatics inspired by the early short silent film by Segundo de Chomón (1907). It was performed first in *Abracadabra*, and then in Cirque du Soleil's show *Iris* which Decouflé directed. See Bill Marcks (2013, September 27). Les Kiriki Acrobates Japonais. [Video file]. https://www.youtube.com/watch?v=szOBDjUf550

77 For video links to extracts of Jo Lancaster and Simon Yates' work with Acrobat see https://www.acrobat.net.au/current-shows

78 See Katie Lavers (2018). It's not for everyone. *ArtsHub*. Retrieved from https://performing.artshub.com.au/news-article/reviews/performing-arts/katie-lavers/its-not-for-everyone-255027

79 Tim Barrass is an Australian musician, composer, and sound scientist who has performed as a musician with Acrobat since the mid-1990s.

80 For video links to Jennifer Miller's work with Circus Amok, see https://www.circusamok.org/circus/

81 Mark Sussman (2016). A queer circus: Amok in New York. In P. Tait & K. Lavers (Eds.), *The Routledge Circus Studies reader* (pp. 198–206). Abingdon, Oxon & New York, NY: Routledge, p. 200.

References

Acrobat (2019). Acrobat performance research farm, current shows. Retrieved from https://www.acrobat.net.au/current-shows

Alexander Whitely Dance Company (2019). Retrieved from http://www.alexanderwhitley. com

Allsopp, R., & Lepecki, A. (2008). Editorial: On choreography. *Performance Research, 13*(1), 1–6.

Arratoon, L., & Arratoon, A. (2017). Philip Rosenberg, hand-balancer and acrobat, Cirque Le Roux. *The Widow Stanton* [Blog]. Retrieved from http://thewidowstanton. com/post/155291187143/philrose

Banes, S. (2011). *Terpsichore in sneakers: Postmodern dance*. Middletown, CT: Wesleyan University Press. (Original publication 1987).

Batson, C. R. (2016). Les 7 doigts de la main and their cirque: Origins, resistances, intimacies. In L. P. Leroux & C. R. Batson (Eds.), *Cirque global: Québec's expanding circus boundaries* (pp. 99–121). Kingston-Montreal: McGill-Queen's University Press.

Bill Marcks (2013, September 27). Les Kiriki Acrobates Japonais. [Video file]. Retrieved from https://www.youtube.com/watch?v=szOBDjUf550

Browning, T. (Director) (1932). *Freaks* [Motion Picture]. USA: Metro-Goldwyn-Mayer

Cage, J. (1991). Autobiographical statement. *Southwest Review, 76*(1), 59–76.

Circa (2019). Shows. Retrieved from https://circa.org.au/shows/

Circus Oz Living Archive (2018). Roof walk, from a 2004 show in Melbourne. [Video file]. Retrieved from http://archive.circusoz.com/clips/view/56923

Cirque du Soleil (2019). Retrieved from https://www.cirquedusoleil.com/shows

Cirque le Roux (2019). Retrieved from http://www.cirqueleroux.com/en/

Company 2 (2019). Retrieved from http://www.company2.com.au

Cousin, G. (1994). An interview with Mike Pearson of Brith Gof. *Contemporary Theatre Review, 2*(2), 37–47.

Dragone (2019). Retrieved from http://dragone.com/en

Gandini Juggling (2009). Mike Day Solo 2 from CAUGHT - STILL /HANGING. [Video file]. Retrieved from https://vimeo.com/2157079

Gandini Juggling (2019). Shows. Retrieved from http://www.gandinijuggling.com/en/our-shows/

Gravity and Other Myths (2019). Our work. Retrieved from https://www.gravityandothermyths.com.au

Hamish McCormick/Carnival Cinema (2012). Carnival chronicles: Lady Torpedo and The Big Swing Brothers – 'Toss the Girl' – National Circus Festival 2009. Retrieved from https://vimeo.com/45183460

Hutchison, D. (2015). Philip Rosenberg: 'Circus training is bitter but rewarding.' *The Stage*. Retrieved from https://www.thestage.co.uk/features/interviews/2015/philip-rosenburg-circus-training-bitter-rewarding/

Jacob's Pillow Dance Festival (2019). Retrieved from https://www.jacobspillow.org/about/pillow-history/jacobs-pillow-story/

Konyot, T. (2018). Induction into the Circus Ring of Fame – Konyot family. Retrieved from http://tinakonyotdressage.com/HTML/Family.htm#Family

Kostelanetz, R., & Flemming, R. (1999). *Writings on Glass: Essays, interviews, criticism.* Berkeley: University of California Press.

Kwint, M. (2016). The circus in late Georgian England. In P. Tait & K. Lavers (Eds.), *The Routledge Circus Studies reader* (pp. 331–348). Abingdon, Oxon & New York: Routledge.

Kwon, M. (2002). *One place after another: Site-Specific art and locational identity.* Cambridge, MA: MIT Press.

La TOHU (2010, July 13). Nofit State – Première Tabu Premiere. [Video file]. Retrieved from https://www.youtube.com/watch?v=O29Wqxql4r4

Lavers, K. (2018). It's not for everyone. *ArtsHub*. Retrieved from https://performing.artshub.com.au/news-article/reviews/performing-arts/katie-lavers/its-not-for-everyone-255027

Lavers, K., & Leroux, L. P. (2018). The multiple narratives of Cirque du Soleil. In B. Sellers-Young & J. R. McCutcheon (Eds.), *Narrative in performance* (pp. 111–132). London: Red Globe Press/Palgrave Macmillan.

Lehmann, H-T. (2006). *Postdramatic theatre* (K. Jürs-Munby, Trans.), London & New York, NY: Routledge.

Magnusson, B., & Tiemann, B. (1989). The physics of juggling. *The Physics Teacher, 27*(8), 584–588.

Magnusson, B., & Tiemann, B. (1991). A notation for juggling tricks. A lot of juggling tricks. *Juggler's World, 43*(2), n.p.

Mally, L. (2003). Exporting Soviet culture: The case of agitprop theater. *Slavic Review, 62*(2), 324–342.

Merce Cunningham Trust (2019). Merce Cunningham, past, present, future. Retrieved from https://www.mercecunningham.org

NoFit State (2019). Shows. Retrieved from https://www.nofitstate.org/en/shows/

Pearson, M. (2010). *Site-specific performance*. Basingstoke: Palgrave Macmillan.

Reich, S. (2019). Steve Reich. Retrieved from http://www.stevereich.com/

Reich, S., & Hillier, P. (2004) *Writings on music, 1965–2000*, Oxford: Oxford University Press.

Robertson, T. (2001). *The Pram Factory: The Australian Performing Group recollected*. Carlton, VIC: Melbourne University Press.

Ross, A. (2010, October 4). Searching for silence, John Cage's art of noise. *The New Yorker*. Retrieved from https://www.newyorker.com/magazine/2010/10/04/searching-for-silence

Roy, S., & Lee, R. (2011). Gill Clarke. *The Guardian*. Retrieved from https://www.theguardian.com/stage/2011/dec/20/gill-clarke

Rush, M. (2007). *Video art*. London: Thames and Hudson Ltd.

STEIM Amsterdam. (2012). Preview: Juggling balls. Retrieved from https://vimeo.com/29421406

Sussman, M. (2016). A queer circus: Amok in New York. In P. Tait & K. Lavers (Eds.), *The Routledge Circus Studies reader* (pp. 198–206). Abingdon, Oxon & New York, NY: Routledge.

Tanztheater Wuppertal Pina Bausch (2019). Retrieved from http://www.pina-bausch.de/en/

Teicher, H., & Berger, M. (Eds.). (2002). *Trisha Brown: Dance and art in dialogue, 1961–2001*. Cambridge, MA: The MIT Press.

The 7 Fingers (2019). Shows. Retrieved from http://7fingers.com/shows/

Théâtre Sénart (2017, June 26). SECRET (TEMPS 2) // Johann Le Guillerm. [Video file]. Retrieved from https://www.youtube.com/watch?v=Eqd6f_KrEUM

The Wallendas (2018). The world famous Wallendas. Retrieved from http://wallendaenterprises.com/

Thomas, J. (Producer), & Wenders, W. (Director) (2011). *Pina*. [Motion Picture]. Germany: IFC Films. Retrieved from https://vimeo.com/31227698

Tisch School of the Arts (2019). Retrieved from http://tisch.nyu.edu

Trisha Brown Dance Company (2019). Retrieved from https://www.trishabrowncompany.org

Vaughan, D. (1999). *Merce Cunningham: Fifty years*. New York, NY: Aperture.

Wright, T. (2018, March 12). Circus Oz at 40: From self-made tent to global success in many tricky moves. *Sydney Morning Herald*. Retrieved from https://www.smh.com.au/entertainment/circus-oz-at-40-from-selfmade-tent-to-global-success-in-many-tricky-moves-20180309-h0x8vw.html

Wright, C., & Lipson, A. (1996). SiteSwaps. Retrieved from http://www.juggling.org/help/siteswap/ssintro/

Further Reading

Baston, K. (2010). Jacques Brel and circus performance: The compiled score as discourse in *The Space Between* by Circa. *Australasian Drama Studies, 56*, 154–69.

Boudier, M., Carré, A., Diaz, S., & Métais-Chastanier, B. (2014). *De quoi la dramaturgie est-elle le nom?* Paris: L'Harmattan, Univers théâtral.

Bouissac, P. (2012). *Circus as multimodal discourse: Performance, meaning, and ritual*. London: Bloomsbury.

Deleuze, G., & Guattari, F. (1987). *A thousand plateaus: Capitalism and schizophrenia* (B. Massumi, Trans.). Minneapolis: University of Minnesota Press.

Fischer-Lichte, E., & Wihstutz, B. (2013). *Performance and the politics of space: Theatre and topology.* New York, NY: Routledge.

Goudard, P. (2005). *Anatomie d'un clown.* coll. Scénogrammes, série Canevas. Montpellier, France: L'Entretemps.

Goudard, P. (2005). Lire et écrire le cirque. In *Anatomie d'un clown.* coll. Scénogrammes, série Canevas. Montpellier, France: L'Entretemps, 2005, 47–93.

Guyez, M. (2018). Hybridation de l'acrobatie et du texte sur les scènes circassiennes contemporaines. (Unpublished doctoral thesis). Université de Toulouse, France.

Harvie, J., & Hurley, E. (1999). States of play: Locating Québec in the performances of Robert Lepage, Ex Machina, and the Cirque du Soleil. *Theatre Journal, 51*(3), 299–315.

Leclerc, A. (2013). À la recherche d'un corps vide. *Recherche, 7*(January), 1–9.

Leroux, L. P. (2009). Le Québec à Las Vegas: pérégrinations postidentitaires dans l'hyper-Amérique. *L'Annuaire théâtral, 45*(Spring), 9–20.

Leroux, L. P. (2009). *Zumanity:* la spectacularisation de l'intime, ou le pari impossible d'authenticité au Cirque. *L'Annuaire théâtral. Revue québécoise d'études théâtrales, 45*(Spring), 69–91.

Lievens, B. (2009). Dramaturgy: From Aristotle to contemporary circus. *Disturbis, 6.* Retrieved from http://www.disturbis.esteticauab.org/Disturbis567/Bauke.html

Lorant, T. C. (1986). *The Pickle Family Circus.* San Francisco: The Pickle Press.

Mullet, J. (2014). Australian New Circus in the 1980s. *Australasian Drama Studies, 64,* 97–108.

Poulain, A. (Ed.) (2011). *Passions du corps dans les dramaturgies contemporaines.* Villeneuve d'Ascq, France: Presses Universitaires du Septentrion.

Schechner, R. (1994). *Environmental theatre.* New York, NY: Applause Books.

Stoddart, H. (2000). *Rings of desire: Circus history and representation.* Manchester: Manchester University Press.

Wallon, E. (2013). *Le Cirque au risque de l'art.* Arles, France: Actes Sud/Papiers. (Original publication 2002).

Wilson, T. J. M. (2016). *Juggling trajectories: Gandini Juggling 1991–2015.* London: Gandini Press.

INDEX

Note: *Italic* page numbers refer to figures and page numbers followed by "n" denote endnotes.

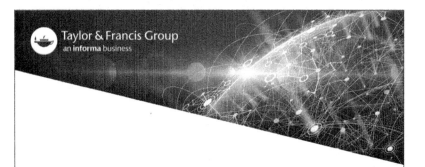